YEARS *of*
the MODERN

An American Appraisal

YEARS *of* *the* MODERN

An American Appraisal

Henry S. Commager
Alan Barth
Walton Hamilton
Alvin Johnson
David Riesman
J. K. Galbraith

Perry Miller
Harrison Brown
Erwin D. Canham
C. T. Lanham
Sumner Welles
Norman Cousins

JOHN W. CHASE
Editor

NEW YORK • TORONTO

Longmans, Green and Company

1949

LONGMANS, GREEN AND CO., INC.
55 FIFTH AVENUE, NEW YORK 3

LONGMANS, GREEN AND CO.
215 VICTORIA STREET, TORONTO 1

YEARS OF THE MODERN

FIRST EDITION

Printed in the United States of America
VAN REES PRESS • NEW YORK

PUBLISHER'S FOREWORD

This book is an interpretation of America and the American people in mid-passage; as such, it is also an exploration in ideas and ideals.

From its inception by the editor early in 1947, the publishers have regarded this volume as a major editorial and publishing project. Both the general plan and the step-by-step development of the book involved discussions with many persons representing a cross-section of our national life. Their response, sympathetic and serious, has played an important part in moulding *Years of the Modern*.

Particular acknowledgment should be made of the important contributions given in the early stages of the project by an informal group which met as a body to consider the special problems presented by an undertaking of this character. Members of this group consisted of Norman Cousins, Philip C. Jessup, Archibald MacLeish, J. R. Oppenheimer, and Beardsley Ruml. They were generous of their time and interest.

Frank Ernest Hill contributed the prefatory note to the reader, as well as the commentaries preceding each chapter.

v

CONTENTS

vii

CONTENTS

YEARS OF THE MODERN

Years of the modern! years of the unperform'd!
Your horizon rises, I see it parting away for more august
    dramas,
I see not America only, not only Liberty's nation but other
    nations preparing,
I see tremendous entrances and exits, new combinations, the
    solidarity of races,
I see that force advancing with irresistible power on the
    world's stage,
(Have the old forces, the old wars, played their parts? are the
    acts suitable to them closed?)
I see Freedom, completely arm'd and victorious and very
    haughty, with Law on one side and Peace on the other,
A stupendous trio all issuing forth against the idea of caste;
What historic denouements are these we so rapidly approach?
I see men marching and countermarching by swift millions,
I see the frontiers and boundaries of the old aristocracies
    broken,
I see the landmarks of European kings removed,
I see this day the People beginning their landmarks, (all others
    give way;)
Never were such sharp questions ask'd as this day,
Never was average man, his soul, more energetic, more like
    a God,
Lo, how he urges and urges, leaving the masses no rest!

His daring foot is on land and sea everywhere, he colonizes
the Pacific, the archipelagoes,
With the steamship, the electric telegraph, the newspaper, the
wholesale engines of war,
With these and the world-spreading factories he interlinks all
geography, all lands;
What whispers are these O lands, running ahead of you, passing under the seas?
Are all nations communing? is there going to be but one heart
to the globe?
Is humanity forming en-masse? for lo, tyrants tremble, crowns
grow dim;
The earth, restive, confronts a new era, perhaps a general
divine war,
No one knows what will happen next, such portents fill the
days and nights;
Years prophetical! the space ahead as I walk, as I vainly try
to pierce it, is full of phantoms,
Unborn deeds, things soon to be, project their shapes around
me,
This incredible rush and heat, this strange ecstatic fever of
dreams O years!
Your dreams O years, how they penetrate through me! (I know
now whether I sleep or wake;)
The perform'd America and Europe grow dim, retiring in
shadow behind me,
The unperform'd, more gigantic than ever, advance, advance
upon me.

—WALT WHITMAN

FOR THE READER

Years of the Modern *is a project carried out by a group of Americans gravely concerned about the state of the modern world. It was undertaken with the assumption that there would be time, although not too much time, in which to survey the continuing crisis and perhaps to prepare for action. The group responsible for this book is much larger than the list of contributors. More than eighty men and women, representing a cross section of every important activity of American life, were consulted about the volume-in-the-making. In many cases they have continued to give generously of their time and advice. Their deep and persisting interest would seem to dispel any idea that Americans are unconcerned about the fate of their country.*

What is the meaning of this project called Years of the Modern *and for what reasons have the dozen men whose names appear as contributors been chosen to carry it through?*

In a large sense the project is a report, a story. The story has a hero: modern man. All the contributing authors are concerned with him and the dangers he faces; they themselves are modern man, along with their two billion fellow world-citizens. The authors are deeply interested in the continuity of modern man's life. They are no less concerned with its spiritual and materialistic aspects. Above all, they are concerned about man as the potential master of his environment and government, both of which have often mastered him.

What, more precisely, is the story which these contributors tell? It might be called a creative inventory of our times. For to those who embarked on the project it was clear that if man was to deal successfully with the grim challenges he faced, he must first of all know what he was and what resources he had. Judgment, action, could only follow on understanding. Without that, effort might well be futile. With it, there was hope of success. To bring into focus this vital process of self-assessment, the twelve contributors tell of modern man in a number of illuminating areas. They have tried so to testify that man may face the future with greater awareness and perhaps with greater confidence.

This project has intentionally been limited to an exploration of the American scene. A single land and people are easier to study than an entire world. Furthermore, the study of one land by men who are familiar with that land is more likely to produce a vigorous and specific report than would a study of a broader and less familiar scene. In the case of America the survey of one nation and people might also be said to be strategic; for both the power and primary obligation to meet the present crisis lie with this land and its citizens. They more than any other group must be responsible for decisions. They must act. Responsibility and action alike demand self-knowledge. That other friendly peoples associated with us are equally involved in the present crisis, and that we should understand them better than we do—these are facts that need not be argued. But in the project at hand the authors have placed emphasis upon the problems of their own land and of their fellow Americans.

This book makes no pretense of presenting all aspects of the American story. Rather, the effort has been made to take a limited number of strategic aspects of the nation. All sub-

jects have been chosen with the idea that they are crucial, not only because they show great changes but also because the changes in question are vital and are even now shaping the future.

Men who could report on such areas were hard to find. Each of the contributors was chosen because, whether known or unknown to his fellow Americans, he was an authority in his field. Each was chosen also because he had an alertness to the meaning of that field in relation to the rest of life. Each was chosen because he had convictions about what he had seen and felt in the course of his own work. Finally, each was selected because of an ability to phrase these convictions with clarity and imaginative force.

There was no effort made to limit the activity of any contributor in his relationship to the activities of his fellow contributors. There was only an effort to make sure that each writer understood the greater situation about which he was reporting—that he saw and felt the world crisis and perceived the relationship of his own experience to this continuing challenge. It was felt that this common understanding would promote a unique, exciting unity.

The purpose of the twelve contributors to YEARS OF THE MODERN *has not been to seek and state categorical answers. Often the reader will find answers implicit or direct. But the aim has been to cast a light, not to give directions.*

For this project is designed to open up larger activities, to induce tens or hundreds of thousands to join in the process of self-knowledge.

It is frankly a challenge.

1

The American is under summons and challenge. By the implacable force of events, he is being asked to write history, to take the leadership of a racked and divided world. The varied fibres of race and experience that have been woven into the man he is today—these he has need to understand. He has need to assess his faults and his virtues—to look at them as if they had appeared in some specimen of life brought from a newly charted continent. He has need to consider whether or not his past has prepared him for his future. That future will lead him to activities he had previously avoided, and for which he has had little training or experience. It is certain that he will find them both exciting and rewarding.

1

Henry Steele Commager

PORTRAIT OF THE AMERICAN

I

The important questions about any nation, as about any individual, come back to character. "What kind of people do they think we are?" asked Winston Churchill at a momentous crisis in history, and Britain—and the democratic world —survived, not because the English Channel held the Nazis at bay, but because of English steadfastness and courage. Yet it is clear, too, that England's insular position is, itself, an ingredient of the English character, just as the protection of the Atlantic and the open frontier have been ingredients of the American character. The broad question, what kind of people are we? inevitably takes precedence over any particular questions of government, economy or sociology, of domestic or foreign policy, but it cannot be separated from the elements that give rise to such questions. Character is intangible and unique but it is neither abstract nor isolated; it is both cause and consequence, creator and creation. It is the product of a thousand factors of geography, history, and economy, and it determines, in turn, the manifestations of those factors.

3

What kind of people, then, are we Americans? What have we inherited, and what have we created? What values do we cherish, what standards do we maintain, what fears do we confess, and what hopes do we avow? What are our motivating interests, sentiments, and passions? What are our instinctive habits of conduct and what our calculated principles? How do we view ourselves, and how do we view others? How have we responded in the past, to the various crises of economy, politics, and war, and to the challenges of philosophy, culture, and science; how may we be expected to respond, in the future, to the implacable demands that will be made upon our understanding, our courage, and our virtue?

These are questions that cannot, in the nature of things, be answered comprehensively or conclusively. No biographer, not even a Boswell, a Lockhart, or a Freeman, has exhausted the possibilities of an individual character, nor can the historian hope to do more than suggest the broad outlines of a national character. Certainly in a people so mixed as the American, scattered over so broad a territory, coming from such varied backgrounds, professing such different faiths, concerned with such diverse interests, there is no single pattern, however rich. Yet from Crèvecœur to Brogan, the most judicious foreign visitors have concluded that America has fused its human ingredients into something approaching a type, and observation of the American soldier overseas confirmed the conclusion that somehow the homogeneous had triumphed over the heterogeneous and the general over the particular.

The American character is an amalgam of inheritance, environment, and experience. The inheritance is chiefly British, but it is, in a broad sense, that of western Christendom. Con-

4

tributions from Germany, Scandinavia, Italy, Bohemia, Poland, Russia, and—above all—Africa made an impact on special groups and regions; but their total effect on American institutions was negligible, and only the African had a lasting influence on the American character. The environment, like the inheritance, is varied—varied both in time and in space, for Americans lived in different environments in different eras of their history. The diversity of the environment, however great, was less important than its general character—spaciousness, richness, beauty, and isolation. For over two centuries the environment was a challenge and a reward—a succession of wildernesses that demanded the utmost of those who braved them, and of soils and minerals that rewarded industry and ingenuity richly.

Fully to appreciate the American experience—the third factor in the formation of the national character—would require a rehearsal of the whole of American history. Certain elements of that experience were to prove of special importance to white Americans: Puritanism and the principle of the dignity of the individual; the Enlightenment and the sovereignty of Reason; the Revolution and the doctrine of the subordination of government to man; education in self-government through a constantly expanding electorate and in democracy through voluntary association; the absence of feudal institutions of church, state, and society, and the necessary practice of social and religious tolerance; freedom from hard and fast class distinctions; the combination of abundant natural resources and of individual industry which made possible a high level of material prosperity and the indulgence of women and children; the traditions of immunity from European entanglements, of victory in war, of inexhaustible resources, of moral superiority, and of Providential favor—traditions none the less effective even when not consistent with reality.

The Old World inheritance persisted into the late nineteenth and twentieth centuries, when it was augmented and, in part, transformed by the new immigration and by the reception of new scientific and philosophical ideas such as evolution, determinism, and Freudianism. With the passing of the frontier in the 'nineties the peculiar impact of a wilderness environment disappeared, and as technology enabled men to master their environment, the role of geography and climate was diminished. Yet the varied forces of weather, soil and water, of mountain, prairie and forest continued to make themselves felt. A larger uniformity embraced striking sectional divergencies, and the American scene presented as richly differentiated an economic pattern as that of all Europe. And to almost three centuries of history—often overlaid with romance or transfigured by legend—Americans added half a century of experience which by contrast seems almost wholly contemporaneous. This recent past, merging imperceptibly with the present, has had a decisive influence on the shaping of the American character.

The watershed that divides the historic past from what we may call the modern era can be located, with some assurance, in the decade of the 'nineties. That decade witnessed important changes in the material scene: the passing of the frontier, the completion of the transcontinental railways, the coming of the "new" immigration, the decisive shift of population from country to city, and of economy from agriculture to industry, the rise of trusts and of modern labor organizations, the emergence of the New South, and the advent of the

United States to world power. And during these years, too, the intellectual and psychological world in which Americans lived underwent a comparable change. The doctrine of evolution challenged religious orthodoxy and profoundly affected science and the social sciences, philosophy, literature, and art. Catholicism emerged as a major force, threatening to compete with the Puritan and the evangelical tradition. A new physics gave scientific sanction to the principle of uncertainty, and currents of thought stemming from Marx, Nietzsche, and Freud introduced radically new elements into the pattern of thought. The rise of sensational journalism and of a more popular press accelerated that tendency towards the vulgarization of ideas already notorious in America, while pragmatism, regarded by unfriendly critics as a comparable vulgarization in philosophy, provided Americans with a philosophical method highly congenial to democracy.

The twentieth century introduced not only new material circumstances and philosophical concepts, but novel techniques, experiences, and challenges. Among the new techniques it is sufficient to mention the moving pictures, the radio, television, and modern advertising, with their vast and almost unexplored potentialities for molding opinion. Among the new experiences the most important are the most obvious: a depression which left permanent scars and should have taught permanent lessons in economy and government, and a world war which violently wrenched life from its normal course, confronted millions of Americans with perplexing problems in conduct and morals, and placed upon the American character unprecedented responsibilities. Among the new challenges are the growth of the welfare state, the attainment of world power, the advent of a permanent military organiza-

7

tion, and atomic energy. All these, together with the deeply-
rooted and permanent factors of inheritance, environment,
and historical experience, condition the American character
as it reveals itself at mid-century.

II

Let us, then, try to delineate that character.

The American is optimistic, self-confident, and self-
satisfied. He takes for granted that his is the best of all countries, the happiest and most virtuous of all societies, the
richest and most bounteous of all economies. He knows that
Providence has favored him in the past and he takes for
granted that he will continue to be the object of special dispensation. Collectively he has never known defeat, or prolonged misery, and only colored Americans—who are usually
left out of calculations—have known oppression. He is not
indifferent to the past, as long as it is American, and is inclined to believe that history began in 1607 or—if he is a
Yankee—in 1620. Mostly, however, he lives in the present
or the future. Although less sure of progress than his fathers
or grandfathers, he is confident that if there is progress, it
will be under American leadership and bear the American
imprint. Accustomed to seeing his boldest plans and most
sanguine anticipations realized, he believes that they will
continue to be fulfilled—but with that belief goes a suspicion
that in these matters he is no longer the free agent he was
during the period of relative immunity from European
affairs.

The American has boundless faith in the new generation
over the horizon, is willing to make almost any sacrifices
for it except those required by self-restraint. Education is his

religion. It is commonly said that the United States is a young country. That is true only in part, and in a special sense, but it is indubitably true that it is above most others a country whose society and economy are organized for children and young people—again, so long as they are white. That indulgence of children, which most foreign commentators have remarked, is rooted, in part, in good fortune and prosperity, and, in part, in the confident assumption by each successive generation that the period of true greatness lies ahead.

In one important respect, confidence in the future has led the American to a characteristic disregard of the interests of his children and of his children's children. Because he believed that his natural resources were inexhaustible, he used them recklessly, taking little care for soil or forest or stream, or even for the less tangible but no less important element of the beauty of carefully tended trees and roads and lawns. Because he trusted his own individual strength, he was hostile to planning, especially by any governmental agency. Because he was easy-going and heedless, he piled up staggering public debts for future generations to pay, and was unwilling to burden himself, even in times of prosperity, by a speedy retirement of that debt. The twentieth century saw improvement in the attitude toward conservation and a decline in hostility toward planning. Belatedly shocked by the rapid exhaustion of his resources, the American approved a conservation program that at least arrested, if it did not reverse, that process. Confused by the complexity of modern economy and wounded by the great depression, he undertook, somewhat gingerly, a series of experiments in economic planning, of which T.V.A. is easily the most ambitious. All this was a sign of maturity.

Enraptured with his life in the New World, the American is inclined to disparage or ignore any other. Confident of the superiority of what he calls, with naive vagueness, "the American way of life," he is confident, too, of the superior intelligence, competence, and virtue of his own people. Whatever quality is admirable he promptly dubs "American," and he is inclined to think that nowhere but in America do doctors save children or newspapers print honest news or women wear nylons. This is an attitude by no means unique to the American, and more easily excused in a people who have been so favored by nature and history in their attempt to make something new, than it is in some others. Neither familiarity with the history and institutions of Old World nations nor contact with them during two wars disabused the average American of his feeling of superiority or of his tendency either to indulge other peoples for their quaintness and charm, or to disparage them for their backwardness or their wickedness. Yet if the tendency to equate civilization with plumbing is childish, it is perhaps no more childish than the Old World habit of equating it with titles or monuments or traditions.

Because he has a long tradition of victory over the wilderness and over foreign enemies, the American is inclined to regard any set-back to his success or qualification of it as contrary to nature. He looked on the great depression of 1929 not as the logical consequence of his own political and economic follies, but rather as an aberration, and for over a decade his business and political leaders have been busy trying to forget it or to pretend that it never really happened. He has never willingly admitted defeat in war, nor quit while there was still some purpose in fighting: in this he is closer to the British and the Russian than to any other peoples. First and Second Bull Run, Fredericksburg and Chancellorsville, did not fatally dishearten the North; nor Gettysburg and Vicksburg the South. Pearl Harbor seemed not so much a defeat as an indignity; it did not depress the American, but astonished and outraged him.

Much of the American's optimism is rooted in innocence. Less virtuous—certainly less moral and law-abiding—than his British cousins, he is at the same time less sophisticated and consequently less disillusioned. Notwithstanding an inheritance of Puritanism, he has never really subscribed to the doctrine of the natural depravity of man, and despite the efforts of generations of revivalists, he has never taken the Devil seriously. Nor has he ever comprehended corruption, as have, for example, the French and the Germans. His philosophers early abandoned those problems of evil which had engaged the anxious consideration of philosophy since the days of Plato. Emerson remained his favorite philosopher, and after him, William James. Josiah Royce, who did wrestle with the problem of evil, was largely ignored. Of his major writers only three—Hawthorne, Melville, and E. A. Robinson—concerned themselves with sin. His imagination, which is lively enough in the realm of humor or fantasy, seems incapable of penetrating to the depths of human depravity. By comparison with French novelists like Jules Romains or with English ones like Graham Greene, his hard-boiled novelists and tough mystery-story writers seem like adolescent boys scrawling naughty words on walls. Even World War II, even the German and Japanese torture camps, failed to bring home to him the full reality of evil, and he remains, therefore, psychologically disqualified for appreciating the fears and despairs that today afflict so large a part of the world.

11

This attitude affects even his foreign and his military policy. He is confident that in a third world war his side would win, and impatient with the misgivings of some western European states about the outcome of such a war. When he takes thought, he realizes that, win or lose, a third war would destroy western Europe, but he does not always take thought. So, too, with his control of the atomic weapon. He feels that his intentions are good, and assumes that his country will not misuse atomic bombs, and he expects other countries to trust him, too. He is perpetually astonished and outraged by Russian suspicion of his motives. He is sure that in the event of atomic warfare his country will have the most and the most effective bombs, and that it will inflict more damage on the enemy than the enemy can inflict on it. He does not commonly appreciate that the damage to Britain or Scandinavia, for example, might be incalculable and irreparable—to say nothing of the fact that equally sinister weapons may suddenly be turned on him.

III

American culture is predominantly material, its thought and its standards quantitative. The normal American tends to compute almost everything in numbers, even qualitative things such as religion or art. He takes pride in statistics of population growth, automobile production, magazine circulation, and college enrollment, and is inclined to put a financial value on objects of public interest—houses, or bridges, or works of art—not because he is primarily interested in money but because money furnishes the most convenient quantitative yardstick. He is proud when his company

12

builds the highest office-building, or his city the most miles of boulevard, or his college the largest stadium.

This passion for quantity is looked upon as naive, even as vulgar, by outsiders; it has given acute pain to such different critics as Matthew Arnold, Knut Hamsun, and de Madariaga. Yet it has certain advantages. Oftentimes quantity is meaningless, but oftentimes, too, it contributes directly to human welfare and happiness. The American wants the highest standard of living, and knows that telephones and libraries and boulevards contribute to that standard. Only rarely does he delude himself that twenty thousand students at the State University guarantee a higher standard of education than five thousand students at Oxford, but at the same time he is prepared to maintain that two million students in colleges and universities do make for a more enlightened citizenry than, say, one hundred thousand. He is not to be dissuaded from his pride in keeping twenty-seven million boys and girls in his public schools or in the handsome buildings he commonly provides for them.

His respect for numbers contributes to the maintenance of the two-party system, and to a more cheerful acquiescence in majority decisions than is to be found in many other countries. It may even be argued that there is a connection between majority—or quantitative—rule and economic and social progress. It is suggestive that the section of the country where minority control is indulged has made least material progress, and least progress in social and intellectual tolerance. Nor is the quantitative standard wholly without significance in international relations. The American can fight when outnumbered—witness the history of the Confederacy

13

—but prefers to fight with the largest numbers and the best equipment, and the ability of America to muster large numbers and produce superior equipment is a basic consideration in world affairs.

The American is ingenious, inventive, and experimental, though less so in the twentieth than in the eighteenth or nineteenth centuries. This ingenuity is in part an inheritance from life on successive frontiers, where almost everyone was a jack-of-all-trades, in part a concomitant of an equalitarian society where rewards went to the most enterprising. It is, in addition, a consequence of the important fact that America came to maturity during the era of the industrial revolution. The American likes to tinker, and his passion for gadgets is notorious—the very word has come to be an Americanism. He has carried this aptitude for tinkering over into the whole field of science and technology, and to a lesser degree into the realms of education, libraries, journalism and sports. Except in law, he is unimpressed by precedent, and has little use for tradition. He prefers to do old things in new ways, and the fact that something has never been done before is more a challenge than a discouragement.

His proclivity for invention and experimentation does not carry over in any substantial form into the political or cultural fields. Here the American is conservative by instinct rather than by conviction. Those who are prosperous, successful, and powerful are generally conservative, and the American is no exception. Most of his political inventions date back to the eighteenth and early nineteenth centuries— the federal system, the written constitution, the constitutional convention, the colonial system formulated in the Northwest Ordinance, and judicial review; since that day political inventions have been largely confined to the less spacious realms of party and administrative techniques. Although he permits changes in his unwritten constitution, he does not want to change his written one, and he is inclined to regard criticism of that document as heretical. It is remarkable that no basic change has been introduced into the written constitution since 1868. Of the three branches of his government the judicial, which is least democratic in character, is the most exalted, and the legislative, which is most democratic, is most condemned. Tocqueville's observation about the aristocracy of the robe in the eighteen-thirties was equally valid a century later. Although the federal system permits wide experimentation in forty-eight state laboratories, few states have in fact ventured beyond familiar political arrangements and techniques. On the other hand, much of the New Deal program showed audacity, the T.V.A. revealed both boldness and originality, and lend-lease was probably the most ingenious invention in the history of modern international relations.

The twentieth-century American does not display hospitality to new or radical ideas in non-political realms. In economics he still prefers the dogmas of Spencer to the experiments of Keynes: it should be added that the verbal expression of his preference here is sentimental and nostalgic. His attitude towards such institutions of property as the corporation, the stock market, land tenure, patents, and labor organizations, is predominantly conservative. In religion he is a conservative, if not a fundamentalist, and the only churches that show a positive decline in membership are the Unitarian, Universalist, and Quaker. Neither his movies nor his radio nor his advertising—the three most popular media of culture—show any weakness for innovation. Some artists

15

and poets experiment, but it is not they who command
the favor of the public or of patrons, but rather those who
are content with traditional forms. Three decades of agitation
for modern housing have produced chiefly colonial or Eliza-
bethan or Spanish reproductions. Even in the automobile,
where American productive skill is supreme, the boldest experiments come from abroad. In the realm of science,
medicine and technology, Americans have retained considerable intellectual boldness, but not, on the whole, in the social
sciences, and the growing popular complacency about American society and economy augurs ill for any bold ventures in
that arena.

The American is pre-eminently practical. He is the enemy
of all abstractions, theories and doctrines. Franklin is his
favorite philosopher, and after him, William James—James
who asserted that it was only minds debauched by learning
that ever suspected common sense of not being true. The
American requires that everything serve a practical purpose
—religion, education, culture, science, philosophy, even art.
He has produced great speculative scientists, but he admires
Edison rather than Willard Gibbs; he has produced speculative philosophers, but exalts William James above Josiah
Royce; he has produced no great political theorist since Jefferson, no major social theorist since Lester Ward; and both
Jefferson and Ward were practical as well as speculative
philosophers. His education, too, is practical, and only in
America do graduate schools of architecture and journalism
and engineering flourish.

This strain of practicality is regarded by many Europeans
as lamentable, but it is not without merit. It means that philosophy has been levied upon for practical and democratic

purposes. Transcendentalism, in its German and English versions, was private and remote, but in its American, it became a powerful instrument for social reform; pragmatism, the most characteristic and most popular of all American philosophies, requires that all truths prove themselves by their consequences. It also means that religious leaders have largely abandoned theology for humanitarianism and reform; that education has broken away, in part at least, from its classical mold and been called on to serve the needs of a business society; that in the realm of politics the American will give his vote to a third party only rarely and reluctantly, and is not tempted by speculative theories. Many foreigners are distressed that there are no discernible differences between the Republican and the Democratic parties, but Americans know instinctively, as well as by experience, that parties are organizations to run the government, not to advance theoretical principles, and, on the basis of results, the American party system appears to be as efficient as any in the world.

What is true of philosophy and politics is certainly true of industry, but distinctly less true of agriculture and of business. The efficiency of American technology is unparalleled, but the efficiency of farming is spotty and that of business circumscribed. Agricultural inefficiency had its origins, and its justification, in the abundance of cheap land on successive frontiers, thus making extensive cultivation more profitable than intensive. But with mechanization, the application of science and the contributions of government bureaus, farming is becoming every year more productive and, outside the South, compares favorably with that of Britain and Scandinavia.

American business prides itself on its organization, man-

17

agement, publicity, profits, and other characteristics that
advertise a high degree of efficiency, and American universities alone teach business administration as a science. Yet
what is perhaps most striking about American business, as
distinct from industry, is not social or economic efficiency,
but the disproportion between effort and result. Random com-
parisons with British business are relevant. Probably no
banks are more elaborately equipped with devices to keep
track of accounts and in particular to control overdrawals
than the American, but the several million depositors who
lost their savings in American banks during the twenties and
thirties might well feel that British banks, for all their shab-
biness and their apparent casualness, are substantially more
efficient. The machinery of Hollywood is incomparably more
elaborate, and more expensive than that of British studios,
but Hollywood does not produce pictures as good as the best
English films. The total production-costs of American radio
run into astronomical figures, but many impartial auditors
prefer the less expensive product of the BBC; and American
radio has yet to produce anything as good as the "Ideas and
Beliefs of the Victorians" series. Or, to look to other fields,
the personnel, machinery, and appropriations of the Information and Education division of the American Army were
ten-fold as elaborate as those of the British Education program, but it could be argued that the British did a better
educational job. What all this suggests, so far as it is tenable,
is that the American has faith in machinery, admires bigness,
is inclined to mistake the effort for the product and to judge
the product by the effort—and the cost. This is natural enough
in a people whose genius is inventive, who enjoy abundance,
who delight in quantity, and who have learned to rely on

machinery to do work ordinarily done by people. What is interesting is that the American businessman should persist in regarding himself as a paragon of efficiency.

Another qualification on the efficiency of the American is his deep-rooted and pervasive carelessness. He is careless about his work, his trade, his profession, about speech, manners, and social relationships. In part this is a consequence of generations of rural and frontier life, in part of the absence of distinct social standards or a clear-cut social pattern; in part it is a manifestation of equalitarianism, individualism, and good nature. It reveals itself in countless ways, some deplorable, but mostly amiable. The American slurs over his words, leaves sentences unfinished, cheerfully ignores the rules of spelling and grammar. He is lawless in small matters, as in large; disregards rules and regulations, endures public litter, disorder and noise, and the invasion of privacy. His manners, like his dress, are informal, and informality characterizes the relations of superiors and subordinates in the various hierarchies of education, business, the professions, and even the Army. Compared with the Scotch or the Swedish working-man, he takes little pride in a finished job, and does not prize craftsmanship. His roads and his railway roadbeds needed to be relaid every few years. Neither his houses, nor his furniture, nor his automobiles are made primarily to last.

The American pays dearly for the luxury of carelessness. He pays in wasted resources of land and of forest, in heavy costs of governmental administration, in excessive bills for continuous repair and replacement of his most elementary requirements. On any system of accounting, it costs more to run the machinery of a city whose inhabitants are contemptuous of law than that of one where the whole population is a

19

cooperative law-enforcement agency; more to run a library whose patrons steal, mislay, or deface books than one in which books are respected; more to maintain public parks and monuments ravaged by visitors than those which are respected. Whatever else may be said of such disparate things as American state and local government, the armed services, the radio, the moving pictures, and advertising, it can be said that they are the most expensive in the world. Nor is the cost of carelessness economic only: the cost in time and energy is heavy.

Yet wastefulness and carelessness are not absolutes; they are characteristics rooted in and modified by other qualities. Good-nature accounts for generosity as well as for extravagance; individualism encourages independence as well as wastefulness; hostility to discipline contributes to political liberty as well as to lawlessness. It is sobering to remember that the Germans were good workmen and good craftsmen, careful of the proprieties, respectful of rank and position, orderly, law-abiding, disciplined, and prudent.

IV

The American tradition was of necessity one of tolerance. The late-eighteenth-century American knew that his country had been founded in dissent and born of Revolution, and his nineteenth-century successors did not forget this, for nonconformity and dissent were encouraged by subsequent historical experience. State and federal constitutions guaranteed free speech, press, and worship; successive frontiers shattered traditions and encouraged experimentation; the transcendental and the pragmatic philosophies, for all their differences, exalted individualism; a decentralized political system invited a wide latitude in political experiments; a heterogeneous population required toleration of social differences; the habit of voluntary association in a thousand organizations provided the most varied outlets for individual energies and interests. Had the nineteenth-century American wished to be a traditionalist, he would have found it difficult to know what tradition to honor, unless it was indeed the tradition of toleration and of individualism.

The decline of the inventive and experimental spirit in the twentieth century was accompanied by a growing impatience with nonconformity and a growing circumscription of the arena of individual activity. By mid-century the average American was inclined to think of his country as a finished product, its character fixed and its standards formed, and to insist upon conformity and upon outward manifestations of unity. World War I encouraged this attitude; World War II crystallized it; with the inauguration of the cold war against Russia, it received sanction from state and federal governments. The drift towards conformity revealed itself in many ways: in the standardization created by moving pictures, radio, advertisements, schools, patriotic and fraternal organizations; in the popularity of guides to good conduct, business success, friendship, home making, love and marriage; in the censorship of books, plays, and motion pictures; in the emphasis upon gestures and ceremonies of loyalty; in the mounting hostility to criticism, even from such agencies as political parties and universities, whose professional function was that of the critic.

Intolerance was no new phenomenon in American history, but not since the days of the Federalists in New England—not even in the ante-bellum South—had it been as indiscriminate as it became in the nineteen-forties. It found expression, then, in the antics of state and federal committees on un-American activities and in the requirement of loyalty oaths from groups whose record of loyalty was unimpeachable. It manifested itself in legislative purges of schools and universities, and in the bold intrusion of churches into the realm of politics. It assumed blatant character in anti-Semitism, in the nullification of constitutional guarantees of civil rights to Negroes, and in the emergence of doctrines of racism that had been thought peculiar to the Nazis. In the economic arena, it took the form of hostility to "alien" doctrines by those who subscribed to laissez-faire, Manchester liberalism, and social Darwinism, under the curious misapprehension that these were native. With the Alien Registration Act of 1940, the doctrine of guilt by association entered American law, and various executive and Congressional loyalty tests extended that doctrine to extreme lengths: at mid-century the credentials of a United States Senator, long distinguished in academic life, were openly challenged in Congress on the ground that he had associated himself with an organization designed to advance human welfare in the South. Equally unprecedented, and equally pernicious, was the doctrine of guilt by intention, which likewise made its way into American law in these years. A people who had traditionally cherished liberty no less than order, and who had distinguished themselves as champions of freedom throughout the world, began to whittle away the constitutional guarantees of free speech, free press, and free assembly. Since the conquest of Greece by Rome, history had frequently recorded instances where the vanquished imposed their ideas upon the victors; would history record that American democracy, at the moment of its greatest triumph, had yielded to the racial ideas of the Nazis, the thought-control techniques of the Japanese, the police-state psychology of the Russians?

Less ominous, but not without significance, and certainly not without interest, is the apparent growth of class-consciousness in twentieth-century America, especially during the second quarter of the century. By Old World standards, nineteenth-century America, except in the South, had been largely class-less. Such class distinctions as obtained were based on mixed considerations, partly economic and partly social, associated with race, family, and education as well as with wealth. But in those years classes merged almost imperceptibly into each other and, for whites, especially if native born, the transition from one class to another was natural—a matter of years rather than of generations. After the Civil War, large scale immigration, internal migration, the rise of cities, the weakening of the planter class in the South, and the emergence of the new rich in the North, all contributed to a new blurring of class lines.

Although large-scale immigration ceased after the outbreak of World War I, and though a new planter-class arose on the ruins of the old, these influences persisted into the twentieth century, and several, like internal migration and urban growth, were even sharpened. By mid-century it was proper to say that except for Negroes, Mexicans, the foreign-born of southern and eastern Europe, and possibly the share-croppers of the South—a sizeable group to be sure—most Americans belonged to the middle class. Certainly few admitted that they were of a lower class, and just as few professed to belong to an upper; the distinction which Americans themselves made was between upper and lower middle.

Yet along with this general levelling of classes came an

emergence of class consciousness at once ostentatious and pervasive, and artificial. It appears in the growing importance of the Social Register, and of society pages in newspapers, in a new and flourishing interest in genealogy and in filiopietistic organizations like the Colonial Dames and the Sons of the American Revolution, in the mounting influence and popularity of private schools, in the spread of Old World practices like tipping, in the hierarchy of country clubs, and in the preference for French on menus and in school curricula. It appears most blatantly in advertising, with its deliberate appeal to snobbery. Yet it is worth noting that advertisers, who have the largest stake in class consciousness, find it worth while to publicize not only the preferences of the first families of Boston and Philadelphia, but of the stars of the movies and the radio, of the ball park and the gridiron, who constitute the most widely-acknowledged American aristocracy.

Clearly these outward manifestations of class consciousness are an effort to proclaim publicly what no longer proclaims itself. In Britain, for example, social position is relatively fixed, and acknowledged, by such unmistakable indications as titles, or a public-school accent, or professional status: no one can doubt the social credentials of a Lord, or a barrister, or a graduate of Eton College. But in the United States, the distinction between classes had always been narrow and uncertain. Church affiliation had been free from class connotations, accent had foregone its ancient prerogative, there was no special social merit in any profession—not even in the clerical—and almost the only method of distinguishing social position had been through manifestations of what Thorstein Veblen called conspicuous wealth and conspicuous waste. But while the gap between the rich and the poor widened in the twentieth century, the gap between what the rich and the poor could buy with their money has narrowed steadily, until by mid-century it has all but disappeared. Material display is no longer an indication of social status. With the difficulty of getting and keeping help, big houses have been abandoned, and—from the outside—almost all flats look alike. The difference between cheap and expensive cars, too, are imperceptible, as Fords and Cadillacs try to look alike. Every shop-girl can afford ready-made clothes that are good copies of Worth or Paquin, nylon stockings, and smart accessories, and bankers and clerks dress so nearly alike as to suggest a business uniform. The poor as well as the rich can afford vacations in Florida; the poor as well as, or more often than, the rich drive to work in their own cars. All buy the same canned goods or frozen vegetables or bottled drinks, the same imitation Sheraton or Hepplewhite furniture, the same radio and television sets. Almost all read the same newspapers and magazines, see the same movies and listen to the same radio programs. Rich and poor enjoy essentially the same social services, and amenities—colleges, hospitals, libraries, and entertainment.

It is against this background of social and economic levelling that we must reflect the calculated efforts to revive or to create social distinctions. As such distinctions no longer speak for themselves in accent, education, dress, food, or luxuries, they have to be asserted in more ostentatious ways. For clearly no calculated efforts to preserve social or class distinctions can succeed. None can resist, in the long run, the cumulative effect of intermarriage among people of different backgrounds, internal migration, a fluid economy, high income-taxes, and the levelling influence of the public school, the athletic field, and military training. What is significant, then, is not that social and class distinctions are invoked and applied, but that so many people yearn for them and that so many businesses have a stake in them. Just as two generations earlier the rise of the "local color" school in literature was a confession of the passing of genuine provincialism, so in the mid-twentieth century the energetic celebration of class distinctions is an expression of wishful thinking and of nostalgia rather than a description of reality.

V

Notwithstanding political and social intolerance, the American remains, as in the past, democratic and equalitarian. Both democracy and equality had roots in his philosophy but both, like toleration, were largely the product of experience. Nothing in that experience suggested that democracy worked less effectively than other forms of government, or that an equalitarian society was less wholesome than one that maintained class distinctions and, if the American looked to his own history rather than abroad, the experience of the ante-bellum South suggested the opposite conclusion. After the last quarter of the nineteenth century, American economy and society experienced profound changes, but those changes were mostly quantitative rather than qualitative, and there was no general inclination to reconsider either the philosophy or the practice of democracy. In so far as the mid-twentieth-century American subscribes to a social or political philosophy, that philosophy remains Jeffersonian.

Yet there are serious qualifications on his democracy, qualifications of which he is ignorant or to which he is indifferent. His political system is more democratic than its framers intended, but less than he imagines. The written constitution, the separation of powers, the federal system, and judicial review, are all designed to restrain the excesses of democracy, and all function according to design. The American achieves majority rule, but with greater mechanical difficulty than the peoples in other English-speaking countries. He believes in universal suffrage, but millions of his fellow-citizens are debarred from voting, and only half of those entitled to vote trouble to do so, even at Presidential elections.

Democracy is most effective in the non-political realm, and especially in the innumerable voluntary organizations which the American maintains. Nowhere else, except in Britain, do men and women associate so readily or so energetically for common purposes. Where, in most countries, the state establishes colleges or libraries, builds hospitals or playgrounds, reforms the law or the civil service, in America it is, more often than not, private organizations that take on these activities and responsibilities. A thousand organizations enlist the energies and loyalties of men: associations of manufacturers and bankers, of workers and farmers, of scholars and scientists, of parents and teachers, associations of vegetarians and stamp collectors, fishermen and horseshoe pitchers, associations for the perpetuation of circus street-parades and for the reform of the calendar—the list could almost be extended interminably. It is through these organizations that the average American makes his interest, and in some cases his will, known; it is through them that he learns to organize, participate, and lead; these, rather than the party headquarters or the much advertised town-meeting, are the instruments which train him in the business of self-government.

Voluntary associations are not only democratic, they are,

with some notorious exceptions, equalitarian. Most of them are open to all who are interested or qualified by experience, and leadership generally goes to the most active and most generous. In the eighteen-thirties, Alexis de Tocqueville concluded that equality was the most pervasive and effective single factor in American society, and the passing of more than a century has not modified this conclusion. The sense of equality permeates American society: language and literature, education and religion, entertainment and sports, all testify to its effectiveness. Equality is accepted, as a matter of course, even where it is not observed. Southerners who "keep the Negro in his place," northerners who tremble at the prospect of inundation by foreigners or Jews, subscribe sincerely enough to the philosophy of equality. What seems palpable insincerity to the outsider passes unobserved by the American or, on occasion, is considered only an embarrassing exception to the rule. It will be admitted that the exceptions are numerous and flagrant, but it is important to remember that no respectable groups suggest changing the rule.

Both democracy and equality presuppose respect for the individual, and individualism flourishes best in a democratic order. Traditionally the American is an individualist, impatient of restrictions on his conduct or his personality. He is anti-authoritarian, dislikes rules, regulations, formalities, and precedents, prefers to do things his own way, and wants to be let alone. His own experience has given him little reason to distrust either government or the military, but distrust of both is deeply engrained. Children are not ordinarily exposed to discipline either in their homes or in their schools, and there is less emphasis on discipline in the American army than in most others.

Yet individualism, so marked in the nineteenth century, is less pronounced in the twentieth. Illustrations come readily to mind. The reform movement of the eighteen-thirties and forties rested on a highly individualistic philosophy and sought private salvation; that of a century later was social and governmental. Pragmatism as formulated by William James was individualistic, almost eccentric; the pragmatism of John Dewey is primarily social. The individual editors of an earlier day—Greeley and Dana for example—have given way to large impersonal organizations, and for most newspapers, press-services have supplanted reporters. The emphasis in scholarship and science is on cooperative enterprises; so complex is modern science and technology that few individuals are able to master any one part of it. American books are directed less to individual or special tastes than to the mass market; with a population three times that of Britain, American publishers bring out fewer titles, except for reprints, and even here British publishers show more respect for individual tastes. Although the census lists over two hundred religious demoninations, actually over three-fourths of all church members belong to the largest five, and the larger churches are growing steadily at the expense of the smaller.

The causes for the apparent decline of individualism are complex. It is in part the result of the passing of the frontier, and of a rural society, for urban life offers less scope to the individual character. It is in part the product of universal public education, of standardization, and of the growing emphasis on social and intellectual conformity. It is in part the consequence of the triumph of that very principle of equality which originally encouraged individualism, for individualism flourishes most luxuriantly in an aristocratic society like that in the Old South where the requirements of conformity were more limited and eccentricity more easily indulged.

It is in the realm of economics that individualism is most aggressively asserted—and most effectively limited. President Hoover used the term "rugged individualism" to describe private enterprise, and soon private enterprise became identical with "the American way of life." But in fact, as the inexorable statistics of corporation growth reveal, American economy has become less individualistic with every passing year, and private enterprise less private. What is interesting, however, is not so much the gap between reality and ideal, as the almost religious fervor with which many Americans celebrate the ideal. It is as if the American, who no longer indulges himself freely in the individualistic expression of religion, or social reform, or culture, or even politics, as he did in the nineteenth century, finds in the economic realm the last refuge of an individualism which he still associates with the heroic period of his history.

Yet if in consequence of these political, economic, and psychological influences, the scope for the expression of individualism has been circumscribed, the fundamental philosophy, which regards each human being as an end in himself rather than merely as a means to an end, is unimpaired, and reappears at every great crisis of American history.

VI

It would be folly to suggest that what we have described is the American character. All we can say is that the qualities which we have delineated seem to be some of the more pronounced traits of the American of the mid-twentieth century as they appear to one observer. No other observer would draw quite the same portrait; many would draw one altogether different. Yet some features, it is safe to say, even some apparently incongruous ones, would probably be common to all portraits. No analysis of the American character could omit optimism, amiability, energy, self-confidence, enterprise, materialism, idealism, practicality, sentimentality, progressivism, conservatism, inventiveness, carelessness, intolerance, equalitarianism, individualism. These characteristics are not, in themselves, profoundly different from the characteristics of some other peoples—the English or the Norwegian, for example. It is not so much the particular elements as the juxtaposition of all the elements that gives them peculiar interest. Nor is it realistic to lose sight of the obvious fact that it is the combination of these qualities with immense power that gives them significance.

For, in large measure, the destinies of mankind are, for the moment, committed to this people. Not ambitious for power, they have achieved power. Not eager for responsibility, they have been unable to escape responsibility. Inclined to parochialism, they have been thrust into world leadership. Fundamentally peaceable, they have been led by circumstances to become the arsenal of the western world. Only the future will reveal whether they will find, in their heritage, their history, and their character the resources to quicken their minds, embolden their spirits, fire their imagination, lift up their hearts, and fit them for their duties and their destiny.

"To secure the blessings of liberty to ourselves and our posterity" was advanced by the founding fathers as one of the six reasons for devising the American Constitution. The founders were literal and not rhetorical in this declaration, for the entire framework of the government they designed was so built as to guard and preserve freedom.

In its more than one hundred and sixty years of life the American nation has changed radically. The country that in 1787 was one of land-holding farmers with a sprinkling of shopkeepers is now one of corporations, industries and mighty labor unions; of corn, cotton, tobacco and fruit-growers. The government itself is in business and controls and promotes —as well as prosecutes—business. Lobbyists swarm over the Capitol and propagandists push their causes by pamphlets, motion picture, the press and the radio.

In this America of bigness and almost frantic activity, one must study anew the place and functions of freedom. In our larger and more complex society we still pay tribute to the "blessings of liberty."

Is our praise a mere nostalgic gesture, or is freedom in America today a living and working force which pays greater dividends than ever before?

Alan Barth

AMERICAN FREEDOM: A METHOD

Freedom has worked well for the American people. Under its stimulation and release, a continent has been opened and exploited; the greatest human migration in history has been encompassed; a stable political order has been developed in which men have managed to live together in a high degree of harmony and to produce for their own enjoyment an extraordinary volume of goods and services. Lately, moreover, the American pattern of freedom has given fresh proof of its vitality in surviving two major shocks. In the thirties, it weathered and overcame economic disaster born in part, it must be said, of its own excesses. In the forties, it won a mortal contest against a totalitarian system which denied all the values of freedom.

It has been the utility of freedom on the basis of such pragmatic tests which has made it at once the dominant motif and the most pervasive symbol of the American political structure. Whether or not freedom, in the sense of "the rights of man," is "natural"—that is to say, ordained by God—as political philosophers of the seventeenth and eighteenth centuries believed, it is useful. And it is on this utilitarian ground that it has found its validation. It has been valued by Americans, idealistically, as an end in itself; but even more, pragmatically, as a means to the attainment of other more material ends: it has proved itself as a tool and a technique.

Freedom in this sense concerns the relationship of the individual to the State—a relationship which is never static and which in the United States has evolved in conformity with emergent needs. The American premise respecting this relationship is that the final end of the State is to make men free to realize their own potentialities and that minimal governmental interference is most hospitable to this end.

There are two distinct strands in the American pattern of freedom. Individualism—relatively unfettered initiative and enterprise—has been its warp; tolerance has been its woof— tolerance of heterodoxy, and even heresy, in religious belief, in political theory, in social ideals.

The tradition of individualism may be said to embrace freedom of action, necessarily conditional and qualified, since one man's freedom may be another man's fetters. The tradition of tolerance embraces the more subtle area of freedom of the mind and is much more nearly an absolute, since the free formulation and expression of ideas by every individual inflicts injury on none and is indispensable to the freedom of all. It will be useful to examine these twin strands separately in terms of their adaptability to the real conditions of contemporary life and of their significance respecting the relationship of the individual to the State.

I

The years of the modern have ushered in dramatic changes in the social environment of the American people. We, and the world of which we are a part, have become irremediably integrated. The integration, bringing individuals into intimate relations with one another, has correspondingly enlarged the role of government in harmonizing these relations and in giving effect to collective purposes. The tradition of individualism has had to undergo severe modification in the process.

The government of the United States which in the administrations of Washington, Adams and Jefferson, required the services of slightly more than one thousand civilian employees today has slightly more than two million on its payroll. It is not uncommonly said that the size of the contemporary bureaucracy could profitably be reduced. But those who say this are rarely specific as to where the reductions should be made and, generally speaking, would be horrified at proposals to eliminate existing government services. Anyone proposing that the Department of Agriculture could dispense with, say, its Bureau of Entomology and Plant Quarantine, would find that a great many of his fellow-citizens love it and rely upon it. The Commerce Department's Coast and Geodetic Survey, the Interior Department's Fish and Wildlife Service, the Treasury Department's Bureau of Narcotics, the Labor Department's Bureau of Veterans' Re-employment Rights, all perform services which a substantial number of Americans consider important. The Hoover Commission has recently recommended a considerable rearrangement of the Federal Government's multitudinous agencies but it has not intimated that the scope and variety of their services can be significantly curtailed.

It is a truism that the government is engaged today in activities never dreamed of in the philosophy of Thomas Jefferson and most of his contemporaries. What was instituted as a government of jealously limited powers, having only a remote relation to the individual, has come to have some of the aspects of a Leviathan, trenching in myriad intimate ways upon individual action.

The federal government builds houses and subsidizes schools, electrifies farms and guarantees the price of farm products, insures citizens against the hazards of unemployment and old age, underwrites banks and regulates stock exchanges, fixes maximum hours and minimum wages for labor, produces and distributes electric power. It exercises an absolute monopoly over what may be a revolutionary new source of power through its exclusive ownership of all fissionable materials and its authority to control all the means of producing atomic energy. It is undertaking at present to finance the reconstruction and stabilize the economies of a dozen European countries. And it is scarcely to be doubted that most Americans want these services to be performed.

When the government renders services, it also imposes restraints of a sort on individual initiative and enterprise. But it would be a doctrinaire view indeed that could contend that such restraints necessarily constitute a loss of liberty. There was something more than prophetic in Walt Whitman's vision of

> Freedom, completely arm'd and victorious and very haughty,
>   with Law on one side and Peace on the other,
> A stupendous trio . . .

The image expresses an acute insight into political science. The trio is indivisible, freedom without both law and peace (which is to say, order) being no more than anarchy. John Locke said about all there is to say on this subject some three centuries ago:

For law, in its true notion, is not so much the limitation as the direction of a free and intelligent agent to his proper interest, and prescribes no farther than is for the general good of those under that law. Could they be happier without it, the law, as a useless thing, would of itself vanish; and that ill deserves the name of confinement which hedges us in only from bogs and precipices. For liberty is to be free from restraint and violence from others, which cannot be where there is no law; and is not, as we are told, "a liberty for every man to do what he lists." For who could be free, when every other man's humour might domineer over him?

In a crowded community, men's humors are rather more likely to seem domineering to their neighbors than where abundance of space permits relative isolation. Thus in cities, if men are to be free to move at all, they must move in accordance with the dictates of the traffic cop standing on the corner.

Americans have been slow to look upon the traffic cop, or any other agent of the authority they have vested in government by law, as a friend of freedom. As Frederick Jackson Turner observed, "To the pioneer, government was an evil." The conditions of the frontier and the existence of free land made liberty seem synonymous with individual independence; the men who expanded the frontier asked only that they be let alone in their conquest, and spoliation, of the wilderness. They enforced squatter rights and made their own law—even to lynch law. Their individualism, for all its enrichment of the democratic tradition in America, was headstrong, selfish, reckless. Carried forward by the descendants who capitalized their conquests and came into possession of vast wealth and power, this rugged individualism served as a pretext for wielding despotic private control over the economic life of a people to whom free land was no longer available. The democracy born of this individualism had to turn increasingly to the government for its preservation.

No doubt there was a certain crude utility to haphazard distribution of the public lands through pre-emption and graduation laws, bounties to war veterans, extravagant land grants to railroads, and all the other invitations to outrageous land speculation, when the interest of the nation lay in the speedy settlement of the West. But with the West settled, the interest of the nation lies in afforestation, in soil conservation, in land reclamation, in rehabilitation of the rural slums created by the profligacy of the past. These can be accomplished only through government aid and intelligent land-use planning. We have embarked on such a program belatedly enough, and shall have to continue with it far into the future.

Equally, the industrialization of America made imperative the checking of irresponsible private power by public authority. When production was relatively atomized and when transition from the status of employee to the status of employer seemed feasible to any persevering aspirant, the doctrine of "Every Man in His Humour" had validity enough. But a man's humor can become dangerously domineering when it shapes the fortunes of a hundred thousand employees and affects a national economy delicately balanced and intricately interdependent.

Moreover, so far as millions of wage-earning Americans are concerned, there is not much room for the expression of individualism in the dehumanizing techniques of modern manufacturing. Men engaged in mass production have become scarcely distinguishable from machines. Consider, for example, this description of his job by a Ford Motor Company

worker who was on strike in 1949 and who was quoted as
follows in the *Boston Sunday Herald* of May 8:

> My job is to put fenders on the new cars coming down the assembly
> line. I stand in one place, and 346 times a day, if the line is running
> right, I put a fender on a new car. That's all I do—just fenders.
> Other fellows on the line put on wheels, hub caps, bumpers, put the
> motors in the cars, adjust the steering wheels. That's all they do.
> They just stand, like me, in one place, and the man with the steering
> wheel, why, all he does in a day is adjust 346 steering wheels. . . .
> Now, shooting off the main assembly line are sub-assembly lines that
> deliver the parts of the car to the right spot at the right time, so that
> the body men have to be sure that they have 346 fenders delivered
> to me in exactly the right order to match the cars coming down the
> final assembly when they reach me. So, we say the speed is 346.
> That's fine. Everybody is happy. Nothing goes wrong along the line,
> and at the end of the day, Mr. Ford has 346 cars and I have eight
> hours pay. But suppose something breaks down along the line and
> we are shut down for 40 minutes. That's where the rub comes in. We
> say that the speed should continue at the rate of 346 a day. But the
> company says it has the right to speed up the line so that as much of
> the lost production can be recaptured the same day as possible. So
> maybe for a couple of hours I'm putting on 380 fenders a day. See! It
> wasn't our fault the line had to be shut down for 40 minutes. So
> why does the company have the right to penalize me for it?

In addition to intervention for the peaceful settlement of
such conflicts, there are other areas as well in which governmental action is inescapable—the harnessing of rivers, the
encouragement of scientific research, the bolstering of the
public schools, the provision of hospital and medical care. The
federal government will act in these areas because they entail
problems beyond the capabilities of individual initiative, even

of concerted local initiative—continued neglect of which will prove altogether too costly to the community.

For a long, long time, to be sure, the Supreme Court, vested here as in virtually no other country with the power of judicial review of the constitutionality of legislative acts, interpreted the Constitution of the United States as rendering the federal government powerless to deal with many of these national problems. But the contemporary Court has wrought a revolution by a more realistic construction of interstate commerce. The effect of what it has done has been, in point of fact, nothing more than a reversion to John Marshall's view that Congress is empowered under the commerce clause of the Constitution to do almost anything that genuinely needs to be done for the maintenance of the national economy.

The contemporary Court seems to be accomplishing a revolution no less significant in the realm of civil liberties and civil rights. By interpreting the Due Process clause of the 14th Amendment as requiring the states to observe the guarantees of the 1st Amendment, it has put the federal government in the position, somewhat ironically, of championing and defending those very "natural rights," against federal violation of which the Constitution was originally designed to guard. The Court has also sanctioned recently some federal efforts to protect Negroes in the South from violence, intimidation and denial of political rights by state officials. Thus, the Constitution, to use Mr. Justice Jackson's illuminating metaphor, intended initially to serve as a shield for the protection of individual liberties against national encroachment, is now being construed as a sword arming the federal government for affirmative action to safeguard the liberties of Americans from violation by the states and perhaps even by their fellow-citizens. "We cannot be content," said President Truman in an address at the Lincoln Memorial in 1947, "with a civil liberties program which emphasizes only the need of protection against the possibility of tyranny by the Government. . . . The extension of civil rights today means not protection of the people against the Government, but protection of the people by the Government."

Mr. Truman's view is not a novel one. It was advanced explicitly nearly three-quarters of a century ago by Mr. Justice Harlan and was implicit in much that was said and thought long before him. But its enunciation by a President of the United States marks a dramatic step in the transformed relationship of the individual to the state made logical by changed social conditions.

This transformation will not be undone by those who deplore it, looking nostalgically back to an irrecoverable past, even though they use the symbol of liberty and the shibboleth of States' Rights to plead for its undoing. Men who have experienced an improvement in the conditions of life as a direct result of governmental action are not prone to be dismayed at hearing such action stigmatized as regimentation or paternalism. Men who have found new dignity through governmental protection of their rights and interests will not be disposed to see in this protection any substantial threat to their freedom.

Big government, powerful government, has been made a necessity by the complexity of the domestic economy and by the emergence of the United States as a great international power. There will be ample room and urgent need under such government for a high degree of individualism—for exercise of the resourcefulness, energy, and initiative which have been the great contributions of the individualist tradition to American democracy. But there will not be room for the kind of individual conduct which closes the door of opportunity in the faces of other men—which, in the name of freedom for a few, denies freedom to the many. The preservation of freedom in the future will not be found, in any case, in diminution of the powers of government. It will be found in democratic control of the uses to which these powers are put.

II

Democratic control is indisputably the key premise of the American society, no matter with what sophistry it may be argued nowadays that because the founders designated the country a republic they did not intend it to be a democracy. These founders took as self-evident what John Locke had said a century before and what Thomas Jefferson restated as "the common sense of the subject" among men of his own time— that governments are voluntarily instituted among men in order to secure certain "natural rights" and that they derive their just powers from the consent of the governed.

Of course, all governmental powers, just and unjust alike, are derived from the consent of the governed. But consent can be coerced, as it has been in authoritarian states ancient and modern. It can be coerced by terror and the direct application of military force, or somewhat more subtly by suppression of speech and control of the instruments of communication. The fashion in present-day dictatorships is the mastery of men's minds through manipulation of all the information reaching them.

Diversity of opinion is the distinguishing characteristic of a free society. Where it exists and is afforded uninhibited expression, popular consent, even when bemused or mistaken, may reasonably be considered voluntary; and the powers of government to which such consent is accorded may fairly be termed "just powers." The business of politics in a free society becomes, then, the mobilization of consent.

Ambrose Bierce once defined politics as "the strife of interests masquerading as a contest of principles." The varied and conflicting interests of the American public—which make of it a congeries of publics—find expression through a multitude of voluntary associations, some of them committed to the advancement of particularistic and no doubt selfish purposes, some of them dedicated to broad policies which their members believe conducive to the general welfare. In either case, they tend to make their appeals on grounds of principle. Thus, those who oppose, as well as those who seek, grade-labeling, or governmental distribution of public power, or the 160-acre limitation of the Reclamation Laws, or rent ceilings, or public housing, are rarely so crude as to profess any sordid economic motivation; their stand is always in the name of some lofty abstraction, such as free enterprise or States' Rights. Many of the same people may at the very time belong to organizations working assiduously and quite selflessly for promotion of the nation's health or education, for aid to Europe, for world government, for disarmament or for a more powerful army, navy, and air force.

Such groups are the real levers by which public opinion is moved. Their fulcrums are the newspapers, the radio, the films, the pulpits, the public meetings of the country. There is a consistency, a coherence, a sense of direction within these voluntary associations which is not to be found in the major American political parties. For the major parties are loose agglomerations, successful in competition with each other to

45

the extent that they nurture the hopes and enlist the support of a preponderance of the special interest groups. Their aim is universality; they strive to be all things to all men. For this reason, their principles are necessarily generalized and stated with as much ambiguity as expediency seems to permit. Their interest, as Odegard and Helms have pointed out in *American Politics,* is not in policies but in jobs. They conduct election campaigns, to be sure, with great gusto, vulgarity, personal abuse and idealistic appeal; and no doubt a great many voters cleave to them on grounds of loyalty and tradition. But in the mobilization of consent they constitute more the outward form than the inward reality of a process dominated by considerations of group interest. The point was well illustrated in the 1948 presidential election where the decision turned less upon the votes of men and women as Republicans or Democrats than upon their votes as farmers, industrial workers, Negroes or members of other minority elements in the population.

In attempting to put their policies into effect in the form of legislation, the interest groups work with, and upon, the members of legislatures through agents known opprobriously as lobbyists. They function under one of the most fundamental of all constitutional guarantees—the right to petition. And although very often they abuse this right, they fulfill a vital role in the legislative process, representing legitimate competing claims of the American people in ways that valuably supplement elected representation on a geographical basis.

The effectuation of national policy confronts peculiar difficulties in the United States because of the precautions taken by the authors of the Constitution to prevent any despotic exercise of power. These authors not only limited the government's jurisdiction, absolutely barring it from certain specified areas, but they also divided the powers of government in order to frustrate tyrannical action by any of its branches. Sometimes the frustration produces sheer stalemate.

The Constitution says that "all legislative powers herein granted shall be vested in a Congress of the United States." But it grants to the President a limited veto power and a joint responsibility with the Senate in the making of treaties and the appointment of officials; it authorizes him to recommend to the Congress "such measures as he shall judge necessary and expedient" and it enjoins him both to "preserve, protect, and defend the Constitution of the United States" and to "take care that the laws be faithfully executed."

From the early days of the republic, presidents and congresses have been at odds, each jealous of the other's powers and prerogatives. Strong presidents have always sought to lead Congress; strong congressional leaders have always sought to confine the President to mere administration of their acts. The authority of the President has been powerfully bolstered by his position as the one national official (along with the Vice-President) who can claim the entire nation as his constituency, and in the twentieth century, executive leadership has been promoted by the expanding role of government in relation to the people.

Theodore Roosevelt made affirmative leadership a candid function of the Presidency, using his relationship to the whole people as a means of bludgeoning Congress into acceptance of his views. "The White House," he said, "is a bully pulpit." Aided by the growth of the press as a mass medium, he used newspapers effectively both to evoke popular sympathy and to make the expression of it audible on Capitol Hill. Woodrow

Wilson conceived of his relationship to Congress more or less as that of a British Prime Minister to Parliament. It was in his administration that the practice began of having legislation openly written in the executive departments and submitted to Congress for enactment. The practice was perfected by Franklin Roosevelt, who declared at the very outset of his first term: "The presidency is not merely an administrative office. That is the least of it. It is pre-eminently a place of moral leadership. . . . Without leadership alert and sensitive to change, we are bogged up or lose our way."

There are important considerations of logic and common sense to support presidential guidance of legislation. The President presumably has in mind a rounded program of action for his administration. In foreign and domestic affairs alike, he must seek the cooperation of Congress, and, considering the hydraheaded character of that creature, cooperation must take the form of initiative on his part. Party responsibility is certainly not today one of the attributes of the American political system; the major parties, as has been previously suggested, strive so much for catholicity as to be incapable of national coherence. Only the President can assert any discipline over the members of his party; and the only disciplinary weapons at his command are patronage or the use of his prestige to appeal directly to the people.

To call a President a dictator because he uses these weapons to carry to fulfillment the pledges he made while campaigning for office is to equate freedom with political irresponsibility. A President can be indifferent to the conduct of Congress only if he is devoid alike of conviction and of conscience. So long as Congress remains free to reject or modify laws recommended to it by the executive, and, in addition, to initiate legislation within itself, the constitutional balance of power would seem to be unimpaired by forceful presidential leadership.

Yet such are our political traditions that every presidential prodding of Congress evokes cries, at least in the press, of despotism and dictatorship. President Truman in the spring of 1949 was excoriated as a veritable Caligula for indicating that he would withhold patronage from those members of his party who continued to thwart redemption of the campaign promises by which his recent election was obtained. Woodrow Wilson was roundly scored for his appeal to the people in 1918 to give him a Democratic Congress which would support his views in respect of the League of Nations. Franklin D. Roosevelt was even more vehemently denounced for his attempt in 1938 to purge the Congress of Democrats acting in direct opposition to his leadership. These "chiefs of state" could scarcely have acted otherwise in the face of their own convictions as to what was right.

Mr. Roosevelt made a classic, if quixotic, statement of the moral imperatives involved when he went to Barnesville, Georgia, on August 11, 1938, and asked the people of that state to replace Senator Walter George, who was on the platform beside him:

Let me make it clear that he is, and I hope always will be, my personal friend. He is beyond question, beyond any possible question, a gentleman and a scholar; but there are other gentlemen in the Senate and in the House for whom I have a real affectionate regard, but with whom I differ heartily and sincerely on the principles and policies of how the Government of the United States ought to be run. . . . To carry out my responsibility as President, it is clear that if there is to be success in our Government there ought to be coopera-

tion between members of my own party and myself—cooperation, in
other words, within the majority party, between one branch of
Government, the Legislative Branch, and the head of the other
branch, the Executive. That is one of the essentials of a party form
of government. It has been going on in this country for nearly a century and a half. The test is not measured, in the case of an individual,
by his every vote on every bill—of course not. The test lies rather in
the answer to two questions: first, has the record of the candidate
shown, while differing perhaps in details, a constant active fighting
attitude in favor of the broad objectives of the party and of the
Government as they are constituted today; and, secondly, does the
candidate really, in his heart, deep down in his heart, believe in
those objectives? I regret that in the case of my friend, Senator
George, I cannot answer either of these questions in the affirmative.

This was scarcely the language of dictatorship. It was a
moderate, candid appeal to the rationality of the voters—
without rancor, without personal abuse. It reflected on the
President's part nothing but a profound sense of the urgency
and importance of the program he had in view. But the people
of Georgia, at least those permitted under its poll tax requirements to vote, resented this "outside interference" and sent
Senator George back to Congress to obstruct the President
whom they had previously sent back to the White House.

If it is a part of the President's function to lead Congress,
it is even more an obligation of his office to give a sense of
direction—which is to say, of leadership—to the people themselves. The image of the nation as "a ship of state" is an apt
one. The ship cannot sail unpiloted. The job of piloting belongs
properly to the President. Nothing is more necessary to national morale and to the sense of unity indispensable to
national security than general recognition of a firm hand at
the helm. One of Mr. Roosevelt's great services to his country

certainly was the sense he supplied in the frightening days of 1933 that he had a course charted and knew how to steer it.

Indeed, one of Mr. Roosevelt's greatest qualities was his extraordinary understanding of the function of leadership in a free society. Stated in its simplest terms, this function entails creation of a public opinion sympathetic to the course which the leader believes the country ought to pursue. It involves a tremendous educative task, an exposition of policies in terms meaningful to the people and evocative of their support. A public of one hundred and fifty millions cannot formulate policies or even make clear its own aspirations; it can only accept or reject policies formulated by those to whom it has entrusted leadership.

There should be no need to distinguish this role of leadership in a free society from the *fuehrerprinzip* in a totalitarian state. The essence of the *fuehrerprinzip* is the infallibility of the leader. The essence of democratic leadership is persuasion on the basis of reason. The vital consideration is that the leader remain responsible to the people and replaceable by them.

It is, of course, equally a *sine qua non* of a free society that leadership in opposition to the President or his party be accorded the fullest opportunity to make its own appeal to the reason of the people. This presupposes a free press—free in the sense of having, so far as its content is concerned, absolute immunity from government control. The men who insisted upon the addition of a Bill of Rights to the original Constitution conceived of the press as one of the vital elements in the system of checks and balances they erected to keep government from becoming tyrannical. So far from sanctioning censorship of the press by the government, they affirmatively sought censorship of government by the press. This gave the

51

press as an institution, it is true, a peculiarly privileged position—one that invites the irresponsibility of which it is so
often guilty. Perhaps this irresponsibility is the inescapable
price which must be paid for the indispensable function it
performs.

The democratic process is a process in which irresponsibility
cannot be outlawed so long as it is confined to expression; in
which a Babel of voices, some of them expressing nonsense,
must be tolerated; in which the only antidote for poisonous
ideas is healthy ones; in which the sifting of truth from false-
hood, of wisdom from folly, must be left to the good sense of
the people. It is not an infallible process. But it is the only
process by which the powers of government can be derived
from the voluntary consent of the governed.

III

The crosscurrents of the American system, the pushing and
pulling, the division of authority, the reliance on persuasion
rather than coercion of consent, the denial of plenary power
even to the majority, all tend to make it seem at times cum-
brous, lethargic—even inefficient. It may be all these; but it
works. And when one has looked critically at some of the
Utopian formulas for government, or observed the actual
operation of other governmental systems, he may be forgiven
if he concludes that the American system, for all its defects, is
at least peculiarly adapted to the geographical extent, the
sectional variations, and the economic circumstances of the
American people.

A casual critic might complain with some logic that in the
long period of human gestation and the painful hazards of
childbirth, nature had devised a senselessly difficult arrange-

ment for perpetuation of the human species. There is a good deal of evidence, however, that the difficulties serve extremely useful purposes. They help to shape an emotional attitude on the part of parents to offspring which has made the family so enduring an institution.

Equally, the delays and impediments of the democratic process contribute significantly to a sense of national unity. They have a powerfully cohesive influence. For when the process has been fulfilled, it affords a widespread feeling of participation in the decisions reached. The minority, if not persuaded as to the wisdom of the majority, has at least had a chance to speak out, and knows that it can go on in conformity with the rules of the game, still hoping to transform itself into a majority. There are, to be sure, irrevocable steps in national policy to which dissidents must submit. But if numerous they are usually able to modify the prevailing view in some measure.

Thus, when the Lend-Lease Act, a radical innovation in American foreign policy, was first broached by the President in December 1940, it touched off a debate that was carried on not only in Congress but in public meetings and the press throughout the country. The issue was contested with logic, with emotion, with invective; was pressed on either side with all the arts of propaganda; and was finally resolved only after the opposition had been accorded full opportunity to state its case. Three months seemed a long time to spend in adopting an emergency measure. But as a result, the country embarked on the Lend-Lease program, with all its terrible implications of involvement in the war, aware of America's stake in Britain's survival and prepared as it could have been in no other way for the events which were to follow. This process of resolution through conflict yields a national unity impossible in totalitarian societies where decisions are taken by fiat—a unity which has proved one of the formidable sources of American strength.

Diversity is much more likely than conformity to prove a source of unity. For men can be brought into strict conformity only by the most stringent social and institutional compulsions. Genuine unity has its roots in common allegiance to fundamental values and is cemented, rather than disrupted, by mutual tolerance.

Tolerance of diversity has another useful consequence. It affords a safe outlet for opposition to national policy. Dissent which is free to express itself is likely to expend its force in expression; repressed, it may develop explosive potentialities, erupting in forms which cannot be countered by reason. The victims of repression all too frequently gain converts not to their ideas but to their martyrdom.

Tolerance has its greatest utility, however, in the challenge it presents to conventionality and complacency. Only through uninhibited criticism can official error be exposed and corrected. It is far better that criticism be captious, unreasonable and unfair than that it be absent altogether. For it is the most powerful of goads—even if dangerous—to those entrusted with authority. It requires them constantly to justify their conduct to the public. It is the trigger of innovation and improvement.

The pragmatic value of free criticism was never better demonstrated than in the course of the war. Successive failures on the part of the administration to mobilize production, for example, were disclosed and ultimately corrected. Precisely the opposite was the experience in Germany. There, where the concept of total war was first developed, it was never, in fact, put into practice. One of the most interesting discoveries of the United States Strategic Bombing Survey, which studied the physical and psychological impact of the American air offensive immediately after Germany's collapse, was the fact that German resources were never fully employed. The most monolithic of all totalitarian states fell far short of the democracies in organizational efficiency. Production of luxury goods unnecessary to the war effort and wasteful of strategic materials was permitted almost to the war's very end. Women who might usefully have been employed in war plants were allowed to continue in domestic service—generally in the homes of Nazi officials and party members—in striking contrast to the stringency with which women were recruited for industry in democratic Britain. Germany's fat Luftwaffe commander was permitted to continue making the wrong types of airplane.

The reasons for this are even more interesting than the facts themselves. The Strategic Bombing Survey came to the conclusion that inefficiency was widespread in Nazi Germany precisely because no one felt free to complain about it. Subordinates did not dare to criticize their superiors; the press was an organ of the government; and so far as the public was concerned, it was without access to information and without vehicles for opposition—save for the underground and bomb plots to eliminate the Fuehrer. Since mere questioning of the Fuehrer's infallibility amounted to treason, the result was the compounding instead of the correction of error.

Yet one still hears it said that democracies are, by their own nature, fumbling and wasteful in comparison with the streamlined efficiency of dictatorships!

It is, indeed, one of the astonishing paradoxes of our day that liberty has become most suspect just when it has proved itself most successful. There is a marked tendency to treat it as a luxury to be enjoyed only in untroubled times. The whole of the American experience contradicts this notion. The essence of that experience is that the broadest tolerance of ideas is a positive source of strength. Such tolerance is needed most, and most urgently, precisely in those times when the society is most subject to stress.

But the country is suffering at present from a kind of national neurosis, grounded in irrational fears. The prime object of these fears, of course, is Communism, a way of life so alien in origin and so at variance with American traditions that one cannot help wondering why there should be any apprehension at all of its general acceptance. As long as there is ample legislation forbidding overt acts against the security of the State, there is scarcely need to punish mere advocacy, which is so unlikely to have any practical effect that it cannot reasonably be considered incitement. Mr. Justice Holmes stated the case very simply: "If in the long run the beliefs expressed in proletarian dictatorship are destined to be accepted by the dominant forces of the community, the only meaning of free speech is that they should be given their chance and have their way." Given their chance in accordance with the pattern which has for so long safeguarded the American society, it is in fact almost a certainty that they will not have their way. The method of denying them their chance is incalculably more dangerous than the evil at which it is aimed.

The most serious threat to the American system today lies in the reckless zeal of fearful men who would forfeit the essential values of that very system on the pretext of assuring its safety.

It is commonly in the name of national security that liberty is lost. National security may require a wide variety of restraints on individual action. But it cannot require restraints on freedom of expression. For freedom of expression is its fountainhead.

Nevertheless, it is in the name of national security that sober proposals have been advanced in Congress to penalize and, in effect, to proscribe not only Communist organizations but what are called "Communist Fronts"—that is, any organizations whose purposes and opinions may be deemed communistic in connotation. In the name of national security, a committee of Congress, the House Committee on Un-American Activities, has stigmatized as Communists or "fellow-travelers" all manner of groups and individuals whose ideas happen to be at variance with the narrow notions of Americanism held by certain members of the committee. In the name of national security, the executive branch of the Government has instituted a "Loyalty Program" under which the Attorney-General is authorized in his absolute discretion to designate as subversive voluntary associations of American citizens, affording them no hearing and no opportunity for judicial review of his decision. Further, a Loyalty Review Board is empowered to declare individual employees of the Government disloyal to their country without even allowing them to confront their accusers—an elementary safeguard guaranteed by the Constitution to persons charged with mere pocket-picking. The principal effect of this program has been to put a premium on mediocrity and conventionality in the Federal service and to establish a kind of means test for Government employment—a test under which only the indigent in ideas need apply.

The consequence of all this heresy-hunting has been a widespread tendency to equate dissent with disloyalty, a kind of hardening of the arteries of the democratic process. Nonconformity has become hazardous; it is liable to be identified with Communism. On account of it, men have been thrown out of their jobs in private industry, even out of pulpits and university faculties. Ironically, those responsible for such intolerance commonly profess that they are not repressing freedom but are acting in its behalf. They deny freedom to preach or teach to individuals whose ideas they distrust, because, they say, these cannot be free men. Thus freedom itself is put into the straitjacket of orthodoxy.

In the aftermath of World War I, when there was a similar consternation over Communism, the late Senator Borah made an observation no less apt today. "The safeguards of our liberty," he said, "are not so much in danger from those who openly oppose them as from those who, professing to believe in them, are willing to ignore them when found inconvenient for their purposes; the former we can deal with, but the latter, professing loyalty, either by precept or example, undermine the very first principles of our government and are far the more dangerous."

Happily, the American tradition provides powerful correctives for hysteria. They are to be found in a homely, underlying pattern of fair play, in a respect for the mavericks who can take derision, in a still widespread willingness to defy convention and authority, in an irreverent questioning of cant, in a tough self-reliance not readily panicked or stampeded. These are enduring bequests of the individualist tradition. The American people have been through other periods of hysteria; their fundamental sense of proportion has always reasserted itself.

Moreover, the democratic process has recently undergone a tremendous and significant revitalization. Fresh forces have begun to participate in it with fresh vigor. Organized labor has learned how to make itself politically effective. Farm groups are concerning themselves with issues beyond their own special interests. Women are now playing an active and powerful role in the mobilization of consent through such groups as the League of Women Voters. Liberals and intellectuals have ceased to sit on the sidelines viewing with alarm, and have undertaken to make their collective influence felt through organizations such as Americans for Democratic Action. Scientists have moved actively into the political arena. Political debate has become an important part of university life for students and faculty alike. Politics is again, as it once was in the early days of the Republic, the business of the people.

These diverse elements will serve as healthy checks on one another and on latent tendencies toward reaction and repression. They have already exerted a decisive influence in the reorientation of the United States from isolationism to enlightened responsibility in international affairs. They demonstrated in the course of the war a capacity to resolve differences in the light of larger common purposes—a capacity for cooperation in crisis which can grow only out of freedom and which has been a wellspring of American security. Out of the conflict they create will come the only kind of unity capable of enduring the tests of the future. They will not be allergic to innovation or fearful of new ideas—even of heretical ideas—because they themselves have emerged out of ideas not long ago considered heretical. They will have faith in the democratic process because they are its essence.

Heresy frightens only those whose own faith is feeble. The original and "natural" right of Americans, the right on which their society was founded, to advocate a change in their economic system or in their government—even, in the words of the Declaration of Independence, "to abolish it and to institute new government, laying its foundation on such principles and organizing its powers in such form as to them shall seem most likely to effect their safety and happiness"—this right is no mere luxury. It is what makes the United States today, in the vital sense of the term, a union.

The Revolution of 1776 abolished, along with the political tyrannies of George III, the system of royal monopolies and discriminatory commercial laws which American colonists had cursed for generations. In their place the revolting Americans welcomed the freedom of the market extolled in England by Adam Smith. Buying, manufacturing, selling were to take their natural course; they would be self-regulatory, ran the theory, self-purifying. The one evil to be feared was interference by the state.

The climate of the ensuing era was favorable to the "radical"—the scientist, inventor, manufacturer or man of business with a "root" product or process. For three quarters of a century the young Republic fostered and grew under this competitive economy.

How the techniques of combinations and monopolies were rediscovered, and how the government was summoned to preserve, not to restrict, competition, are a part of the story. How effective or ineffective has regulation by the state been? Has it provided a free field for the radical, the man with a new idea?

Have we come back to something akin to the royal monopolies that our ancestors destroyed in 1776?

Walton Hamilton

THE GENIUS OF THE RADICAL

The digits 1 7 7 6, properly arranged, fix a date of some significance in our annals. For in that year a series of events conspired to give a strange twist to the will of Nature's god and to shunt American culture onto its own distinctive track. Then, as always, time moved with stealth; disguised its changes behind ancient forms; and introduced its novelties without revealing their identity. A number of things which made a difference happened off stage; a few were remarked at the time, although their meaning was only dimly sensed. And only slowly was a grim—and rebellious—movement against established authority converted into the legend of "the spirit of '76."

It was, as the record came to reveal, a most prophetic year, even though men of the times could not have said for what. There was, first, the signing of a radical document, penned by a bookish country squire of thirty-three, called the "Declaration of Independence." There was, second—although it caused no ripple over here—the appearance of a radical treatise written by a long-headed Scot who knew what the books said but had also dared to go outdoors and look around. This book

63

bore the sensational title of *An Inquiry into the Nature and Causes of the Wealth of Nations*. There was, third—completely unheralded on this side of the water—the firing of a verbal broadside by one of those sons of Old England who refuse to breed true and who, comfortably fixed themselves, storm at the prevailing order. It was, of course, Bentham's *Fragment on Government*. And then there was a scion of a Scot *émigré* in Prussia, one Immanuel Kant, busily putting together a somewhat blasphemous theory of moral obligation called *A Critique of Pure Reason*. And in another realm an instrumentmaker—note the appropriateness of the term—a certain James Watt, quite oblivious of the Twentieth Century Limited which he was helping to create, was seeking a patent for his multitubular boiler in a toy called the steam engine. In such diverse ways a barrage of words, ideas, and things done was being hurled at the rock of ages.

Names, documents, even events, erupted from the great deep upon the placid face of the eighteenth century. You can keep faith with the spirit of history, and yet make Jeremy Bentham speculate on the Wealth of Nations; explain how Adam Smith came to scribble the Declaration of Independence; and make the Fragment on Government flow from the inkwell and quill of Thomas Jefferson. These protests, whether polemic, document, or declaration, were kindred things. For a host of protestants, refusing to praise what God had ordained, were joined in a grand chorus of rebellion. They had lost faith in a neat and tidy world operated from above; in an establishment in which every man had his appointed station; in the primacy of order and obedience among the cardinal virtues. They called for the release of the human spirit; the proof of accepted truth; the return of adventure; the right of man, as well as of the nation and the race, freely to elect for himself to be saved or damned.

It is impossible to say by what doom or dodge three such upstarts as Bentham, Jefferson, and Adam Smith were given so much leeway in shaping the course of events. It may be providence was asleep at the switch. Or that advantage was taken of a temporarily unoccupied celestial throne—the best authority has it that the Old Testament deity was being deposed in favor of Nature's god about that time. Or the width of the Atlantic may have been too much for the prestige of Church, Crown, and the old Colonial System to cope with. But whether by the negligence of heaven, the backwardness of transportation, or the edict of the frontier, *vox populi* succeeded to the prestige and trappings of *vox dei*, and for the voice of the people the radical called the tune.

In any event, the prelude to American history was written in a radical key. And the nineteenth century, that great lull in history from Waterloo to Sarajevo, is the day of the radical. Throughout this period, the voice of protest was mighty, not in word alone but also for action, in all the land. Not a strand of the fabric of culture did it leave untouched. In the physical world, as well as in human affairs, the rule of the mighty is succeeded by the reign of law. The force which causes the apple to fall holds the stars within their celestial courses. The national economy is conceived of as an analogue to the Newtonian universe; attraction and repulsion are replaced by utility and disutility which, under the free play of economic forces, held the industrial system in an equilibrium, in which the optimum replaces the conservation of energy. In the political domain, the true path for policy is found through an automatic system of checks and balances between interests. In ethics, a credo of individualism leads to the ultimate right and the true good. In the rarified sphere of theology, a personal god is replaced by a deistic god, who having wound up the clock in the beginning, is content to allow it to run on without further intervention. It is an easy step to atheism; to take away faith, the lord of all has only to throw the key away.

Such principles, whether of physics, economics, politics, ethics or divinity, were elaborated into systems of thought by the schoolmen. These principles rang true because the intellectual climate gave them life. For they recited in erudite ways, with an adequate supply of therefores and polysyllables, the simple lesson taught by common sense. God is in his heaven; everyone's minding his own business makes the world go around; learned statesmen do not—or at least ought not—to interfere with matters which they do not understand.

II

The radical we have always had with us; not every era has been tolerant of his genius. The Middle Ages boasted a world of authority, feudal ties, and Christian unity. There was one church, many states, and a myriad of local economies of dubious status. The church professed to be, and often was, overlord of all temporal sovereigns, however great. As guardian of the moral order, it imposed its ecclesiastical discipline upon all Christian souls and through penance and kindred institutions exerted its spiritual influence upon secular institutions. It held princes and kings to a code often higher than their own wishes; and thus, without controlling government, the church exercised its dominion over the agencies of government. The dominant economy was made up of self-sufficient manors, upon which personal relations of lord and villein were governed by use and wont. The money economy, the frailest sort of cash-nexus between trades, was operated largely by persons outside the fold of Mother Church and little concerned to secure Christian burial. In so integrated a society, institutions were not distinct, and the words Church, State and Economy had little of their modern meanings.

In time the Protestant movement, an aspect of a protracted cultural revolution, dissipated the power of the church, and the rising political order fell into a pattern of rival nations, each seeking to enhance the repute and extend the limits of the realm. In this game of empire-building—which after the discovery of the New World was played for high stakes—each nation attempted to build and create a commercial system which would fulfil its high purpose. As a result, economies became instruments of war and diplomacy. The American colonies were caught up in the struggle, first as a partisan of England, and later as rebels against the old colonial system.

It is out of this rebellion that the "American philosophy" sprang. Its dominant theme has been the separation of state and economy. The two are conceived as distinct institutions; each has its separate province; if their functions are mixed, chaos becomes lord of all. As for industry and commerce, the role of the state is to prevent force and fraud, see that the rules are fair, and leave all business to the actors themselves. The market, open to all comers and free of all privilege, becomes the dominant industrial and agricultural control. If there is need for pins, or fertilizer, pinwheels or plastics, cash in the hands of buyers will bring out the product. If the public loses its liking for top hats, home organs, or cast-iron lions on lawns, lack of demand will dry up the supply. Price cannot for long be too high, for the competition of sellers will drive it down;

nor can it endure at too low a figure, for the competition of buyers will force it up. As tastes change, that is, if backed up by purchasing power, resources will be shunted from industry to industry in response. With economic forces at all times in free play, the industrial system will forever be tending to an equilibrium which it never quite attains. And at any given moment it will be using to the fullest the limited material resources of society. The sin, the grievous sin against the economic ghost, is to restrain trade, to rig the market, to erect a monopoly. All of this has been explained over and over again in the learned tomes which tell in half-a-thousand pages what Poor Richard set down in a dozen old saws.

But what the good books fail to recite is the opportunity which the market process accords to the radical. For the market has no committee on credentials; no standards for insuring that the entrant be a good fellow; no test of loyalty and no ban because of race, politics—or we-don't-like-his-looks. It is scornful of tradition and prestige, and the traditions from the past are not among its currencies. All who go to market are free to do as they please; to sell or buy as they like, to produce wares by whatever device and to sell by whatever method they wish. The game is arranged so that the marketeer must "make good" if he wants to survive. He may, of course, have his fling, and, when his shillings are gone, depart. But if he is to abide and to prosper, he must induce others to purchase his goods—and at prices in excess of their cost. If he can do that simple thing, he is free—and continues to be free—to do as he eternally pleases.

In fact, the invitation to be radical is inherent in the institution. The market has pitted seller against seller in a deadly combat. If the man of business keeps faith with the past, at best he can only break even. If he wants to get ahead he must be bold. He is not only at liberty but under a strong incentive, to come across with a new wrinkle, to perpetrate a new gadget, to invent a new method of production, to make use of a new market dodge. If people, or enough of them, will take to his novelties, he is paid, not punished, for disrespect to the ways of the past. And if a new trick enables him to shade a cost, that is nobody's business but his own. The individual alone, thinking, contriving, ever alert, blazes the trail. He may, of course, fail; but if he succeeds, there is no one to stop him. On the contrary, whether the novelty be in style, product, organization, technical process, or merchandising method, he makes obsolete that which was once good. In time, a few daring souls will follow and presently that which was strange will become the usual.

No such liberty to think, and by thinking, to shake the foundations of society, is afforded by the political process. In days of old a respect for custom was among the most exalted of virtues; and it was determined by proper sequence: what was good for gild, town or realm. Under such a regime, an innovation had little opportunity to make its own way. It had to win the approval of the gildsmen, burghers, or ministers of state before it was given its chance. Its very promise of success was an argument against its approval; for it would prove a nuisance, or perhaps even a menace, to the good men of a system set in its way. For, whereas the market process asks only "will it pay?" the political process ponders, as often as not with a parade of horribles, "what will it do?" And from schoolboys to the sanctified of earth, men do not vote for schemes which threaten doom to their dominions. The market blocks off ruler and multitude and allows the individual—

always at his own peril—to be as disrespectful of the way of sages of old and of his fellowman as he pleases.

Nor is there respect or even awareness of the claim of the future. In the market, the trader is not much concerned with posterity or humanity. The novelty is released to do its work, goodly or dirty, in the economy, on the sole condition that it demonstrate its capacity to enlarge a profit or to cut a cost. Further than this, no evidence of its fitness for society and for survival is demanded. What is implicit in the innovation is a matter of no mercantile concern. Its innate power to make its way, to change the habits of men, to blast at creeds and orders and systems, is beside the point. Once given the run of our culture, there is usually no time to arrest its creative impact. It is voted in by a minority; yet all, in spite of a lack of conscious choice, must live with it. A minority, beguiled by appearance, lets the novelty in; the majority must endure in consequence all that lies implicit within it.

III

Although the nineteenth was the century of the radical, we did not accord to the market complete sovereignty. Too many other values were to be served, too many institutions were there to serve them. And history is the creature of too many masters to accord absolute rule to any agency of combat. But the market did win and for some decades did hold a dominion beyond the dreams of Adam Smith; and during long years it did command the gate to our way of life and did decide what should come in. Now that it has passed into decline, and other authorities are mighty where it once held sway alone, we can in retrospect see the character and magnitude of the work which it did. It is not for us to call its work good or bad; for

we have neither moral gadgets by which to assess it nor a
known alternative to put in its stead. The age of Victoria and
the moving frontier elevated human reason to a high pinnacle
—and found the market and all its works good. We today look
back and wonder that it was given so much freedom to shape
our culture. But, after all, who can tell before the event what is
wise and what is foolish? Or who could prophesy with historical sense a better time?

But, good or bad, the way of the market—unlike the political process—gave to novelty a chance to prove itself. In our
great age, when a simple faith in "the progress of mankind"
was more than national security, it offered the radical—the
man who seeks to get to the root of the matter—an opportunity
to release his creative energies. The real radicals who rose to
the opportunity, and without intending to do so transformed
American culture, were scientists, technicians, businessmen,
alike impatient of what they had been taught and to the havoc
their creations might bring to the deep folkways of the nation.
With tapeline, microscope and crucible they challenged the
cry of scarcity of Nature, which had made of the world a
great penitential, where the threat of lack of sustenance was a
trying-ground for men's souls. They discovered that Nature
offered to mankind no more than stuffs of one sort and another.
It was knowledge, reduced to the precisions of technical process, which converted these stuffs into resources. There had to
be a way of turning it to account before an inert material could
become even a potential resource. As a result, the catalogue
of Nature's offerings gave way to an exhibition of the current
state of the useful arts. It became impossible to know what
innovations of matter, process and product the adventure into
knowledge would provide next. And so, as the world of

71

scarcity became the world of abundance, long-range planning went out of the window and the national blueprint was halted before the question mark of the test tube.

A flood of innovations, such as the Christian-tradition community had never before known, came from drafting room, laboratory, and executive office through the gate opened by the market into a somewhat startled society. Novelties in general were called by old names—witness steamboat, sewing machine, hydraulic ram, motorcar—and thus deceptive words were used to cushion shock. The capacity of the people to assimilate the strange and even outrageous was put to the proof. For the new things out of the fiery furnace and off the assembly line refused to stick to their appointed tasks, and insinuated themselves into alien matters. In replacing craft of hand by machine process, bold men did not directly aim at erecting the factory towns of Lowell and Lawrence or of setting the stage for a story such as *The American Tragedy*. In giving the steam engine a glorious ride on the rail, the primary aim was not to build cities and to propel skyscrapers toward the heavens. Old Cyrus McCormick did not say to himself, "Let me invent a reaper and binder, to be followed by a miscellany of farm machinery, to the glorious end that a trend towards concentration shall be turned loose on the farms." The telegraph, with its antediluvian alphabet, and the telephone—to this day we still do not know who invented it—were not brought into being to break local barriers or to rob the first families in small towns of their social primacy. Nor did a certain Ben Franklin, never warmly received by the respectables of Philadelphia, fly a kite in order that many decades later General Electric and the T.V.A. should be mighty in the land. It was the misfortune of the internal combustion engine, a small

72

mobile instrument of transport, to come along too late to
scatter our cities over the landscape.

So, too, with the skills and techniques plied upon stuffs less
material than iron, tungsten and magnesium. The corporation
was not elaborated into a hierarchy of dodges, equities, and
powers to turn into a quaint antique a survival of feudalism
called the law of real property. The modern marketing structure, with its serried ranks of functionaries and factotums, was
not created to absorb the labor which the economies of machine production had displaced. If Marconi invented wireless
—the Supreme Court says he didn't—his primary aim was
not to regiment entertainment for the American people. We
have without doubt somehow created mass consumption; but
one hunts in vain through legislative annals for the decree by
which it was brought to pass. The mark of the radical is on all
that was dear to our fathers; yet we cannot trace its origin to
the will of "We, the People."

The sharp contrast between the automobile and the building
trades reveals the market at its pragmatic best. The automobile is a cultural upstart; at its coming, social conventions
did not hedge it about. The building trades are hoary with
age; mores of assorted kinds have long ago possessed them.
The polite restrictions of building codes, of finance companies,
of covenants which run with the land, of the usages of the
building trades, hem in on all sides the erection of a house.
And even before the war decreed a higher plateau for costs,
a home that should have sold for ten thousand dollars, if
efficiency had had half a chance, was priced at twice that
amount. It is true that before the automobile got well on the
highway, respectability got in a few feeble licks. The select
circle of licensees under the Seldon patent—which was for a

car with a motor and all its works—refused to admit a certain
Henry Ford to its fellowship; and, because the aforesaid individual could not present satisfactory personal, financial,
and technical credentials, the bankers gave him and his high-
faluting plans the go-by. As a result he was driven to resort
to the chisel, a weapon indulged of old by the market, but
under an anathema when gentlemen of a trade get together.

As a result, the automobile as we know it had its beginnings
in a shed and is a product of the assembly line. Ford had the
parts made for him, on credit, naturally; sold his cars for
cash—a percentage with the order, of course, the balance on
delivery; and, with assembly reduced to routine, he contrived
the quickest of all turnovers. Thus he had monies in hand with
which to pay before ever the bills for the parts rolled in—and
distilled an enduring contempt for the noble office of the
investment banker. The new vehicle which in bankers' eyes
might have made a real appeal to rich men too far inland to
use a yacht, had by a narrow shave escaped the luxury class.
Ford set out deliberately to bring his car within the means
of lower and lower income groups. The horseless carriage—
note the early necessity for the word—came gradually to
reflect its motor power; in two decades it converted all self-
respecting Americans into mechanics, and imposed a network
of concrete highways upon the several states. And students of
society now dispute its uncertain and significant effects upon
mating and morals and its capacity to decentralize the population.

The free market allows the adventurer to crash the gate. It
makes bold ideas the price of success. The daring soul, practical enough to make good, leads the way. There follows the
imitator, and the few who accept become in time the many.

And in turn the people accept the novelty, for the time at least, as that which is, has always been, and ever more shall be. Such is the true way of the radical.

IV

The market, even in its golden age, exercised a qualified, rather than an absolute rule. As time went its inexorable way, the voice of protest was heard in complaint. The chief count was that the results produced were not in accord with the canons of a Christian order; that the processes of production were not in strict accord with the moral values. The market, it was charged, put children to work too soon, arrested their talents, and exploited their bodies. It worked females—and perhaps males in full possession of all their faculties—for overlong hours. It allowed the machine, which had entered the factory as a labor-saving device, to take its toll of human flesh. The system of competition took the savings of the people, including the widow's mite, without holding them in sacred trust. And, in general, it used up its labor force, as well as its families, without affording security against the great hazards of life. Nor was it solicitous to the moral quality of the product. It allowed impure to be served up as pure food, permitted intoxicating liquors freely to be bought and sold, and made woman's ancient coinage an ordinary ware of trade.

Protest, however, rang out with more than a single voice. It was suspected that in oil, steel, tobacco, meat-packing, brotherly love among members of the trade was carried further than the law allows: that at a Gary dinner, where the talk was all of art and old masters, a remark about the price of steel occasionally slipped in; that in disregard of the rules of fair play, the big boys were not above ganging together, and

by driving up costs and cutting prices, putting the squeeze-play
on the little fellow. It was admitted that there were depressed
industries, such as bituminous coal and women's dresses,
where rivalry among a multitude of small firms had become
deadly and the workers were called upon to bear in lower
wages the costs of competition. It was discovered that a city
is better served by a single street-railway, waterworks or
electric power plant than by many, and that a pair or trio of
telephone companies serving the same community is a nuisance. In a word, it dawned slowly and with horror that within
the economy Nature had created its own zone of monopoly.
So there arose a demand, not to depose it, but to subdue the
market to a constitutional sovereign.

So it came about that, as a result of scattered promptings,
the government was invoked. The great American sport of
trust-busting was off to an early start. Here the attempt was to
employ the state, not to break down, but to preserve the market
as an agency of control. The state was to step in to break
"restraints," to maintain a free economy, to help competition
over the hard places. The idea of antitrust was a little blasphemous; for it indicates a lack of faith for man to attempt
to underwrite and reinforce a law of Nature. But modern men
of a trade, like gildsmen of old, were becoming aware that
they were being pitted against each other to the good of
nobody except the public, and so they were beginning to
wonder if in union there wasn't plunder as well as strength.
Accordingly, the initial antitrust law was written in the faith
it professed to serve.

The next move, in fact it was already under way, turned
toward making a moral institution out of the market. Man
was a selfish beast; the acquisitive instinct was a mighty thing.

76

The bother was that it was mighty by itself when it ought to be mighty with a purpose. Keep the market open, let the urges of the Old Adam run strong, but cut a channel for it. Or, to borrow again from the mixture of metaphor which attended the legislative drive, set rules of fair play for the business game, subdue the pursuit of gain to public purpose, and lift the struggle to an ethical plane.

Theodore the Great, finding the law good but impotent, had created an antitrust division of five lawyers and four stenographers to police the national economy. His unwilling subjects had called it "the big stick." But meanwhile the idea of a regulating agency had come to the front; and Woodrow Wilson bade the Congress create a Federal Trade Commission, all complete with monies and a proper code of behavior for business and inquisitorial powers. A breach in the wall which held the state and the economy apart had been made three years before the passage of the first antitrust act, by the setting up of the Interstate Commerce Commission. But that was an act of grace, not of impiety; had there not been repetitions of "Erie" all over the country? And were not the railroads, as a natural monopoly, to be set down as an exception?

But when Woodrow Wilson proceeded to establish the Federal Reserve Board, a new faith was coming into practice. The Democrats, true to the humanitarian ends, abandoned the technique of Jefferson and Jackson and boldly called upon the state to assume new burdens. The Republicans timidly ventured on their own; and Herbert Hoover, rather insensitive to the problem of unemployment, saw nothing amiss in putting capital on the dole. So the Reconstruction Finance Corporation, responsible to no one and with sufficient power, through lending, to shape the pattern of the national economy, came into being. Since the collapse of the great bull market in the late twenties, the nation had been in a condition of perpetual emergency; and F.D.R. had enthroned regulation with a galaxy of alphabetical agencies.

This has all occurred, not by design or according to plan, but by the good old rule of catch-as-catch-can. But it has come as the result of necessity and in service to the most worthy ends. Its spirit has been: let there be a law! and there was a law. As the legislature has piled statute upon statute, the old guard has not been content to surrender. Instead, it has carried the battle into the courts where the law, made of the stuff of common sense and not always up-to-date, offered prospects of a rear-guard victory: acts regulating hours of labor were struck down in the name of liberty of contract—for surely a free man who has reached years of discretion "knows when he is tired."

It was only through an assumption that no regulation is the rule, thus making possible an exception in respect to women workers because of maternity, and eventually the inclusion (forgetful of maternity) of adult males within the exception, that legislative control of hours won its final victory over the judiciary. A minimum-wage law for women was declared null and void by the courts as denying the inalienable right of the Lizzie Smiths of this world to work for a starvation wage. And it was not until the shift of a vote made at a critical time by a discreet justice that a majority of one was found for the legislation. In a twilight display of heroics, the Supreme Court struck out lustily at the measures of the New Deal. But even justices are not made of everlasting stuff; and, as the old court gave way, the new men passed a self-denying ordinance and pledged themselves as good boys to stick to their judging and

78

to shut up shop as a super-legislature. And it took some time for the learned bench of nine, with the help of a court-packing —or unpacking—plan and a change of faces, to discover that the creed of laissez-faire had not been written into the Constitution by the founding fathers.

As a result, the rigid frontier between state and economy, which had once been holy doctrine, was well-nigh obliterated. In ordinary commerce, gentlemen of a trade must not love each other enough to come into agreement. A code of "fair labor standards," with authority to back it up, received the sanction of the law. Recently, without batting a judicial eye, the Supreme Court read a corpus of labor law into a contract voluntarily entered into between a corporation and its employees. Many of the provisions of law were contrary to arrangements mutually satisfactory to the parties and therefore had to be replaced. As with labor, so too with the other interests in the commonwealth. The stocking and mattress were robbed of their financial function by the guarantee of bank deposits. An array of blue-sky laws appeared, aiming to protect hard-earned savings against investment in lots in Lake Michigan, or perpetual motion machines. Even the consumer was accorded some legal protection against the glib words and slick tricks of the salesman.

A standard for weights and measures, together with a pharmacopœia common to the trade, are a legacy from the old days. But the market has now been closed to all meats that do not pass government inspection; drugs must attest their purity or they cannot be sold; false and misleading advertising is under a legal ban. Oleomargarine must avoid a yellow color, lest the buyer confuse it with butter—to throw a protective tariff about the wares of the cow. Narcotic drugs, save as the

doctor prescribes, are taboo; and, as respects intoxicating
liquors, the several communities which make up the nation
have tipped the scales towards wet or dry in terms of the
distinctive capacities of their several peoples to withstand
temptation. In instances in which private enterprise is hesitant
or unsuited, the state has ventured into the production of goods
and service. Thus it has made highways public roads; taken
command of the mails and schools; and in projects like T.V.A.
and Bonneville has ventured into public power. And, most
sacrilegious of all, through an assortment of agencies it has
manipulated discount rates, intervened to support the market
and otherwise tinkered with natural economic laws.

To such worthy and disturbing ends, a vast hierarchy of
agencies and authorities, commissions, boards and state-owned
corporations has been brought into being. The point is that our
various industrial activities are to be operated by private
persons—that is, by artificial beings created by the law and
called corporations; that since these corporations would carry
on with a single eye toward money-making, it is necessary to
create an authority to assert the public interest. Accordingly,
as the years have passed we have added board to flourishing
board. The administrative agency has in our law acquired a
sanctity almost equal to that which our fathers visited upon
the courts.

Yet, as an instrument for subduing the turbulent pursuit of
gain to the useful and the good, the commission is not a spectacular success. Its timid will is no substitute for the checks
and balances by which acquisitive souls are ruthlessly pitted
against each other. It cannot with feeble licks do the work it
is assigned to do. The business to be regulated takes the
initiative, moves at a quick staccato drive to a single goal.

The commission, in a decorous procedure in which every step must accord with meticulous rectitude, follows afterward with a review that in the fullness of time approves, corrects, or sets aside what has already been done. A hearing on a rate case may shuttle up and down the track between commission and court of appeals for a score of years. And, when a lawfully correct answer is at last forthcoming, the facts which once upon a time gave it validity may have departed the scene. No line could better attest the two distinct systems of time in the world of action and in the world of judgment than the lament of a great jurist that running of hot oil had refused to abide the stately and ceremonial processes of the law.

Nor is the agency neatly shaped for the task it is called upon to perform. The dispatch which a single head could offer becomes dissipated into the collective wisdom of five or seven or eleven men, and here, at the expense of boldness, that dull invention of mathematics—the least common denominator— gets in its deadly work. The forward look is often enjoined by a rotating chairmanship and buried beneath a deluge of immediate detail which had better be left to subordinates. Members of the trade pour into political channels the energies once spent in minding their own business; and the trip to Washington does duty for the drive upon inefficiency and high costs.

Offices along the Potomac may be air-conditioned, but they are not insulated against moth and rust. A crusade creates a militant board and, after some years, the vitality of youth begins to ebb. Service to the public has no certain copy-book reward; a bright young man who proves himself "realistic" can step out to a career in industry; the civil servant who accounts security the chief of virtues abides and avoids hazards to his neck. The public official discovers that men of the trade are made of the same human stuff as himself. As the same issue recurs, the temporary measure, at first tentatively worked out, soon becomes a routine for disposing of the matter. The oldest agency, the Interstate Commerce Commission—popular opinion to the contrary—has never had plenary power to fix railroad rates. The carriers initiate all rates which, if not challenged within the period appointed by law, automatically go into effect. Moreover, no individual road is free to move until its proposed tariffs have been cleared through a series of rate bureaus, a situation which unkind persons sometimes refer to as monopoly.

The Maritime Commission is a socialistic institution which, though a government corporation, owns and operates ships. In recent years it has exhibited its devotion to free enterprise by selling boats as junk and buying them back as precious vessels. The Civil Aeronautics Board has read a mandate from the Congress to create a transport industry adequate to the commercial and military needs of the country, into a command to guard the financial interests of a few chosen lines. What is the result? It has frozen an industry in its infancy into a high-price luxury service; it is busily engaged in barring the gates against so radical an idea as the spirit of enterprise; and it is denying transport by air to the great mass of American citizens. It has allowed low-cost service only to irregular carriers; and, as they have built up business, by rule and regulation the Board has decreed that they are not to carry it. It has in effect made the old adage now read, "Nothing fails like success." And in a series of agency regulations, the commission has become mixed up with foreign policy and is being projected into overseas' affairs.

A real critique of government by administration—the major political phenomenon of the twentieth century—remains to be done. The truth—though as yet it has provoked no systematic treatise—is that "the felt need" and the call for an effective control are imperative; but that, as yet, the art of politics has failed to contrive the right answer. For devices for insuring responsibility have not been invented and woven into the structure of controls. The agency operates outside of representative government and far removed from the political process.

Above all, regulation by commission and rule tends to stifle initiative within an industry and to establish privilege. The chance of the radical to think boldly and to submit his innovations to the arbitrament of the market is abridged or even denied. In trucking, air transport, and radio broadcasting, the right of a "grandfather" vests a concern with the route or channel over which it operated when legislation went into effect. In trade after trade, to the benefit of those already there, the gates are closely guarded against the newcomer. The radical has been denied his opportunity—yet the problem of control has not been solved. An institution marked by such infirmities is not good enough for America.

v

The campaign for regulation has provided its counter-revolution. For business, intent on its own advantage, did not take this turn of events lying down. If it could not stop the trespass of the state on its preserves, it could at least impose its own will upon all that came within its reach; and sooner or later it could clothe in its own livery the prætorian guard set up to keep it in order. The first move in this direct action

83

was to appeal from the Congress to the courts—a strategy which in the old court met with success. But as the bench had now assumed a new look and the words "null and void" passed out of fashion, a change in business strategy was decreed. The judicial siege was lifted and the forces now released were deployed along the legislative front. The informal techniques of pressure replaced the formalized processes of law, and the Congress was called upon to harass civil servants and to encumber the administrative process with solemn and needless procedures. At last, wiser and simpler counsels prevailed: it was easier to capture an agency than to fight it; it was better to convert a control into a sanction for what the man of affairs wanted to do than to endure it.

The new strategy made its own way in the economy with amazing ease. In the learned professions, an examination was deemed necessary to test the competence of novitiates—and to protect the public. Arts not so fine could become professions by the election of the legislature; and would-be realtors, morticians and beauticians might or might not be lawfully licensed to practice by an official committee drawn from the tradesmen with whom they hoped to compete. A building code, without doubt, served the cause of public safety—but it could be made to secure the work of construction to local contractors and local labor. Inspection had once served to keep milk pure but along came pasteurization to rob it of its function. Still it had to be retained; for, through its code, an elaborate system of private government could be imposed upon the milkshed. This system limited entrance to the market to the elect, permitted the maintenance of a high price for fluid milk, while surplus milk of like kind was sold at a lower figure; and, deposing the market, converted the industry into a neat and tidy political domain.

Agencies of control, under the commission system, are ripe for capture. The interest to be regulated is compact, organized, mobile, alert to every move, able to concentrate all its forces with neatness and dispatch at its point of decision. The public interest is general, sluggish, diffused, unable to effect a united front or to move in time. It is small wonder that the American Association of Railroads has an office within the building which houses the I.C.C.; that the Milk and Sugar Divisions of the Department of Agriculture look upon their industries as constituents; that C.A.B. is intent to shield against all free enterprise its "certificated" lines. The War Production Board was generally viewed as a house of delegates from American industry to the government. It is no stimulus to surprise that such things are; it would be a miracle—and a slur upon the zeal of men of affairs in the acquisitive game—if they were not.

The attempt all along the line has been to convert regulation into a weapon of business enterprise. If politics meddles with business, business can take a fling at politics; and, at political invention, Babbitt, at least by the agency of his attorney, has been rather better than the statesmen. No senator or commissioner, or any conclave of them, has produced a kit of techniques comparable to the effective array built around the exclusive right conferred by the United States upon the inventor. The very vocabulary of umbrella-, dragnet-, blocking-, fencing- and trap-patent attests the fact that the patent system is on the march. Among the inventions which make up the politics of industry, the most brilliant is the patent license

whose origin, nature, and use is on this wise: a corporation
dedicated to the making or vending of business machines,
detergents, light metals or ethical drugs, sets a group of
salaried technicians to work. Letters-patent are taken out for
the resulting inventions, always in the name of employees, who
assign all their rights to the corporation. The latter, meanwhile, by purchase, by resort to law, and by other practical
devices which here need not to be inquired into, acquires as
large a coverage of a technology as possible. The result is an
accumulation of an "arsenal" of patents, useful alike for defense and for aggressive warfare. Since the legal life of a
patent is seventeen years, the arsenal is constantly being de-
pleted; since new letters are always coming along, it is constantly being augmented. Since "improvements" are subject
to patent, numbers can be made to make up for the dying
"flash of genius." The important thing is to have and to hold
so large and so strategic a part of technical knowledge upon
which the practice of an art depends that no one can carry on
except by leave of the patent owner.

Such an arsenal, by grace of the patent license, provides the
foundation for the empire. A large corporation asserts dominion over a province within the economy; or a number,
aware that respect for each other's domain's pays dividends,
set up an authority for the industry. The authority does nothing
so obvious as to license the members to make, vend and use the
inventions for which the government has given its grants. Instead, by divorcing its license from particular patents, it
authorizes the recipient to use any, a certain number or kind,
or all the inventions covered by the patent pool. And such permission, in no wise tied to seventeen years, runs for an agreed-
upon period. It may be set down as for five, twenty-five, fifty-

five years, since the life expectancy of the ever-changing arsenal is undetermined. The license, however, is severely defined in scope; the recipient can employ it only within a defined area of production, or in the manufacture of enumerated commodities, or at certain stages of the fabricating process. Even more important, the licensee's access to the know-how covered by patents—as well as to that not so covered and also called know-how—is hedged about with conditions. The operating company cannot carry on without access to the necessary useful arts; the essential knowledge is in the exclusive possession of the holder of the patent pool; access is at the pleasure of my lord.

Here, then, is the most brilliant of political inventions. With ease, it at once liberates an area of the economy from the rule of the market, puts it under a single political authority with no public responsibility, and allows an enterprise which would otherwise be called by a nasty name such as combination, monopoly or conspiracy, to carry on under cover of law. The domain marked out by the grant of licenses becomes a private province of a law and order of its own. A character committee scrupulously examines the credentials of all who, by applying for licenses, knock at the door of the industry. It turns down all applicants whose lack of integrity is attested by lack of funds; and in general it keeps newcomers out. A design, neat and compact enough to satisfy the most rigid planner, is frozen into the structure of the industry. Each concern occupies its appointed place within the industry. The wares to be made, the quantity of output, the capacity to produce, the price to be charged, the markets to be sold, are all set forth in detail in the license. The series of licenses constitute the law of the trade, a breach of which is not to be tolerated. A concern which ex-

87

ceeds its quota, applies the chisel to its price, or shows disrespect for another's preserves, becomes subject to discipline.
The authority is not unversed in the fine art of reprisals; and
there are formal ways of bringing the sinner to repentance.
The industry's system of justice is speedy and sure. But, if,
perchance, rebellion raises its head, there is a last resort. For
to act in violation of the license is to invade the rights of its
overlord, and exposes the offender to a suit for infringement.
Thus the federal courts are called upon to underwrite and to
police a private system of government. A while ago before a
congressional committee, an attorney for a corporate imperium
was asked if, in regimenting the industry, his client had not
gone further than the Supreme Court had been willing to indulge the commonwealth of Oklahoma. He answered "yes" but
added the gloss that his corporate empire did these things
much more neatly than did a sovereign state of the union.

In neatly plotted and tightly hedged domains of the corporate imperium, the freedom to adventure is gone. In putting
on the ancient mask of free enterprise, the corporate estate
asserts its independence of the state whose favors it regards
itself free to accept. Its mark is dominion over an area of the
economy and supremacy of the private law within its province.
In the illustration given, that dominion was rested upon the
patent grant; in examples given above, it is rested upon inspection, the building code, the license to trade or profession.
It can be grounded upon a trade-mark, a public franchise or
exclusive ownership of a source of supply, such as borax or
sulphur. In the late thirties the tide was running so strong as to
prompt a joint inquiry by executive and legislative into the
concentration of economic wealth and power. The war years
provided conditions favorable to the trend: the bulk of war

orders went to large corporate estates; the little fellows, as sub-contractors, became feudal retainers. The trend towards "self-government in industry," fed by government orders and subsidies, today moves faster than ever. The industrial imperium may have many virtues; it is not, in any way, American.

The usual way of history is to answer questions before they are put. If it is asked whether or not we will accept a new order of society, the only possible reply is, "Why ask? The damn thing is here." Certainly the issue of living with—and probably under—the corporate estate has never been squarely presented at the polls. Its coming has been so omnipresent that it could never be cast into terms to permit a plebiscite. It is bringing with it many things which puzzle, which invite distrust. The solo inventor long ago departed his garret; invention is only one phase of organized research. Scientists are becoming technologists—and consequently are engaged primarily in the service of big business. Their current task is not the uncompromising "progress of science and the useful arts," but the creation of improvements at a rate and in numbers just sufficient to keep alive an armament of patents adequate to the defense and the enlargement of the corporate estate.

In competitive economy, like that of old, the urge is to boldness and the fresh creation. The incentive is to get the jump on, to take the market from, rivals, to keep more than a step in the van. In a system in which the corporate overlords reign by prescriptive right over an area of the economy, the great discovery or basic invention threatens to wreck the established. You cannot mix a world of neatness and order with a drive to capture the unknown. The corporate estate does not rest upon economy and efficiency. Instead, it is founded upon and held together by the appropriation to its own ends of sanctions uttered by the state for another purpose. It lives, expands and exercises dominion by artificial means; it has as yet failed to demonstrate its capacity to make its own way in the world.

The life history of an institution, like that of a plant, presents its mutation, and it is probably too early to assess the species by what it is now. Evidence abounds that, for all of its orderly omniscience, the corporate estate has not yet reached a stabilized form. Its structure and practice are out of accord with the prevailing body of popular belief. As we demand that the potential capacities of man be fully developed, it assigns to the individual an appointed place. As we insist that we will not be regimented, it provides an irresponsible collectivism. It is beaten upon by the course of human events which never has done—and so far as we know, never will do—the bidding of any collection of men, however mighty. Nuclear physics, which the corporate estate would never have considered promoting, has opened fresh vistas and has shown anew that the resources of nature are what the human understanding makes of them. As a result, the government is putting large monies into the art of finding out. At the moment, military objectives are in the ascendancy. The spending is not in the hands of scientists, but of scientific politicians unversed in the social studies; thus, appropriations are going largely to well-established industrial imperiums. Such ventures may possibly get out of hand and become instruments of progress in service to the common good.

Nor does the closed and well-ordered imperium provide a suitable environment for the advance of a culture. If art, music, literature is to have its chance, not only must the human spirit be free, but the individual must have a chance at a rich and distinctive exposure to the experience which only a society of unlike ways can give.

Thus, at the moment, the drive for regulation and the rule of the corporate imperium have united to create a crisis which threatens to destroy the radical and to deny to American society his genius. At such an hour we turn back to the spirit of 1776. The bookish country squire from Virginia, the Englishman who would dare to reform even the law, and the wide-awake Scot who was bold enough to ask what made nations and their people well-off, were probing to the roots of the matter. They understood that there could be too much neatness and order. They dared to challenge the status of authority and obedience as among the cardinal virtues. They knew that change is inevitable; that that which is established can only decay; that the dynamic urge which drives towards the unknown is a condition of life. As all that is new must be put to the proof, so must the spirit of inquiry be released to come upon the new. The way of progress is the way of the radical, who dares to think and to act alone, to blaze the way for the minority, in order that, if it is a better way, all may follow. For the digits 1 7 7 6 properly arranged will cease to hold true significance when we forget that national salvation comes by allowing every man to choose his own primrose path to the everlasting bonfire.

4

"Assyria, Greece, Rome, Carthage, where are they?" Byron asked the enduring ocean. The record prompts the question of what we can hope of our own civilization. Particularly, is there any reason why we can expect its social patterns to last where earlier patterns crumbled?

To the eyes of the Western liberal, the outlook has its aspects of darkness. A large segment of the world's peoples has sought refuge in a totalitarian regime. That regime asks the surrender of the individual to the State in return for the promise of economic security. The driving faith of Communism is that its own rigid patterns can be imposed on an entire world.

The western democracies must look for a double strength. They must find the force to endure where other civilizations failed. They must also demonstrate a superiority to a totalitarian system which seeks to draw all doubtful lands into its orbit.

Have the democracies the vitality that the era demands?

4

Alvin Johnson

THE FAITH OF A SKEPTIC

Whether I qualify for the title skeptic I leave to the philosophic reader. But it is my persistent habit to look beyond the conclusions, optimistic or pessimistic, to the facts, real or fictitious, on which they are based. This habit was known to the Greeks as skepticism. Let me stand then, provisionally, as a skeptic, in the Greek sense.

Every man who thinks at all is concerned about the present condition and the future of the Western civilization under which we have built our lives and our hopes for the future. Within the span of a single generation we have seen the two most destructive wars of history, civil wars within the organization of the civilized nations. For the moment there is no war, but neither is there peace. If we conceive that Western civilization as we knew it before 1914 extends to the Urals and the Bosporus, more than half of the area of Europe is dominated by a political system irreconcilably hostile to the traditional systems of Western civilization. It is not because of lack of warlike spirit, nor of competing interests conceived to be vital, that the guns are silent today. The sole force standing against war is the fear of its powers of total destruction. A third world war might indeed topple the artificial structures of Communist rule, structures resting on propaganda and terrorism, with only the enforced consent of the masses. But the struggle would also shake the foundations of the traditional Western polity. It might well leave the great majority of mankind without effective organization, to join in a century-long *bellum omnium contra omnes.*

Within the non-Communist areas of Western civilization, there are manifest stresses of grave import. In every country there are factions dominated by the Communist ideology, and these factions, at least in Italy and France, maintain the character of major minority parties, often powerful enough to block government action and to create an impression of political helplessness under which the Communist following grows luxuriantly.

Moreover, the faith in private enterprise, the economic foundation ideologically of traditional Western civilization, has visibly waned. In England, mother of economic individualism, Socialism has taken over the powers of the State. If America remains true to the principle of private enterprise, it is with an increasing array of reservations. This is even more true of most of the other countries composing the Western bloc.

At the same time the power of organized labor is everywhere in the ascendant; and organized labor does not as yet acknowledge the public-welfare obligations that go with power. It blithely prices itself out of the market, as in the building trades, and looks to subsidized building for employment, or for unemployment benefits if the Government fails to find funds for subsidies. Obviously the time is coming when our political and social life may be thrown into confusion by the struggle between privileged labor and the unprivileged groups, the unorganized consumers and labor in fields where it can not establish strong key positions in the economic structure.

For generations the Western nations could look to the forced labor of colonies to support the status of the business classes and, through the taxes they could thus pay, the Government budget. The colonies could be counted on also to take the products of industry at good prices and supply in exchange raw materials and food at low prices, to bolster the standard of living of the Western working classes.

The colonies are gone. British India and Burma are independent. The Philippines are independent. The Dutch hang on desperately in Indonesia, the bread basket of the Dutch middle-class. But Indonesia is going. Africa remains, but the black man has risen to the consciousness that color does not black out human rights.

Anxiety is the lot today of the statesman, the social philosopher, the responsible journalist. Anxiety lives among the millions as a boon companion. This would be a serious symptom if civilized man had ever lived free from anxiety. For the sake of the argument, I will grant that we are more anxious today than our forefathers were. This cannot be proved, but let it stand.

Arnold Toynbee, the greatest of living historians, has assembled the record of nineteen civilizations before ours that have risen in high hopes, that have grown mightily to significant stature, only to degenerate and fall. Superficially viewed, they fell through attack by superior forces, like the Babylonians by Persian attack, the Persians by the attack of Alexander's Macedonians, the Aztecs and Incas by Spanish attack, Rome by the continuous barbarian attack. But in practically

97

all the cases these civilizations succumbed because the force of life was already out of them. Internal stresses had eaten away their vitals. Had any of them the volume of internal stresses that gnaw at the vitals of our own civilization? We can not say with certainty.

There are, however, a number of characteristics that distinguish our civilization from the nineteen that have gone before and have perished. With the one exception of Greek civilization before the Macedonian conquest, our civilization is distinguished from the rest by the fact that it is a membership corporation of independent sovereignties. Babylonia recognized no independent sovereignty within reach of its arms. Neither did Persia, nor Alexander's Macedon, nor Rome. Nor did Hitler of mephitic memory, nor Stalin, still at large. But Western civilization has never had universal empire on its practical agenda.

Of all the civilizations that have gone before, only one, it seems to me, offers valid lessons for our own. That is the Roman Empire, which, like our own Western civilization, included many peoples in its sway. It controlled an area not much inferior, if we exclude the Americas and Japan. For it embraced more of North Africa than Western civilization ever pretended to control, all of Turkey and the rest of the Levant up to the Euphrates, and in its time of greatest extension, up to the Zagros Mountains beyond the Tigris.

Within that immense area, communications were virtually as free as within our Western civilization. From Ostia, port of Rome, one could go by trireme to Joppa or Alexandria about as expeditiously as by a modern tourist ship. Goods were transported about as cheaply, by the lateen-sailed freighters which thought no more of time than our own freight-forwarding concerns. There were *portoria,* customs duties—as important relatively as our own port duties. There was a system of commercial law which differed from ours mainly in its rigorous insistence on the letter of the contract and in its promptitude of operation.

But in one point—the crucial point, I think—our civilization differs radically from that of Rome, and from all the other civilizations that have perished. That is our concern for the masses of the population, the "underlying population," to use Veblen's apt phrase.

All prior civilizations present the pattern of a cultivated elite forming a structure more or less lofty, more or less stable, resting upon the backs of the underlying population. That population might consist of serfs, as with the Incas, or of peasants, free laborers and slaves, as in Greece and Rome, or almost exclusively of slaves, as in Carthage. In every case the ruling elite lived on the toil of the underlying population, for which it had no concern except that internal disturbances should be effectively repressed.

To this rule the historian may present certain exceptions. The Hebrew Commonwealth did occasionally seek to defend the small peasant against the encroachments of his larger neighbor. The Greek lawgivers endeavored to defend the citizen against the exorbitant charges of the grain speculators. In republican Rome a movement, led by the Gracchi, sought to defend the small peasant against the encroachments of the large estate worked by slave labor. The Roman emperors concerned themselves seriously with the problem of the supply of bread-grain. The successive Chinese empires gave a place of

99

high honor to the tiller of the soil—perhaps the reason why Chinese civilization, though subject to ebb and flow, has held its own, in a sense, through four thousand years.

But with all due allowance for the exceptional instances in which the policy of the ruling elite was favorable to the under-lying population, or a part of it, the evidence is overwhelming that the underlying population was never an important concern of the ruling class in any of the civilizations before our own. The Romans might offer bread and the circus to the turbulent masses of peasants fled to the cities, to the city-bred proletariat forever unemployed, the freedmen, the slaves in hiding—a mob capable of taking fire, and setting fire. There is no trace in Roman thought or in Roman law and administration of any idea that the ruck and muck of the proletariat could be ele-vated to anything useful to the state.

History is mainly a record of civilizations—the cultural structures of the elite supported by the underlying population. It gives us only occasional glimpses of the cultural activities of the underlying population, which produced no written record of its own. From the written record we tend to reach the conclusion that in all preceding civilizations the state of this population was entirely servile. We think of the noble monu-ments of antiquity, like the ruined Colosseum of Rome, as the product of slave labor. Our ideas on this point are so firmly fixed that we hardly pay any attention to the evidence that the free building workers of Rome did not permit a single facing stone to be set in place by slaves. We ignore the evidence that in the Near East, guilds of free artisans were numerous and powerful—although we all learned in our earliest reading of the Bible that the Founder of the Christian religion grew up in the house of a carpenter, a carpenter free enough and pros-

100

perous enough to make a pilgrimage to Jerusalem and to take his family down into Egypt. Peter and his brother were of the fishermens' guild, able to abandon their boats and nets without asking permission of any overlord. Paul the tentmaker could go from city to city and fall in with the local tentmakers, to practice his trade for his living.

Pliny the Younger, in one of his letters to the Emperor Trajan, about the end of the first century, reports that three considerable cities of Asia Minor had been destroyed by an earthquake, and that the building-trade unions of Asia Minor had proposed to rebuild them, at the expense of the unions, if Trajan would recognize the organizations. We have also the reply of Trajan:

"Whether those cities shall ever be rebuilt rests with the gods. In no circumstances will we recognize the unions."

The underlying population of Rome was not altogether an alternately passive and turbulent mob waiting for bread and circuses. It was not altogether a population of slaves and serfs, acting only by upper-class will. It was the carrier of many important elements of culture, not recognized by the poets: the capacity for combination in defence of a trade; the wealth of technique that made the achievements of their civilization possible. It was not the elite but the underlying population that learned the conditions under which wheat could yield abundantly, that trained the poison out of carrots and parsnips, that taught cabbage and lettuce to head and celery to blanch. It was not the elite that taught the potato to give up its hundreds of pea-sized tubers and to concentrate on a few competent ones to sustain man. It was not the elite that discovered that by treatment with wood ashes the poisonous cassava root would yield the bland food item tapioca.

This ancient population knew nothing about nitrates and nitrogen-fixing plants. But the peasants of Vergil's day knew that clovers restored the fertility of soil, and the ancient Inca peasant knew that if you wanted exuberantly productive potatoes in the phosphate-starved Andean uplands, you had to carry to the fields guano from the off-shore islets, hundreds of miles away.

I dwell upon husbandry, because its history is farthest from recorded history. It is almost equally true that recorded history has nothing important to say on the development of the crafts. Again, it was not the elite that taught the women of the Near East and India to spin thread so fine that the woven cloth was too sheer for the use of the wives of stern Spartan moralists. It was not the elite who taught the Indians of the Puget Sound region how to split usable planks off round logs—an art never discovered in the Old World. Out of the underlying population came the arts of stone cutting—even before metal tools were known—and the art of smelting copper ore, and copper and tin together to make bronze. Tubal-Cain, mythical ancestor of the smiths, was certainly not a slave, driven to invention by a master's whip. The African smith-guilds, that probably anticipated the inventions of Tubal-Cain, were free men, popularly endowed with wizard qualities.

No doubt certain ideas of technical value were supplied to the underlying population by the elite, as for example the various applications of the principles of the pulley and the screw. The principles of the arch were no doubt wrought out by the elite, with their mystical appreciation of the qualities of the circle. Such principles were incorporated into the scheme of action of the underlying population, and maintained their place indefinitely. There isn't an Italian stone worker who

102

doesn't know how to construct an effective arch, nor any sailor who doesn't know all there is to know about pulleys.

The late Dean Edwin Gay, greatest of economic historians, used to say that he had never been able to find one single instance of a handicraft technique that had failed to survive the fall of Rome and the blight of the Dark Ages. Neither have I found any instance of lost agricultural technique.

In Vergil's "Georgics" the beekeeper is advised to put his hives near a pool of still water. Since the bees, in the impetuous thirst of a saccharine diet, may miscalculate and plunge themselves into the water, without swimming power to reach the shore, Vergil advises scattering chips over the water, on which the bees may climb to dry their wings. Some years ago, on my way from Venice to Padua, a traffic delay permitted me to walk through a little Italian farm. In the center was a pool with beehives around it, and the pool was scattered over with chips and bits of bark. The peasant explained to me, in Italian I half-understood, that the flotsam on the water was to save the bees from drowning.

Modern orchardists, and one out of every thousand economists, know that fruit bearing rapidly exhausts the soil—even more rapidly than cereal production. Good orchardists fertilize heavily. In Italy, near Brindisi, I watched a peasant digging the soil around a fig tree, and spading in quantities of barnyard fertilizer. I was reminded of a New Testament parable:

The owner of a vineyard had come out to get some figs from his tree and found practically none. He had been similarly disappointed the year before, and the year before that. Accordingly, he ordered his steward to cut down the fig tree and plant something that would yield. "Wait a year," advised the steward. "I will dig the ground around the tree and work in manure. Then if the tree doesn't yield, cut it down."

The ups and downs of "civilization," that is, recorded civilization, do mightily affect the underlying population. Whole provinces may be turned into desert in the course of military operations; whole cities may be destroyed, with their populations massacred or enslaved. When Titus captured Jerusalem, he sold all the inhabitants for slaves, and the glut of the slave market was such that thirty could be bought for one shekel—"two bits" in modern currency.

But an underlying population is protean, wide flung. Always enough of it survives to carry forward the unrecorded but vital items of culture it has developed or acquired.

This fact is characteristic, and of first significance for our problem. For what is evident to every one who cares to think is that our Western civilization, first in history, has been steadily drifting toward the dominance of the underlying population.

This movement began with the early modern Peasant Revolts, in England, France, and Germany, when peasant mobs, armed with scythes and pitchforks, attacked castle and monastery, chanting:

> When Adam delved and Eva span,
> Where was then the gentleman?

The Peasants' revolts were drowned in blood, but not their ideas, which continued to reject the conception of the inborn superiority of the elite. Long before Bobby Burns, the robust peasant was convinced that "a man's a man for a' that." And no country lacked its contingent of poor friars and heretical priests, to spread the doctrine of human equality, as acknowledged in Holy Scripture.

With the expansion of trade in the era of discovery, the merchant rose to a position of power in the state, and scholarship, formerly the monopoly of the Church, became accessible to the merchant's son, who had to train himself for the functions of accountant and lawyer. This rising class came to be more and more impatient of aristocratic pretensions, and in the Age of Enlightenment learned to challenge every claim to superiority by blood. A moderate representative of the Enlightenment, Adam Smith, held to the doctrine that what produces differences among men is Nature and Nurture; and of the two Nurture is far the more important.

"We hold these truths to be self evident, that all men are created equal, that they are endowed by their Creator with certain unalienable rights; that among these are life, liberty and the pursuit of happiness. That to secure these rights Governments are instituted among men, deriving their just powers from the consent of the governed."

It is true, Jefferson was a slave owner when he wrote these words. Many of the signers of the Declaration were slave owners. Were they hypocrites? I think not. It is one thing to see the right as it must be in God's good time, and another thing to act on the right as if that good time had come. But say that the signers were hypocrites. Hypocrisy, Justice Brandeis used to say, is at least a concession to virtue, perhaps the beginning of virtue. "Affect a virtue if you have it not."

The underlying populations of the world, through ages recordless and voiceless, had found in the philosophy of the Enlightenment, the Declaration of Independence and the French Declaration of the Rights of Man, a voice that no succession of reactionary rulers has been able to quiet. It is a voice that echoes today among the American Untouchables— the Negroes of the Deep South—among Hindus and Moslems, in old China and in dark Africa.

Over-refined intellectuals are fond of asserting that the Declaration of Independence is just a collection of platitudes, meaning nothing to anyone. I was seven when I first heard the Declaration read at a Fourth of July celebration. I can not say now whether it was the surge of emotions through that gathering of hard-working farmers that stirred my own childish emotions. But for the first time I conceived of myself, not as a small boy but as a man-child, with all the freedom of the world my private property. Set me down, if you will, as naive. Those "platitudes" of the Declaration mean as much to me still, and more. They are the charter of a civilization that can endure.

Along with the rising self consciousness of the underlying population and its expanding claims, the modern era has been characterized by the triumphant upward surge of free private enterprise, operating at times, as in the American and French revolutions, in reluctant cooperation with the movement toward freedom of the underlying population, but often appearing in the form of a new elite minority, with new and more efficient means for controlling and exploiting the underlying population. For business enterprise was able to appropriate the craftsman and independent peasant and draw them into the cities as a bare-handed proletariat, depending absolutely on business enterprise for work, bread, housing and clothing. Other philosophers besides Marx saw in the triumphant forward march of capitalism a foretaste of a coming system of slavery, with control over life and death in the hands of a ruthless elite, able to bend the power of the State to its purposes.

But capitalism as a governing elite suffered from a fatal inherent weakness. It had no organic unity, like the unity of the medieval aristocratic elite, no symbol like the king, God's anointed. Its principle of cohesion consisted in pecuniary interests, and these could on any occasion blow up a storm of conflict. Under aristocracy a lord or a prince might go bankrupt, but he remained lord or prince, walking ever-erect among men and prepared to come back into his own with the revolving years. The industrial lord or merchant prince, once weakening, received the same consideration from his fellows as the wounded wolf in the famished pack. He got devoured to the bone.

If the state of capitalism within the national boundaries was uneasy, precarious, the state of capitalism in the international field was one of hostile provocation, leading to about one war for every generation. Such wars might be frank commercial wars, as in the brutally frank seventeenth and eighteenth centuries, or they might be wars of national unification, of dynastic ambition, or moral wars "to take up the white man's burden, and civilize the earth," as in the hypocritical nineteenth century.

There were attempts, through international cartels, to weave the great industries of Western civilization into effective wholes. The warp was too weak for the woof, and we had to go through the agony of World War I, which left capitalism a mere shell as a ruling elite. The underlying populations, which had suffered the most but retained the most—the technical skill, the capacity for combination, education, political adroitness—were out of hand.

Inevitably, in this period of the breakdown of the old order, a reaction had to occur toward the conception of the State as the supreme organization of force, a conception that had almost dimmed out under the abortive hegemony of the capitalists. The first fruit of the reaction was the emergence in Russia of the "dictatorship of the proletariat," that is, the dictatorship of Lenin, successor to Ivan the Terrible, with his handful of resolute followers, the Bolsheviks. Next, the dictatorship of Mussolini and the Fascists, drawing into their net remnants of the old capitalistic order at home and abroad. Third in this witch-caldron trinity, Hitler and his Reich of blood, expected to stand a thousand years—the period for which the Devil was to be in chains.

But the new states resting on the organization of force were driven by the logic of the force-state to expand. They were subject to the same logic that made it impossible for Egypt or Babylonia to sit content in their fertile valleys. The Egyptians could not rest so long as Babylonian or Hittite territory was within marching distance. Alexander's Macedon, Caesar's Rome, could accept no limitations on conquest except the diminishing returns from invasion of the Scottish Highlands, the German forests, the drought-burnt Russian steppes and the nomadic deserts east of the Tigris. So Soviet Russia gnaws remorselessly at her borders. Mussolini had to seek conquests that would make the Mediterranean an Italian lake. Hitler had to devour Austria and Czechoslovakia and Poland. He could not be content without the Ukraine, nor would he have been content long with the Ukraine.

Mussolini and Hitler have gone the way to the abyss paved by fate for overweening ambition. Stalin and his dictatorial elite still cumber the earth, but not for long, as history knows time.

For a new conception of the State has been rising upon mankind. Its plan, if one may describe as planning the upward movement of humanity, was dimly outlined in the British labor movement; more vividly in the Danish cooperatives; painfully beset by hereditary defect in German Social Democracy; militant and naive in American Agrarianism and Progressivism; and culminated in the New Deal of Roosevelt and its logical outgrowth—a Welfare State, now supported vigorously by Truman.

The Welfare State—no philosopher or lexicographer gave it the name, but a plain politician rising out of the underlying population; yet, is not the Welfare State a conception of genius, the genius of the whole underlying population?

The Welfare State—still of course a formative and not a completed phenomenon in America—recognizes the need of force to check internal disorder and to ward off foreign foes. But it does not admit that the administration of force is its main business. No! its main business is to see that the underlying population—that is, the whole population, now that the elites have evaporated—has the requisites of the good life: employment, security, education.

The Welfare State does not regard with hostile eye the achievements of other welfare states. We in America, so far as we are not jaundiced by nostalgic yearnings for the good old days of a war-making, peace-oppressing elite, wish well with all our hearts for the British welfare state and are unstinted in our admiration for little Denmark, pattern of the welfare state.

The Welfare State asks for world peace but not (at least in the present) for world government. We Americans know, or should know, what makes for welfare in America. We can not know what makes for welfare in Java or Timbuctoo. We are with Java and Timbuctoo with all our hearts, so far as they are in pursuit of their own welfare, the welfare of all the people, not merely of an elite patterned after the elite that by God's grace we are ourselves getting rid of.

Our Welfare State is eager to join with other welfare states to promote world welfare. Note that our poor crippled League of Nations could yet win successes in suppressing the opium traffic, in making available world statistics on the position of labor, in promoting agricultural technique. Note that powerful private philanthropies like the Rockefeller Foundation, essentially arms of the welfare state, are attacking one after another the plagues that decimate the underlying populations and enfeeble the survivors.

The Welfare State is with us. It is not the state of any elite, but the state of the underlying population, now essentially the whole population. It is a state that can live in glad peace with other welfare states. It is a state that can join in a world union, not of force but of welfare.

We in America are ready to go into our pockets to relieve starvation anywhere. We will make every effort to stamp out malaria and yellow fever and bubonic plague and sleeping sickness. We will pretend that we do it in our own interest, because we are too modest to say that we do it in devotion to the Immortal God whose name we are not fit to pronounce. For all that, we do it in His name.

To be sure, living in this real world, we cannot live to ourselves with our democratic ideals. We must deal with the other nations. We must sell, and we must buy. But first of all we shall sell to our own people, and buy from them. We shall not wish to cram automobiles down foreign throats at times when we Americans often can't get automobiles for love or money. Other nations have much we need to buy. We will buy their products, for our advantage and theirs, and they will take our products in exchange, for their advantage and ours. But we won't hang a sword over their heads, nor come under swords they hang over our way.

This civilization that is rising into control of the world, the civilization of the common man, cannot be assumed to be perfect, for perfection has never walked the earth in broad daylight. Can a civilization of the common man be expected to divert its energies from every-day purposes to set up great works like the Pyramids and the temple of Diana of Ephesus, the Parthenon and the Colosseum, Versailles and Hitler's Sports Palast? Will it subsidize poets as did Augustus, or painters as did Lorenzo the Magnificent, or opera as did the dying Hapsburgs and the perishing New York Four Hundred? In the fashion of those autocrats, no! In its own fashion—by cooperative action, by state and private endowment, by low-priced schools and by regional conferences, yes!

And I have a surmise that within this immense reservoir of what till recently was the world's underlying population, there is one hundred times the creative ability that ever found egress into the sunlight under the elites of the civilizations that have gone before. These creative abilities may not give us Colosseums and Pyramids. Our fifth generation from now will see what they will give us. I see it in my mind's eye, and I bow down in awe.

This is a skeptic's confession of faith. I see great things coming out of the Welfare State, the state of the common man. I

111

know well this state is just dawning. I know well that in the progress of the world toward this state there must be many false leads, under false prophets. It may be that there must be great wars; almost certainly, there must be many revolutions, where antique ideals, crystallized institutions, dare to loom as barriers to progress. God's pity. But we are moving.

The English settlements in North America, and later the new Republic that sprang from them, were favorable to the development of the independent, self-sustaining character. Observation, persuasion by others, ideas encountered in books —all these influenced the "inward-looking" person only as they were instinctively accepted by him and re-made as aspects of his will.

Such a character type had its usefulness in society. It produced valuable workers and leaders in days and lands when confidence and energy were of high practical use—and subject to reward. For many generations this self-directed personality was the ideal toward which most Americans looked.

The intricate life of a technological society now forces upon men and women closer relationships with each other, both in work hours and in those of leisure. A new type of character emerges. Or rather, two new types.

How will they shape the masses of men in the future— and their leaders?

David Riesman

THE SAVING REMNANT:
An Examination of Character Structure

In 1794 the Marquis de Condorcet, in hiding from the French Revolutionary Terror, ill and near death, wrote his *Sketch of an Historical View of the Progress of the Human Spirit*, a great monument to faith in human power to shape human destiny. Condorcet refused to be dismayed either by his own experience of human meanness and savagery or by his wide historical reading in the annals of cruelty and error. For he rested his hopes, not only on "observation on what man has heretofore been, and what he is at present," but also on his understanding of the *potentialities* of human nature.

It has proven more difficult than he had perhaps supposed to develop those potentialities. Today we are aware that the raw material of human nature is shaped by what we call culture into the organized force of a particular character structure; that this character structure tends to perpetuate itself from parent to child; that, largely determined by early experience, it determines in turn the adult modes of life and interpretations of new experience. The combination of character structure and social structure in a given culture is therefore relatively intractable to change. Though in America we are near Condorcet's dream of the conquest of poverty, his dream of the conquest of happiness seems ever more remote. It has become fashionable to sneer at him and other philosophers of the Enlightenment for lacking a sense of the human limitations on improvement. The sneer, however, is unimaginative. Condorcet's scientific, empirical method urges us to see precisely how recent changes in character structure, as well as in the conditions that gave rise to them, have helped to deny utopia. His philosophy then invites us to apply human reason and effort to the improvement of the human condition as thus understood.

My purpose here is to advance such understanding by tracing a shift I believe to have occurred in very recent times in this character structure of modern man: a shift from the predominance of a type I have called "inner-directed," whose source of guidance in life is an internalized authority, to a type I have called "other-directed," dependent on external authorities. We shall further explore the relationship between these two types of character and the changing feelings in people as to their power to resist social pressures. For obviously, given the objectively identical social pressure, the individual's feeling and experience will depend upon his character, in which his previous life-experiences, especially those of mastery and submission, have been crystallized.

While our helplessness in the world is historically the condition of every advance in our mastery of it, the feeling of helplessness may today be so overpowering that regression, and not advance, ensues. But only when we have understood those forces that make for helplessness can we assay the probable outcome, and see what might be required for the new leap to security and freedom envisaged by Condorcet. One requirement is a type of character structure that can tolerate freedom, even thrive on it; I call persons of such type "autonomous," since they are capable of conscious self-direction. The very conditions that produce other-direction on the part of the majority today, who are heteronomous—that is, who are guided by voices other than their own—may also produce a "saving remnant" who are increasingly autonomous, and who find strength in the face of their minority position in the modern world of power.

I

Throughout most of history, people have lived in the bosom of nature, and at her mercy. They have sought a kind of defensive power and command of nature through magic and animism, by which they attempted to personalize and to propitiate the environment. The Pueblo Indians of the American Southwest, for instance, still cope with fear of drought by preoccupation with word-perfect rituals of rain making—and by very practical communal organization of the available water supply. These tribes quiet their anxiety over the weather by substituting for it anxiety over the ritual, which remains in their control. In such a society, as in the feudal past, people live on a relatively unawakened level, with limited life-expectations and limited potentialities for choice. An over-all balance is struck between helplessness and power; institutions mediate this balance, and character structure builds upon it.

This balance altered radically in the West during the age that opens with the Renaissance and closes, to set an equally arbitrary date, with the virtual cutting off of immigration from Europe following World War I. During this period, men were forced to face a world of changed dimensions, changed social relations, and changed meanings. As a result, some felt increasingly helpless and alone: the Calvinist doctrines appealed to them because those doctrines stressed man's helplessness to secure grace, the "chosen" being predestined by a terrifying and inscrutable God. The practical Calvinist, however, did not merely wait for the day of judgment; he tried to force God's hand by a ritual. This ritual, unlike the Pueblo Indian's rain making, was symbolized by hard work in the worldly processes of production—even though the ultimate aim was otherworldly. The result for many was success in mundane pursuits—which was regarded as a sign of election. Thus both hard work and its practical fruits assuaged the feeling of helplessness in the new conditions of life and led to the attainment of a new balance between power and weakness.

This period was the age of the early physical and industrial frontiers—the frontiers of expanding industry and trade, as well as expanding geographical frontiers. This age also enlarged the frontiers of intellectual and emotional discovery, excavating man's past and acquainting him with other cultures. To pioneer on a frontier, whether an external one—at the edge of a white settlement—or an internal one—at the edge of the known in science, art, or industry—requires a somewhat new type of character that is, to a degree, capable of self-piloting, a type that can act when the guidance of custom breaks down or when a choice must be made among several different sets of customs.

I call this type inner-directed, since the source of direction is internalized. By inner-direction, however, I do not mean genuine autonomy, but rather obedience to an internal psychic

118

"gyroscope" which, installed in childhood, continues to pilot the person as he struggles to master the exigent demands of the frontier. This gyroscope is set going by the parents, or rather by their idealized image (the Freudian superego); or by heroes or great men of antiquity or revered elders taken as models. Driven by these internal voices, the inner-directed person is often ambitious—for fame, for goodness, for accomplishment in the world; and this is as true of the bold men of the Renaissance as of the hard, ascetic Puritans. By their own efforts at self-discipline and self-development, these men often helped to "produce" their own characters; the conquering of this internal frontier was accompanied and rewarded by mastery over others and over nature.

In all I have said, I speak primarily of the middle classes, for it was among them that inner-directed types arose; the lower classes moved more slowly out of feudalism. In time, as the doctrine of predestination became attenuated or forgotten, these middle classes developed an ideology of liberalism and individualism that proclaimed for all men the values of freedom and self-reliance compatible with characterological inner-direction. The inner-directed person came to *feel* free and to *feel* self-made: in his psychological innocence, he was not aware how many of "his" choices had been made for him already by his parents and his conditioning generally. He might have read the famous phrase of Heraclitus—"Character is fate"—to mean that he, as an individual, possessed his own fate, working in him through his own self-mastery; while we today would read the same sentence to mean that our own character is not truly ours, but is produced by our social environment, our "fate" of living in a particular place and time —a new, more sophisticated doctrine of predestination.

119

Moreover, the inner-directed person, living in a time of expanding frontiers, could in fact achieve a small degree of the freedom that he felt. Many inner-directed persons achieved a measure of psychic autonomy and independence as theocratic controls declined in the eighteenth and nineteenth centuries.

II

This security of character was reinforced by the experience of a world which itself appeared to be inner-directed. Adam Smith and other late eighteenth-century thinkers saw society as operating "gyroscopically" in a beneficent direction. In general the men who established the industrial revolution in England and America were as unaware of their countries' good luck [1] as of the forces shaping their own characters. A world that seemed to be running on schedule was, of course, an illusion.

A number of great thinkers during this period did not, however, share the widespread optimism of the rising inner-directed middle class.[2] Of these, Malthus is one of the most interesting. He insisted on the entirely temporary quality of any victory over nature, and, contrary to Condorcet, Godwin, and other progressive thinkers, warned that the natural bounty of the earth—now, so it seemed, thoroughly explored —stood in danger of being turned into parsimony by the "natural" growth of population. Yet even Malthus was, by

[1] Karl Polanyi well describes in *The Great Transformation* the series of happy accidents that made liberal capitalism work in the period before 1914.

[2] Most of these thinkers—Brooks Adams, for example, in America—were isolated men. Matters stand very differently today, when the prophets of despair are so popular that they help produce the very catastrophes they herald.

120

modern standards, optimistic; for he saw the world, not as a bad joke on man, but as a meaningful obstacle race designed to develop man's capacities for rational self-restraint. In our terminology, though not of course in his, he advised people to become inner-directed as the sole means of keeping population in line with subsistence: that is, he advised them to plan ahead, to work hard, and to postpone marriage—thus accumulating wealth without accumulating children. Thus, in effect, he proposed a way out of nature's trap by characterological change.[3]

We can see now, with the advantage of hindsight, that such a program never really had much chance of success. Inner-direction was never very widespread, but rather represented the ideal model toward which people strove. We have evidence that many people of that era tried desperately to conduct themselves in the approved inner-directed way, but were unable to conform. Thus, in Vermont of the eighteenth and nineteenth centuries many more people started diaries and account books—perfect symbols of inner-direction of which Malthus would have approved—than kept them up. Such people must have felt helpless in their efforts at self-mastery, particularly since they took as models those pre-eminent men, from George Washington to Andrew Carnegie, who then stood unshaken by disciples of Marx and Freud. Thus, in a very special sense, the feelings of potency were monopolized by those whose inner-direction was relatively stable and successful in the public mind, while a reservoir of hidden impotence existed. Yet for

[3] Malthus' non-ecclesiastic successors substituted birth-control for chastity—which required less, but still something, in the way of character change. Actually, as far as food supply goes, Godwin, with his high hopes for technological change in agriculture, has turned out to be the better prophet. But, to complete the irony of the account, only for those industrialized countries where inner-direction—and Malthusian attitudes toward life—actually made great strides!

many of the unsuccessful, failure never seemed quite final, and so long as the future beckoned, or the belief in grace persisted, helplessness could be staved off.

III

Individual helplessness and collective power play leapfrog with each other throughout history. Today, the helplessness foreseen by a few thinkers, and sensed even in the earlier age of frontiers by many who failed, has become the common attribute of the mass of men. We turn now to discuss some of the factors responsible for this development: in economic and political life, in methods of child-rearing, and in their consequences for character structure.

When immigration from Europe was cut off in 1924, a great symbol of hope in the Western world was destroyed. The "no help wanted" sign had been posted on the American frontier in 1890, but it was now hung out along our borders for all to see. Today, in the advanced industrial countries, there is only one frontier left—that of consumption—and this calls for very different types of talent and character.

The inner-directed type fitted the conditions of essentially open capitalism, which rewarded ability to envisage new possibilities for production, and zeal to realize those possibilities. To a degree, this is still the case. Nevertheless, we think that, on the whole, contemporary society, especially in America, no longer requires and rewards the old enterprise and the old zeal. This does not mean that the economic system itself is slowing down; total production may continue to rise; but it can be achieved by institutionalizing technological and organizational advance, in research departments, management counsel, and corporate planning staffs. The invention and adoption of new improvements can be routinized, built into the system, so to speak, rather than into the men who run the system. Therefore, the energies of management turn to industrial and public relations, to oiling the frictions not of machines but of men.

Likewise, with the growth of monopolistic competition, the way to get ahead is not so much to make a better mousetrap but rather to "package" an old mousetrap in a new way, and then to sell it by "selling" oneself first. People feel they must be able to adapt themselves to other people, both to manipulate them and to be manipulated by them. This requires the ability to manipulate oneself, to become "a good package," to use a phrase current among personnel men. These pressures are, of course, not confined to business, but operate also in the professions, in government, and in academic life.

As work becomes less meaningful and intense, however, leisure grows and men who are discarded as workers are cultivated in the one role that still matters, that of consumer. This is not an easy role, and people become almost as preoccupied with getting the "best buys" as they once were with finding their proper "calling" in the production economy. They turn, then, to the mass media of communication for advice in how to consume; at the same time, these media help make them anxious lest they fail in the role of consumer. We speak here not merely of "keeping up with the Joneses"—this is part of an older pattern—but rather of the much more unsettling fear of missing those leisure-time experiences, including sex, love, art, friendship, food, travel, which people have been induced to feel they should have.

These changes in the nature of work and leisure have made themselves felt most strongly among the middle classes of the

American big cities in the last twenty-five years or so. It is here that we find developing the character type that I call other-directed, a type whose source of direction is externalized. The clear goals and generalized judgments of the inner-directed types are not implanted in the other-directed person in childhood. Rather, he is taught, vaguely, to do the "best possible" in any given situation. As soon as he can play with other children, he is made sensitive to the judgments of this play group, looking to it for approval and direction as to what is best. Parents and other adults come to value the child in terms of his ability to live up to the group's expectations and to wrest popularity from it.

The adult never loses this dependence, but continues to live psychologically oriented to his contemporaries—to what might be called his "peer group." Of course, it matters very much who these others are: whether they are his immediate circle of the moment, or a higher circle he aspires to, or the anonymous circles of whose doings he learns from the mass media of communication.[4] But the great psychological difference from inner-direction is that this modern type needs open approval and guidance from contemporaries. This new need for approval goes well beyond the human and opportunistic reasons that lead people in any age to care very much what others think of them. People in general want and need to be liked, but it is only the other-directed character type that makes others its chief source of direction and its chief area of sensitivity and concern.

These differences in the source looked to for direction lead to different modes of conformity in the two types. The inner-

---

[4] These are some of the "anonymous authorities" of whom Erich Fromm has written in *Escape from Freedom* and *Man for Himself*.

directed person will ordinarily have had an early choice made
for him among the several available destinies of the middle-
class child. What holds him on course is that he has internalized from his elders certain general aims and drives—the
drive to work hard, or to save money, or to strive for rectitude
or for fame. His conformity results from the fact that similar
drives have been instilled into others of his social class. As
against this, the other-directed person grows up in a much
more amorphous social system, where alternative destinations
cannot be clearly chosen at an early age. The "best possible"
in a particular situation must always be learned from the
others in that situation. His conformity to the others is thus
not one of generalized drives, but of details—the minutiae of
taste or speech or emotion which are momentarily "best."
Hence the internalizes neither detailed habits nor generalized
drives, but instead an awareness of and preoccupation with the
process of securing direction from others.

We can find exemplars of the other-directed character in
leisured urban circles of the past, where the preoccupations
were those of consumption, not production, and where status
depended on the opinion of influential others. What is new is
the spread of such an outlook over large sectors of a middle
class that was once inner-directed. Elements of this outlook,
moreover, have now filtered down in America to many members of the lower-middle class.

It is my tentative conclusion that the feeling of helplessness
of modern man results from both the vastly enhanced power of
the social group and the incorporation of its authority into his
very character. And the point at issue is not that the other-
directed character is more opportunistic than the inner-directed
—if anything, the contrary is true. Rather, the point is that

the individual is psychologically dependent on others for clues to the meaning of life. He thus fails to resist authority or fears to exercise freedom of choice even where he might safely do so.

An illustration may clarify my meaning. I have sometimes asked university students why they come to class so regularly day after day, why they do not—as they are technically free to do—take two or three weeks off to do anything they like on their own. The students have answered that they must come to class or otherwise they will flunk, though the fact is that many students get ahead when they finally do break through the routines. It has become apparent that the students cling to such "rational" explanations because, in their feeling of helplessness, freedom is too much of a threat. They fail to see those loopholes of which they could take advantage for their own personal development; they feel safer if they are obeying an authoritative ritual in sympathetic company. Their attendance at class has much the same meaning as the Pueblo Indian's rain-making dance, only the student has less confidence that his "prayer" will be heard. For he has left "home" for good, and all of modern thought teaches him too much for comfort and too little for help.

We can, of course, find far more drastic illustrations of the loss of individual self-reliance by looking to the field of political theory and practice. We may, for instance, compare the attitude which Hobbes held toward state power in the seventeenth century with the attitude of some nineteenth and twentieth century advocates of tyranny. Hobbes, in the *Leviathan,* held that the only intelligent recourse of the individual in a world of power was to surrender to it and to form with his fellows an all-powerful state that could repress internal violence and resist external foes. Above all an individualist, Hobbes saw the state as a necessary evil, useful only so long as it delivered physical security, but without any *ideological* claims. He wrote that a state was entitled to obedience only so far as its strong arm reached, but he did not think kings ruled by divine right nor would he have been deceived today by the equivalent superstition of nationalism. Hobbes believed people needed a strong state as a physical umbrella, not as a psychic altar. For example, he defended the individual's privilege against self-incrimination: the state, he wrote, had every right to kill a subject, with or without reason, if it had the power; but it could not expect cooperation from the victim, who had every right to resist. In his whole outlook, Hobbes spoke for the individual, whose interests, he felt, could be protected in a time of anarchy only by strong, tyrannical rule.

In the last hundred years, many thinkers have echoed Hobbes' desire for a strong, centralized state. But until very recent years their concern has been primarily with an attempt to satisfy psychological cravings—their own or those of the masses—for the sake of unity and emotional cohesion. Comte, for instance, desired a secular state that would match the medieval Church in evoking men's devotion. Freud, who resembles Hobbes in his view of man's aggressiveness, believed this aggressiveness could not be curbed by appeals to self-interest, but only by providing leaders with whom and through whom men might establish emotional ties. (See his *Group Psychology and the Analysis of the Ego.*)

In general—this is not true of Freud—modern reactionary thinkers begin with the society and not, like Hobbes, with the individual. Their fastidious distaste for disunity and "chaos" —their uneasiness in the open rough-and-tumble of democratic

politics and capitalist economics—leads them to a blind worship of group solidarity and the "leader." Modern totali-
tarianism however, exploits these psychological attitudes and
fosters an internal as well as international anarchy far worse
than that which plagued Hobbes. Only on the surface can a
totalitarian movement provide solidarity and emotional cohesion even for its own following. The struggle for power goes
on inside the movement, and the reactionary thinkers who
abetted the seizure of power are among the first to become
disillusioned—and dispensable.

During the last war, the British and Americans captured a
number of Russians who had been taken prisoner by the Nazis.
Most of these men were quite sure that they would be killed if
they returned to Russia. This is not surprising, but what was
striking to us was their complete lack of indignation at the
prospect. Some simply took it for granted; others even justified
it. One man, a schoolteacher, said that Stalin would be entirely
justified in killing him or anyone else who had been in the
West, for such a person could never again be completely satisfied in Russia. The *Leviathan* of Hobbes stands outside the
individual and tells him to join, or else suffer the consequences; but these Russians carried *Leviathan* inside them.

This modern nationalism has a very different psychological
meaning from that of the businesslike nationalism of Hobbes.
It also differs from the more progressive nationalisms of the
pre-totalitarian era, which date from a time when the state did
not exist, or was weak, and had to be created by individual
effort. *Modern* nationalism, on the other hand, insists on emotional submission to a power that is already armed with
unbeatable military force and with immense economic and

propaganda powers. Shortly before his death, Largo Cabal-
lero, former Republican premier of Spain, said:

I would like to see every bricklayer go to work with his rifle slung
on his shoulder. Then I know that nothing could exist in Spain except
the will of the great mass of Spaniards.

For us, in "the years of the modern," the statement has an
archaic ring. We happen to live at a moment when, as Hannah
Arendt has pointed out, the state is so overwhelming that even
martyrdom—the last despairing appeal of the individual
human spirit against the group—is no longer possible.

Americans may feel that all this does not apply to them, but
only to the totalitarian states. The latter, to be sure, are extreme instances, but Americans are perhaps not sufficiently
aware of the current changes in the quality of their own nationalism. For many people, the program of their lives is
determined by fear of a fifth column, and what the Russians
or their allies do is an urgent and an all-embracing preoccupation. To such persons there is little identification with America
in terms of positive aims, but rather a neurotic clinging to a
shadow-war in which our national Superman is engaged.

We may conclude that while the state, through technological
and organizational change, has become immensely powerful,
the individual, through characterological change, has become
less capable of psychological resistance to his contemporaries.
Modern man feels helpless, and justifies this feeling by looking
at the frightening world around him. Like a hypochondriac,
he uses the undeniable threat of real danger to rationalize an
even greater anxiety than a balanced view might warrant.

129

During the long Victorian period, people assumed a danger-free existence as the norm of life; possibly our present hypochondria comes in part from learning the falseness of that assumption. People of a different history have often lived comfortably in the face of impending misery.

IV

Let us examine several further factors that have robbed the middle-class individual of his defenses against the pressure of the group. We shall deal in somewhat more detail with changes in the nature of private property, of work, and of leisure, all of which at one time functioned as defenses.

In the feudal era, the individual was attached to property, largely land, by feudal and family ties. The breakdown of feudalism meant helplessness for many peasants, who were thrown off the land; but for the middle class the result was a gradual gain in consciousness of strength. A new type of relationship between persons and property developed: the person was no longer attached to property, but attached property to himself by his own energetic actions. Property, including land, became freely alienable; at the same time, it was felt to be an individual, not a family, possession. And property was satisfying, substantial—an extended part of the self. Inside the shell of his possessions, the inner-directed person could resist psychological invasion.

Today, however, property is not much of a defense. Taxes and other state activities, inflation and the panicky desire for liquid assets, have made it factually friable. Moreover, the fears of property-holders outrun the actual dangers. Thus, even powerful groups in America feel more frightened of

Communism than its actual power warrants. Property no longer represents the old security for those who hold it, and the fear that it may vanish any day makes it as much a source of anxiety as of strength. The rich no longer dare flaunt wealth, but tread softly, guided by considerations of "public relations." Wealthy students often act as if ashamed of their wealth; I have sometimes been tempted to point out that the rich are a minority and have rights, too.

The change in the meaning of work is even plainer. For the inner-directed person, work seemed self-justifying: the only problem was to find the work to which one felt called. As we have seen, the age of expanding frontiers provided the individual with an inexhaustible list of tasks. Work, like property, moreover, was considered a mode of relating oneself to physical objects, and only indirectly to people. Indeed, the work-hungry inner-directed types of this period sometimes found that they were cut off from family and friends, and often from humanity in general, by their assiduity and diligence. And work, like property, was a defense against psychological invasion, a "do not disturb" sign guarding the industrious man of the middle class.

Today the meaning of work is a very different one, psychologically, though in many professions and industries the older modes still persist. To an increasing degree, the self is no longer defined by its productive accomplishments but by its role in a "Friendship" system. As the "isolate" or "rate-buster" is punished and excluded from the work force in the shop, so the lone wolf is weeded out of management; up-to-date personnel men use deep-probing psychological tests to

131

eliminate applicants, whatever their other gifts, who lack the other-directed personality needed for the job.

To be sure, out of anxiety, a lingering asceticism, and a need for an impressive agenda, the professional and business men and women of the big cities continue to work hard, or more accurately, to spend long hours in the company of their fellow "antagonistic cooperators": "work" is seen as a network of personal relationships that must be constantly watched and oiled. Increasingly, both work and leisure call on the same sort of skills—sociability, sensitivity to others' feelings and wants, and the exercise of taste-preferences freed from direct considerations of economic advantage. Work in this case has a certain unreality for people, since it has almost floated free from any connection with technical crafts. The latter have been built into machines, or can be easily taught; but people must still go to the office and find ways of keeping, or at least looking, busy. Thus in many circles work and leisure are no longer clearly distinguished—as we can see by observing a luncheon or a game of golf among competitors.

The feeling of powerlessness of the other-directed character is, then, the result in part of the lack of genuine commitment to work. His life is not engaged in a direct struggle for mastery over himself and nature; he has no long-term goals since the goals must constantly be changed. At the same time, he is in competition with others for the very values they tell him are worth pursuing; in a circular process, one of these values is the approval of the competing group itself. Hence, he is apt to repress overt competitiveness both out of anxiety to be liked and out of fear of retaliation. In this situation, he is likely to lose interest in the work itself. With loss of interest, he may even find himself little more than a dilettante, not quite sure that he is really able to accomplish anything.

From this it follows that this type of other-directed person is not able to judge the work of others—for one thing, he is no longer sufficiently interested in work as such. He must constantly depend on specialists and experts whom he cannot evaluate with any assurance. That dependence is an inevitable and indeed a valuable fruit of the division of labor in modern society; but the inability even to dare to pass personal judgment is a defect rooted in the character of the other-directed person.

When we turn from the sphere of work to the sphere of leisure, we see again that roles in which the individual could once find refuge from and defense against the group have become stylized roles, played according to the mandates and under the very eyes of the group. The individual in the age of inner-direction had little leisure; often he was so work-driven he could not even use the leisure given him. On occasion, however, he could escape from the pressures and strains of the workaday world into a private hobby or into the resources of culture, either "high-brow" or popular. In either case, the stream of entertainment and communication was intermittent; to come into contact with it required effort. Leisure, therefore, by its very scarcity, provided a change of pace and role. Moreover, beyond these actual leisure roles stood a group of fantasy roles—roles of social ascent, of rebellion against work and inhibition, dreams of world-shaking achievement; the individual was protected against invasion at least of his right to these dreams.

Today, leisure is seldom enjoyed in solitude, nor is it often

133

used for unequivocal escape. Hobbies of the older craft type seem to have declined, and a baseball game is perhaps the only performance where the mass audience can still judge competence. The torrent of words and images from radio, the movies, and the comics begins to pour on the child even before he can toddle; he starts very early to learn his lifelong role of consumer. The quantity of messages impinging on the child becomes increasingly "realistic"; instead of "Just-So Stories" and fairy tales, children are given "here and now" stories of real life, and escape into imaginative fantasy is therefore held at a minimum.

Likewise, movies, fiction, and radio for adults increasingly deal with "here and now" problems: how to handle one's relations with children, with the opposite sex, with office colleagues away from the office. Story writers for the better woman's magazines are instructed to deal with the intimate problems faced by the readers, and soap opera is one long game of Going to Jerusalem: when one problem sits down, another is left standing. Indeed, we might claim, there is no "escape" from leisure. Wherever we turn, in work or in popular culture, we are faced by our peers and the problems they present, including the pressure they put on us to "have fun." A kind of ascetic selflessness rules much of the greatly expanded leisure of the other-directed person: selflessness disguised by the craving for comfort, fun, and effortlessness, but ascetic nonetheless in its tense use of leisure for preparing oneself to meet the expectations of others.

Thus, the newly reached horizons of leisure and consumption made possible by our economic abundance have not been as exhilarating for the individual as the realized horizons of work and production proved to be for many in the age of

134

expanding frontiers. On the frontiers of consumption, limitless in quality and almost equally so in quantity, men stand anxiously, haunted by the fear of missing some consumption-experience which they are supposed to have enjoyed. Young men and women today, for instance, in some urban middle-class circles, often feel they must walk a tightrope in their sex lives: they must have "experiences," yet they must not become involved emotionally on any deep level of human tenderness and intimacy. And the while they are worried lest they are incapable of loving anyone. The word of the "wise" to the young—"don't get involved"—has changed its meaning in a generation. Once it meant: don't get, or get someone, pregnant; don't run afoul of the law; don't get in the newspapers. Today the injunction is more deeply psychological; it seeks to control, not the overt experience, but its emotional interpretation in terms of smooth, unruffled manipulation of the self. This transformation is characteristic of the change from inner-direction, with its clear and generalized mandates, to other-direction, with its emphasis on the process of receiving from others very detailed stage directions in the work-play of life.

To sum up, the inner-directed person had a sense of power as he faced the group because of his relationship to property, to work, and to leisure; and because both he and the group accepted certain specific rights that encouraged any individual to be himself. Such persons often became men of substance and men of the world—they made the world *theirs*. If we look at the portraits of the more eminent men in a centuries-long gallery stretching from Holbein to John Singer Sargent, we can see that they were indeed solid citizens. Today the solid citizen has given way to the "solid sender," the "good Joe,"

not solid enough to risk offending anyone and afraid of dis-
obeying the subtle and impermeable injunctions of the contemporary "peer group" to whom he looks for approval. He
is a sender and receiver of messages in a network of personal
ties which, unlike the personal ties of a folk society, neither
warm nor protect him.

On the surface, it might appear that the individual today
feels powerless because he finds no protection from the hazards
of war and depression. He feels weak because he has no control
over these vast matters that are decisive for him; to avert war
or internal catastrophe he cannot even turn to a ritual. Yet,
granting these objective reasons for anxiety and weakness, we
must nevertheless ask, why is war so likely, when few people
want it? I suggest that one reason—certainly not the only one!
—is simply that great numbers of people do not in fact enjoy
life enough. They are not passionately attached to their lives,
but rather cling to them. The very need for direction that is
implied in our phrases of inner-direction and other-direction
signifies that one has turned over one's life to others in exchange for an agenda, a program for getting through the day.

To be sure, the abdication is not complete. But the fact
remains that the person who is not autonomous loses much of
the joy that comes through strength—through the effort to live
one's life, not necessarily heroically, but, come what may, in
full commitment to it. Modern life, for many people, is full of
tense and anxious relationships to people, to production and
consumption; therefore, these people are prepared to resign
themselves to war which does, after all, promise certain com-
pensations in group companionship and shared meanings.

Thus, we have come full circle from Hobbes' view of man.

For him, people risked war because they were selfish individualists, and he reasoned with them that they were better off in the *Leviathan*. Modern man does not want to risk war, but allows it to come with astonishingly little protest because, fundamentally, he is not an individualist. It is tractable men who operate the intractable institutions that now precipitate war, and when it comes, it is they who conduct it.

V

I do not mean to imply that our society "produces" other-directed people because such people are in demand in an increasingly monopolistic, managerial economy. The relations between character and society are not that simple. Moreover, neither character nor society changes all at once. But it would take us too far afield to trace the many formative agencies in the still far-from-complete shift from inner-direction to other-direction in the middle classes.

Furthermore, I must guard against the implication that I think inner-direction is a way of life preferable to other-direction. Each type has its virtues and its vices: the inner-directed person tends to be rigid and intolerant of others; the other-directed person, in turn, is likely to be flexible and sensitive to others. Neither type is altogether comfortable in the world. But in different ways each finds the discomforts it needs psychologically in order, paradoxically, to feel comfortable. The inner-directed person finds the struggle to master himself and the environment quite appropriate; he feels comfortable climbing uphill. The other-directed person finds equally appropriate the malaise that he shares with many others. Engrossed in the activities that the culture provides, he can remain relatively unconscious of his anxiety and tone-

137

lessness. Moreover, the character type must always be judged
in context. Many persons who are inner-directed and who, in
an earlier age, would have gone through life in relative peace,
today find themselves indignant at a big-city world in which
they have not felt at home. Other-directed persons also may
not feel at home, but home never had the same meaning for
them. It would appear to the envious inner-directed observer,
that the other-directed manage their lives better in a mass
society. Conversely, the other-directed may envy the seeming
firmness of the inner-directed, and look longingly back on
the security of nineteenth-century society, while failing to
see that firmness was often merely stubbornness and security
merely ignorance.

VI

What I have said about the loss of the individual's defenses
is recognized by many thinkers who, however, feel that through
voluntary associations people can attain securities analogous
to those which family and clan provided in the era of primary
ties, and for which work and property made additional provision in the days of expanding frontiers. They see labor
unions as giving a feeling of solidarity to the working class,
and even to increasing numbers of white-collar employees;
they see racial minorities protected by their defense organizations, and farmers by their cooperatives; they see "group
belongingness," in some sort of informal association, available
to all but the most depressed. The advocacy of this as the chief
remedy for the loneliness of the individual is an admission
of his weakness. But it is more than that. It bolsters another
set of power-combinations, only slightly democratized by individual participation. And it adds to the pressure on the

individual to *join,* to submerge himself in the group—any group—and to lower still further not only his feeling that he can, but that he has a right, to stand on his own.

Conceivably, these associations in the future will succeed in strengthening the individual's feeling of his own powers by providing him with defenses, political, economic, and psychological, and by encouraging him to gain, outside his work, a variety of skills, encounters, and experiences. In the meantime, however, with the balance between helplessness and power tipped in favor of the former, the "voluntary" associations are not voluntary enough to do this job.

I turn now to examine another voluntary association, that between the sexes, whose nature, in our age as in any age, provides a profound clue to the state of subjective feelings of power and helplessness. In this context, the rapid change I discern in the denigration by American women of their own sex seems ominous. Eighty years ago, John Stuart Mill (turning to a theme touched on by Condorcet's *On the Admission of Women to the Rights of Citizenship*) wrote *The Subjection of Women* in order to show how attitudes toward this "minority" poisoned all social life; how both men and women suffered from the power-relations that prevailed between them; and how women's potentialities, even more than those of men, were crushed by social pressure. He observed that "the greater part of what women write about women is mere sycophancy to men." But he was gentle with women for he added, "no enslaved class ever asked for complete liberty at once. . . ."

In the intervening period, women did not attain "complete liberty," but they came a long way toward equality with men. In the years after 1890 and until recently, American young women of the middle class insisted on sharing with men the tasks and excitements of civilization. Today there is some evidence that many women of this class have retreated; they have again become enemies of emancipation of their sex; as the weaker power, they judge each other through the eyes of men.

Women today feel under almost as great a pressure to get married as did their pre-emancipation ancestors. In a certain way, they are under greater pressure, since all sorts of psychological aspersions are cast at them if they stay single too long.[5]

Perhaps all this means simply that women have won the battle of emancipation and can relax. I am inclined, however, to think that there is an increasing submissiveness of women to what men want of them, and to the world as men have largely made it. I interpret this, in part, as testimony to the fact that men today are far too anxious, too lacking in psychological defenses against each other, to tolerate critically-minded women. The women they want must be intelligent enough to flatter their vanity but not to challenge their prerogatives as men. Men once complained to their mistresses that their wives did not understand them; now they would complain if they did. For in their own competitive orientation to the world. men would interpret understanding from the side of women as still another, and underhanded, form of competition. This is partly because, since Mill's day, the economic and social power of women has grown; they can no longer be so obviously kept in their places. Hence their gifts, their critical powers, can no longer be patronized by powerful men, but must be subtly destroyed by anxious ones and their willing allies among the women themselves. Men and women, in their weakness, act like those minorities who throughout history

[5] Indeed, men, too, feel under pressure to get married early among other reasons, lest they be thought homosexual.

have kept each other in subjection in the face of an oppressive power.[6]

In sum, men and women eye each other not as allies, but, at best, as antagonistic cooperators. In their roles as parents, they are uncertain of their children and whether they will be liked by them; in turn, this anxiety is absorbed by the children. In earlier epochs of history, events outside the home were interpreted, often somewhat narrowly, through the perspective of family needs and family morality. Today, the situation is reversed, and the home must be adjusted to the values of the outside. As with the state, "domestic policy" and "foreign policy" are interdependent, and the conflicts and strains of each sphere add to weakness in the other.

We come, then, to a conclusion that would seem paradoxical: certain groups in society have grown weaker, but others have not gained in strength at their expense; rather, weakness has engendered weakness. And the state, the beneficiary of individual weakness, is ruled by men who are themselves no less weak than the rest. Even the dictators and their henchmen only seem strong under the imagery of modern propaganda. While the savage believes he will gain in potency by drinking the blood or shrinking the head of his enemy, in the modern

[6] Something of the same transformation has occurred in the relation between parents and children. Even as men are worried lest they might not pass the test with women, so parents are afraid that their children will not approve of them— a problem that would hardly have troubled the person of inner-directed character. While parents appear to be terribly concerned to give their children approval—as they are told by all the textbooks to do—this disguises the parents' own dependence on being approved of by the children, who stand, as Margaret Mead has noted, for the New, for Youth, for the American Way—or, as I might say, for better other-direction. Moreover, parents assume the role of advisors and managers of their children's competitive struggles. This new family constellation is in fact one of the changes that may partly account for the formation of the other-directed character.

141

world no individual gains in strength of character from the weakness of his fellows.

VII

Nevertheless, even under modern conditions, and out of the very matrix of other-directed modes of conformity, some people strive toward an autonomous character. An autonomous person has no compulsive need to follow the other-direction of his culture and milieu—and no compulsive need to flout it, either. We know almost nothing about the factors that make for such positive results; it is easier to understand the sick than to understand why some stay well. It hardly helps to repeat our point that man's helplessness is the condition for his every advance, because this generalization tells us too little about individual cases. However, it seems that the helplessness of modern man in a world of power has been one element in the genesis of some of the extraordinary human achievements of our age. Some of these achievements are the physical and literary productions of men's hands and minds, but other achievements lie in the internal "productions" of men—their characters; it is of these that I speak here.

There were autonomous people of course, in the era of inner-direction, but they were made of sterner stuff; the barriers they encountered were the classic ones: family, religion, poverty. On the other hand, the person who seeks autonomy today in the upper socio-economic levels of the Western democracies is not faced with the barriers that normally restricted him in the past. The coercions against his independence are frequently invisible. An autonomous person of the middle class must work constantly to detach himself from shadowy entanglements with his culture—so difficult to break with because its demands appear so "reasonable," so trivial.

For our study of autonomy, we have drawn freely on Erich Fromm's concept of the "productive orientation" in *Man for Himself*. Fromm shows the orientation of a type of character that can relate itself to people through love, and to objects and the world generally through the creative gift. The struggle for a productive orientation becomes exigent at the very moment in history when solution of the problem of production itself, in the technical sense, is in sight.

All human beings, even the most productive, the most autonomous, are fated, in a sense, to die the death of Ivan Ilyitch, in Tolstoy's "The Death of Ivan Ilyitch," who becomes aware only on his deathbed of his underlived life and his unused potentialities for autonomy. All of us realize only a fraction of our potentialities. Always a matter of degree, always blended with residues of inner-direction or other-direction, autonomy is a process, not an achievement. Indeed, we may distinguish the autonomous by the fact that his character is never a finished product, but always a lifelong growth.

I speak of autonomy as an aspect of character structure, and not in terms of independence of overt behavior. The autonomous person may or may not conform in his behavior to the power-requirements of society; he can choose whether to conform or not. (The Bohemians and rebels are not usually autonomous; on the contrary, they are zealously tuned in to the signals of a defiant group that finds the meaning of life in a compulsive non-conformity to the majority group.) Yet the separation of "freedom in behavior" from "autonomy in character" cannot be complete. Autonomy requires self-awareness about the fact of choice, about possible ways of living. The autonomous person of today exists precisely be-

143

cause we have reached an awareness of the problem of choice that was not required among the Pueblos, or, for the most part, in the Middle Ages, or even in the period after the Reformation, when the concepts of God's will and of duty confined choice for many within fairly narrow bounds.

The very fluidity of modern democratic social systems, that, for the mass of people, results in anxiety and "escape from freedom," forces those who would become autonomous to find their own way. They must "choose themselves," in Sartre's phrase, out of their very alienation from traditional ties and inner-directed defenses which inhibited true choice in the past. However, I think Sartre mistaken in his Kantian notion that men can choose themselves under totalitarian conditions. Likewise, if the choices that matter are made for us by the social system, even if it is in appearance a democratic system, then our sense of freedom also will atrophy: most people need the opportunity for some freedom of behavior if they are to develop and confirm their autonomy of character. Nevertheless, the rare autonomous character we have been describing, the man of high, almost precarious, quality, must arise from that aloneness, that helplessness of modern man, that would overwhelm a lesser person. It is in this quality, and in the mode of life he is groping to achieve, that he has made a contribution to the problem of living in a power-world. Often, in vanity, we judge our own era as the most advanced or the most retrograde, yet the type of perspective on the world and the self that thousands of people have today was probably matched in the past by only a few.

The people I speak of live under urbanized conditions in every land, but they are world citizens in thought and feeling. Sensitive to wide perspectives of time and space, they have

largely transcended prejudices of race or time or class. Their
guides are diverse, and they feel empathy and solidarity with
their colleagues across all national boundaries. There have
been cosmopolitans before, but their horizons were limited by
want of knowledge, and their view of man was necessarily
abstract. There have been internationalists before, but they
have been restricted by class and region. The contemporary
autonomous person has all the sensitivity to others of the
other-directed type: he needs some interpersonal warmth, and
close friends mean much to him; but he does not have an
irrational craving for indiscriminate approval.

In one relationship, that between the sexes, the men and
women who are striving for autonomy are seeking an equality
that takes account of differences, an equality of which Mill
would have approved. Here women are not the subtle slaves
of men, nor do they flatter them as the feminists did by seeking
to adopt men's particular privileges and problems. Though
we have as yet to attain a new model of marriage, grounded
neither in contract nor in sex alone but in mutual growth
towards autonomy, we see new sets of roles developed by
people who have achieved relationships to which both partners
contribute from their productive gifts. It is unlikely, however,
that beyond such families, and small groups of friends or
colleagues, there exist any sizeable institutions or organizations predominantly composed of autonomous folk. It is hard
to imagine an autonomous society coming into being now,
even on a small scale, or perhaps especially on a small scale.[7]

[7] Mary McCarthy describes with humor and insight the fate of an imaginary
enclave of intellectuals seeking autonomy in her story "The Oasis." (*Horizon*,
19, [1949], 75; see, also, for some of the institutional problems, my article, "Some
Observations on Community Plans and Utopia," *Yale Law Journal*, 57, [1947],
173.)

The fact is, moreover, that the autonomous group is hardly aware of its own existence. Those who are to some degree autonomous may not always reveal themselves as such, preferring to conform overtly out of conscious choice. As a result, the potentially autonomous often do not discover each other, though they would in that very process strengthen and defend their own autonomy.

Indeed, the potentially autonomous person tends to bewail as a tragedy his isolation from the masses and from power. He passes by the opportunity of his lot—an opportunity to develop his individuality and its fruits in art and character. Hence he wishes he could undergo a metamorphosis and rid himself of the problem of choice, indeed of his very autonomous strivings; he wishes he were like the others—whose adjustment he often overemphasizes—thus revealing his own other-directed components. By these very tendencies to betray himself and his partially achieved autonomy, he becomes weaker and less autonomous.

The autonomous few can do little enough to reduce the strength of atom bombs and of the hands that now hold them, but some can at least defend their own and others' individuality, and pioneer in various ways of living autonomously. They will enjoy this pioneering to a degree, though it will be held against them by the envious and frightened ones who have abandoned the effort toward autonomy.

If these conjectures are accurate, then it follows that, by a process of unconscious polarization which is going on in society, a few people are becoming more self-consciously autonomous than before, while many others are losing their social and characterological defenses against the group. The latter, though politically strong, are psychically weak, and the autonomous minority, by its very existence, threatens the whole shaky mode of adaptation of the majority.

Nevertheless, joy in life has its own dynamic. We have said that people today are not sufficiently attached to life. We have traced this to their other-directed character structure, and this in turn to large-scale social changes. Yet character structure is not completely fixed for the individual, so long as life lasts, or for the group. Men have some control over the fate by which their characters are made. By showing how life can be lived with vitality and happiness even in time of trouble, the autonomous people can become a social force, indeed a "saving remnant." By converting present helplessness into a condition of advance, they lay the groundwork for a new society, though, like Condorcet, they may not live to see it.

Prophets in Moscow say that America is even now sliding toward a depression, and will soon fall with a resounding crash. Friendly experts in Western Europe label such predictions wishful thinking, yet they are gravely concerned about the future of our economic life. In our own country the so-called free enterprise system provokes decided differences of opinion.

Many business and some labor leaders extoll it. World War II, they point out, proved this system to be the greatest productive force in the world. It has performed prodigies, and will continue to do so, if only government will not shackle or impede it.

The majority of Americans are less convinced. To them the depression is more than a memory. Though they know that measures have been taken to guard against a recurrence, a sense of insecurity still persists.

Back of American uncertainty lies the fact that we have been reluctant to face many of the truths about our economy. Yet we have the information; a realistic picture can be drawn.

But will its significance be accepted by capital and labor? Will they assume the responsibilities which the picture shows to be theirs?

6

J. K. Galbraith

THE AMERICAN ECONOMY:
Its Substance and Myth

I

Apart from Switzerland and one or two of the adult offspring of Socialist England, the United States is the last of the developed countries that finds it politic, or even possible, to call itself a capitalist country. In this sense—and it is to be re-called that in different countries the same institutions are called by different names—the United States is the last of the capitalist countries. This essay is an enquiry into the attitude toward capitalism of the last refuge of avowed capitalism. It is an important subject.

Since the end of the late war, one segment of American com-ment had depicted this attitude in exceptionally brilliant colors. We are presented to ourselves and to strangers as a lone island of youthful confidence and self-assurance in a world that is either searching for a debilitating security or has taken refuge in an all-embracing authoritarianism. Uniquely, we are sure of the quality and durability of our economic institutions.

Unhappily there is much that belies this heroic image. In a week of strictly random selection early this year, the newspapers reported that the retail businessmen of the United States were launching "the largest combined promotional effort in the history of retailing" because, in the words of one of the architects of this somewhat breath-taking enterprise, "We have fallen short of selling our American system along with our products." The President of Columbia University— by tradition a source of grave advices as to our fate—warned the American people that they were threatened by expanding bureaucracy, the disappearance of private ownership, and, more remotely, by dictatorship. The radio sought nightly to rally the citizen's interest in what it termed "your economic system," and it added a plea that he struggle to make it work better. The sickly behavior of the stock market could be explained only by a general foreboding of disaster.

All this, it must be stressed, was in a time of exceptional well-being. Viewed merely as a technical device for providing individuals with the things they want, or are persuaded they should have, American capitalism was and had been demonstrating remarkable vigor. The resulting rewards, if less widely distributed than the most ardent defenders of the system might imagine, were almost certainly leaving more people more nearly satisfied with their livelihood than ever previously in modern history. Anyone who seeks to understand American capitalism must, if he seeks honestly, find an explanation for a pervasive insecurity amid actual or realizable well-being.

II

The explanation begins with the absence of an accepted or acceptable *rationale* of what we still choose, with such semantical variations as "free enterprise," "private enterprise," and the "price system," to call capitalism in the United States. The words accepted and acceptable must be emphasized. The problem begins with the existence of an interpretation of contemporary economic life, which I shall outline in a moment, that is neither accepted by a great majority of Americans nor wholly acceptable as a characterization of things as they are. Broadly, very broadly, speaking, the line of belief and disbelief separates those who have, or are associated with, the responsibility for the direction of business enterprises— a responsibility of undoubted importance in the American community—from those who are not. On the one hand are the businessmen who actively accept the interpretation; on the other, the workers, farmers, and influential and unclassifiable millions of teachers, preachers, civil servants and wage-earning journalists who passively reject it. The consequences are serious for both but especially for those who are adherents. Their interpretation of modern capitalism serves them as a faith; it does not provide them with any usable explanation of the economy of which they are a part. Their eyes tell them that their faith is not shared by what is clearly a majority of their fellow-citizens. Their common sense not infrequently tells them that their faith is not one by which a nation can live. It is scarcely to be wondered that they are troubled men.

What may, for the convenience of a title, be called *the conventional doctrine of American capitalism* now belongs not with those ideas that are communicated through books, lectures, or sermons, but with those that result from simple acceptance of normal and commonplace attitudes. Nevertheless, its antecedents in the realm of ideas are identifiable—and the pedigree is important. The core of what is believed to be true of American capitalism was taught by Adam Smith and, through the nineteenth century, by the succeeding generations of the great English classicists. The United States itself produced many exponents of these ideas but comparatively few innovators. (To some extent the final word as to what is true or not true in economics must still be given by an Englishman.)

In barest essential, the classical *rationale* of capitalism was a theory, first, of how the individual was motivated, and second of how he was limited in the exercise of power to what was good for the community. Man exerted himself because of the prospect of participating in some practical way in the fruits of his own efforts. This share was assured, yet the possibility of profiting excessively was precluded, by the fact of competition. The individual could not misuse power, for he was assumed to have none. If he sought to exploit either those from whom he bought or those to whom he sold, both suppliers (including his workers) and his customers would abandon him in favor of a competitor. Man was made into a social animal by self-interest, and kept so by the man across the street.

The system of economics that was erected on these ideas was a structure of many embellishments and some grandeur. Neither the embellishments nor the grandeur survive, but the doctrine of motivation and limitation of power remain intact in the conventional doctrine of American capitalism. They lie at the root of the most profound source of uneasiness of the American conservative, the fear of the state.

The state, which the Marxians presented as the handmaiden of the businessman, designed to serve his merest whim, has emerged in the United States as the specter that haunts his dreams. Once the basic tenets of the conventional doctrine are recognized and its hold over men's minds conceded, the reasons for the fear become plain. There is little that the state can do that is necessary and much that is damaging. If an individual in pursuit of his own interest can do no wrong, it follows that he need not be guided, directed or coerced by authority. If competition denies power to the individual—if his prices, wages, production and profits are controlled by his competitors—then there is no reason for the state to restrain misuse of private power. Why intervene to control that which does not exist?

Until the nineteenth century, the recurrent experience of man was with the privileged, corrupt, ill-conceived or intellectually presumptuous acts of his sovereign. This was an added reason for decrying intervention. The presumption of an intrinsically evil sovereign also survives in the conventional doctrine of American capitalism.

While little has happened to divorce the businessman in America from the conventional doctrine, much has happened to make it irrelevant for other groups. Most important has been the changing motives of the state. In the United States in the post-revolutionary years, as in England at the same time, the state was either the enemy of the burgeoning business classes or, at best, the capricious friend of those who enjoyed special favors. It was the friend of no other considerable group except its own employees. In nearly all Western countries during the nineteenth century and in the United States more recently, it has appeared as the friend of the many. So far as the New Deal had revolutionary significance, this was it. Although Americans at large may still consider the Federal government awkward, indecisive, and even unreliable, they consider it benign. Yet in the conventional doctrine it remains malignant; such articulators of the doctrine as the spokesmen of the National Association of Manufacturers faithfully so picture it. It is hardly surprising that, to the recipient of social-security benefits, guaranteed farm prices, good roads or R.E.A. power, this aspect of conventional doctrine makes no sense. Within a matter of a century, Western governments have changed from being mainly malevolent to mainly benevolent. The change remains unrecognized in traditional doctrine but not at the polls.

At the same time, there has been a change in the character of capitalism, or in what is known to be the character of capitalism, that has struck at the underpinnings of the conventional doctrine. It can no longer be denied that the modern corporation (and likewise the modern trade-union) has power. Corporations have power not because they have escaped from all competition—the hold of the conventional doctrine is greatly strengthened by the continuance of intense commercial rivalry—but because they have largely escaped the kind of competition that precludes power. The prices and the costs of the individual wheat grower and even the individual small soft-coal operator are given by the market; the amounts they produce and, in the last analysis, the profits they make or the losses they take are beyond their control. Should any one choose to exercise his ultimate sanction against society and go out of business entirely, he would not be missed. Competition in their case—the competition of many small individuals—is still an effective solvent of private power.

But neither the wheat grower nor the bituminous-coal operator is the archetype of capitalist enterprise in America. In the thirties the figure of "200" became a magic symbol in describing the American economy; it was used to denote the number of firms that roughly but unmistakably produced on the order of half of the physical product of the economy. Each of these corporations does exercise power. The United States Steel Corporation exercises unmistakable though not unlimited control over the prices which people pay for steel. It has power to alter these prices in accordance with its assessment of the interests of its owners, management, workers and the public. Such power as the government exercised over these prices in wartime differed in degree but not in kind. One of the most hotly debated questions of the last three years has been whether the steel industry's decisions on prices and on construction of new capacity have been in the public interest. It need hardly be suggested that this debate presupposes that the steel industry has power to govern in, or against, the public interest. As with steel, so with the remainder of the great core of American business enterprise. The presence of such power in private hands is obviously inconsistent with a doctrine that defends capitalism on the ground that it denies power to anyone.

No such ostentatious conflict between doctrine and fact could have gone unnoticed. It has not. And the manner of its recognition has deeply aggravated the insecurity of the businessman. If he denies that he has power—power not accorded him by the conventional doctrine—he stands refuted by the very decisions he must make, for this is not power that can be assumed or divested at will. If he defends his exercise of power as judicious and in the public interest, he admits to having plenary powers to govern the economy. He risks conceding that the state should hold him to account for his stewardship.

The businessman's discomfiture is enhanced by the reaction of liberals to his exercise of power. In a tradition that survives almost alone in the United States, one powerful wing of American liberalism accepts the conventional doctrine as a norm.

157

But, unlike the businessman, it does not assume that the *status quo* approaches the norm. Its all but invariable conviction is that the existing organization of business is sharply inconsistent with the basic requirements of the conventional doctrine. It therefore insists, primarily through vigorous enforcement of the antitrust laws, that the exercise of private power be reduced. Those business practices, most notably collusion between firms, that facilitate the exercise of power must be proscribed. An unremitting, though generally unsuccessful, agitation for the dissolution of existing aggregations of corporate power is maintained. The goal is a business structure that, by dispersing power between many units, denies effective power to anyone. Thus an underlying structure of business, conforming to the logic of the conventional doctrine, would be achieved.

It is possible to argue that the antitrust laws have, over time, been an important source of security for capitalism in the United States. The notion that legislative power resides in private hands—more simply, that one individual exercises authority over the wealth, income or well-being of another— is deeply repugnant to the juridical sense of the American people. To admit of the fact, even though the fact be anything but new, is to demand that something be done. But for a good half-century the counterpart demand for action has been uniformly channeled into an insistence that the antitrust laws be enforced. The latter have thus become a universal lightning rod for liberal emotions. The antitrust laws have not been ineffective. On the contrary, they have probably been a valuable restraint on antisocial exercise of power. And they are a reasonably accurate reflection of what is deemed fair in business relations. But they have not altered the structure of the economy in the direction of the liberal's dream, though oddly enough, they continue to enjoy an all but unique position in the affections of American liberals. The latter concede in effect that past results have been unsatisfactory; they remain fully persuaded that some day enforcement will achieve their goals. Meantime, American capitalism has avoided what, had this dissent taken other forms, might have been a formidable challenge.

Few businessmen have been able to view the antitrust laws with the philosophical calm that they may well merit. On the contrary, in the individual case they pose a peculiarly difficult problem. No businessman can deny their utter consistency with the conventional doctrine; none can enjoy the opprobrium of being charged with violating the law. And as the antitrust laws are now financed and enforced, the responsible heads of every large business in the United States must expect, at least once in their lifetime, to be haled into court to answer for behavior deemed at variance with the very doctrine by which they defend their existence. The shafts of the businessman's friends, in the United States, are no less painful than those of his foes.

III

There is a further way, less by content than by omission, in which the conventional doctrine contributes to insecurity. There is no place in the doctrine for the experienced fact of the devastating depression. Apart from some rhythmic cycles of good business and bad—or less unemployment and more— its norm is full employment. Deviations from this norm are assumed to be self-correcting.

Against this stands experience. The Great Depression without doubt was the most penetrating psychological experience of modern America. World War II involved death or deep sorrow for a few; fear and discomfort for a few more; employment, improved living, escape from dull routine, and unaccustomed and not unpleasant responsibility for others. By contrast the Great Depression was a nearly universal experience in fear and hardship, as well as in the unbearable loss of self-esteem that goes with sudden descent into poverty.

Adherents of the conventional doctrine were no less shaken by this experience than others. It is a measure of the power of the doctrine that a limited number of its adherents were able, by the end of the thirties, to argue that the depression, so far from being an organic breakdown, had really been precipitated and prolonged by unwise government intervention. A considerably larger number, by the end of the war, were willing simply to stand on the flat assurance that any repetition of the earlier disaster was improbable.

A majority undoubtedly thought otherwise, and governed their personal affairs on the assumption of a recurrence of depression. This particular source of uneasiness was reinforced by the sweeping capture of American economics in the late thirties by J. M. (later Lord) Keynes. Scholars whose tendency to exaggeration is not seriously suspect, have unblushingly called it the "Keynesian Revolution."

The achievement of this ivy-covered uprising was the destruction of a proposition that, tacitly and with many dissenters, had ruled American thinking on economics for more than a century, a proposition known to economists as *Say's Law of Markets*. Say's Law held, simply, that the production of goods provided in the aggregate the demand that would seek them out and buy them. Hence, given a little time, a market was assured for all that was produced. It was a comforting theorem: there might be temporary overproduction of individual commodities but not of all products. If a capitalist society always provided a market for all it produced, it obviously was immune to serious or long-continued depression.

It would be hard, though not yet impossible, to find an American economist who still subscribes to the historic dictum of Jean Baptiste Say. Keynes' conquest of Say was less a triumph of primacy than of authority and orderly logic. Generations of greenbackers, populists and proponents of the free coinage of silver had, in effect, rejected Say's Law by citing the advantages of supplying more money—of having the government directly or indirectly supplement the private demand for goods—in times of economic distress. When the ingenious Peter Cooper ran for President in 1876 on the Greenback ticket, he argued the case for his party on grounds that Keynesians would now consider commonplace. Keynes, however, had the advantage of the American habit of accepting British tutelage in economics, coupled with unparalleled intellectual and expository talents. His conquest was all but complete.

The effect of the intellectual repeal of Say's Law was to undermine the assumption that the economy found its equilibrium when it was producing all it could. Very specifically, in their search for personal security, men might seek to save more than would be spent by those who, in response to unrelated stimuli, were investing for future production. The economy could find its equilibrium with men and resources unemployed.

To American intellectuals with few exceptions, Keynes was a hopeful figure. He provided a rational explanation of the Great Depression and its persistence. It was an explanation

161

that proved capable of withstanding, though not without amendment, the most searching attack directed against any writer since Marx. He also offered a formula for securing capitalism against disaster which, although it accorded a prime role to the state, involved no all-embracing intervention. Taxes and public expenditures had always affected the volume of private saving and of total investment; it remained to use these instruments in time of depression to discourage excessive savings and to supplement investment. The scope for independent business decision would remain substantially unimpaired. The person who found the prospect of mass unemployment intolerable no longer had to consider alternatives to capitalism—including the plunge into the cold sea of comprehensive central planning. The exponent of the unorthodoxy of Keynes found, to his comfort, that he could claim to be saving capitalism.

The effect of Keynes on adherents of the formal doctrine was complex. One influential group of businessmen embraced a broad Keynesian view of the American economy. A new business organization, the Committee for Economic Development, made its appearance with a firm though unproclaimed commitment to his views. Others stood firm—but with an added source of disquiet. A depression is a misfortune; to have it proclaimed as in the nature of things is worse. Still more devastating was the emergence of the state, the natural enemy of capitalism, as the instrumentality of its survival.

Keynes had one other unsettling consequence. Capitalism was returned suddenly to the defensive in the ancient argument over profits. The old attack on profits, never quite as acute in the United States as in Europe, was based on issues of social justice and equity. How defend income which made some men rich beyond measure and left others poor; how devise a rationalization that would cover the fortuitous gains of adventurers and heirs, the rewards of pirates as well as the compensation of sober, God-fearing producers?

The concern over the righteousness of profits had been disappearing. The rich speculative returns of the frontier were gone; the progressive income and capital-gains tax were taking a share; the more uninhibited forms of fiscal adventure had been outlawed. In addition, the trade unions had demonstrated their capacity to appropriate some of the share of good earnings, and corporations seemed more disposed to reserve earnings for their own use. Competitive ostentation in private expenditure with its associated irritations largely disappeared as a social pastime in the late twenties. As a result, business profits came to be justified, even among professional dissidents, by a doctrine of expediency. It might not be possible to say that profits bore any close proportion to social contribution. But they obviously energized those who sought them. So be it.

So it might have remained except that profits are intimately associated with the Keynesian problem of saving. Profits provide the major opportunity for that particular saving that might outrun investment and bring a downward adjustment in total expenditure and production. And the worst offender is not the corporation that is open-handedly distributing dividends to playboy heirs, but the one that is austerely acquiring cash reserves to protect itself against some future disaster. The most virtuous businessman by the old standards was in danger of becoming the worst sinner by the new.

The influence of ideas on events was never better illustrated than by the effect of these views on the great postwar debate

163

on profits. Only to a negligible extent was it argued that businessmen were getting more than they earned or deserved. There were no expressions of envy. The issue was strictly whether these profits were the precursor and progenitor of depression. This was Keynes' handiwork.

IV

Clearly the conventional doctrine as a faith has had a severe buffeting both from ideas and from events. Until the outbreak of the war one might have concluded that, under the strain, it was losing its hold on its former adherents. The term laissez-faire had become, among conservatives themselves, one of opprobrium. Even the term capitalism had acquired overtones which careful semanticists sought to avoid. In the war years, however, the American economy recovered its strength. The prestige of wartime achievements accrued on the whole to business. Much flexibility in relating cause to effect is permissible in American economic and political discussion; accordingly, it was possible to point to the achievements of the economy, under what amounted to comprehensive planning, as general proof of the efficacy of free enterprise. This was accompanied by a resurgent energy in the enunciation of the formal doctrine.

At the same time a new tenet was added: the proposition that non-intervention by the state in the economy is a necessary condition for the preservation of freedom. From today's newspaper, one cites what amounts to a standard formulation: "The free exchange of goods has been the forerunner and prerequisite of all freedom among peoples and nations. Slavery and serfdom are the inevitable results of a controlled economy." The stakes in the war on state power, by this

164

extension of the doctrine, became not alone material values. There was now a threat not only to the body but also to the soul.

The notion of a unique association of freedom with free enterprise was taken up by a hardy band of advocates including, even, some former socialists who brought to their new cause the single-minded ardor of the convert. Like devout Marxians, they reserved their strongest condemnation not for their extreme opponents, the Communists, but for such deviationists as British Socialists abroad and New Dealers at home.

It was the good fortune of this group of revivalists to find a prophet of skill and influence in the scholarly Professor Friedrich Hayek whose *Road to Serfdom*, published in 1944, must be counted one of the influential books of the past decade. Professor Hayek, arguing with skill and a certain unconscious selectivity in evidence, held that once a country began to assume collective responsibility for any of its economic problems, it presently assumed responsibility for all life. The irresistible character of this trend he verified mostly by reference to Germany, a country which some might be disposed to consider a special case, and where still others have attributed the rise of fascism to the incapacity or unwillingness of doctrinaire government to rise to the problems of popular welfare. He passed over the apparent survival of individual freedom, as it is conventionally understood, in face of the collective experiments of Scandinavia, England—and the United States. Nevertheless, Professor Hayek did much to rehabilitate the conventional doctrine. Its reverses at the hands of inhospitable ideas and even more inhospitable circumstances during the years of the Great Depression had vastly weakened its promise of material welfare. Professor Hayek added an impressive moral justification for the exclusion of the State. Few authors have ever attracted a more approving audience. Once again, it is interesting to note, the United States had looked abroad for authority in political economy.

The process of complementing and enlarging on Professor Hayek's ideas in the latter years of the war and in the early postwar years has resulted in one of the most fascinating literary eruptions in the entire history of capitalism. In form, it has ranged from vast and nearly unreadable volumes sponsored by the National Association of Manufacturers to succinct treatises designed to instruct in one lesson. Rigorously devoid of either humor or doubt, it is dogmatic rather than persuasive, and based firmly on the view that unbelievers are fools, knaves, or weaklings. Given the basic tenet, namely, that government is the implacable enemy of freedom, it obviously must follow that Communists, Socialists, New Dealers, reformers of every variety, should all be marshaled into one great legion of the damned.

The effect of this literature has, no doubt, been to affirm the beliefs of some whose adherence to the official doctrine was largely subjective. As such, it has helped deepen the rift that divides those who hold to the conventional doctrine from those who do not, for it is certain that there have been few converts among the latter. Education, to succeed, must be reasonably compatible with the experience of the individual toward whom it is directed. A resident of a public-housing project is not easily persuaded that he has less liberty than an inhabitant of an adjacent slum; the farmers of the Tennessee Valley are not easily convinced that the T.V.A. has enslaved them; cotton growers have learned that they can remain at war with Washington while accepting government loans.

Freedom, if it is defined to include the privilege of un-bridled expression, is never really complete: it is imperfect for everyone. A government employee thinks twice before condemning the actions of his superior, and so does a vice-president of the Chase National Bank. In recent times, residents of public-housing projects may have been uniquely privileged in their opportunity to speak plainly about their landlord. If the will to freedom in the United States is so enfeebled that subservience to authority can be purchased by the benevolences of the Federal Government, the prospect for freedom is probably hopeless in any case. Fortunately, there is little evidence of the danger. Even those who are most alarmed are inclined to argue that the danger is the result of aggregating individually harmless or even benign actions. The mathematics involved are reassuring. And they do not assert that the present state of freedom is seriously impaired. The danger has shown a persistent tendency to be always in the future. As we have moved into the future, the danger has remained one year, one bill, or one session of Congress ahead.

Accordingly, the substance of these fears can be discounted; so also can its unflattering reflection on the character of the American people. But the fact of this fear remains important, especially for its contribution to insecurity. It was remarked, once before, that Americans need to take account of fear itself.

V

It would be idle to suppose that the uneasiness about American economic institutions will be resolved at any time in the foreseeable future. The ideas that underlie it are not lightly held. Nor are they, more than any other faith, subject to revision because of evidence, experience or persuasion. One system of the political economy will continue to rule at the business conventions and another at the polls. Washington will continue to be the arena of conflict between the two. Everyone will expect the worst.

Happily, the prospect is far less horrible than the protagonists can allow themselves to suppose. For one thing, the conflict takes place in a context in which the most difficult of all problems have been solved. There is physical barrier to producing a tolerable and even comfortable living for all Americans with, in addition, a considerable margin for serving the whims, social compulsions and neuroses of the well-to-do and something additional for waste. Such a situation is almost, if not quite, a matter of experience. We are the first nation to find ourselves in this happy technological position. No one should underestimate its importance as a solvent of social strains. In other countries the unprivileged must still be helped at the expense of the privileged. In the United States, there is something for both.

We are also aided by the happy circumstance that most of our concerns are in the area of prognosis rather than of experience. The difference is that prognosis can be wrong, and in this instance it probably is. The businessman's insecurity in regard to the state concerns what might happen, not what has— and this attitude needs to be set against the fact that, in the two decades of depression, New Deal, and war, a great deal has happened. The liberal's alarm over the possession by the modern corporation of legislative power that is inconsistent with any available doctrine of government is something he has experienced and survived. If we have begun the descent into serfdom—and no one can deny that government in Amer-

ica is far more comprehensive than it was fifteen years ago
—it has not yet inhibited the speech or action of those who
voice the fear. One would assume that they would be the first
victims.

Only depression is in the realm of experience. And here
there has been further experience of escape to new levels of
employment, production and welfare which reduced radical
dissent in the United States to defending the proposition that
prosperity could not last.

None of this should lead the reader to suppose that this is
an exercise in optimism and reassurance. In the United States
no economic commentator is taken seriously unless he is a
prophet of doom. This essay is meant to be taken seriously.
Yet when we turn to the rules by which we live *in fact* rather
than in ideas, there is some comfort to be gained. Seven propo-
sitions concerning the American economy would seem to be
valid. If they do not assure its survival in the future, they
appear at least to explain its survival to date.

1. In economic affairs there is far more latitude for varia-
tion and even for error than is commonly supposed. A generous
endowment in physical resources and a high development of
intellectual resources increase this latitude. In both respects
the United States is fortunate. We should not flatter ourselves
that we have been wise enough to have survived had this not
been the case. In few matters are Americans so dogmatic as in
their insistence that there is only one path to economic salvation. "Do as I recommend—or face ruin" is our stock argument for a policy. In fact in the usual (though certainly not
in every) public decision on economic policy, the choice is
between courses that are almost equally good or equally bad.
It is the narrowest decisions that are most ardently debated.

If the world is lucky enough to enjoy peace, it may even one day make the discovery, to the horror of doctrinaire free-enterprisers and doctrinaire planners alike, that what is called capitalism and what is called socialism are both capable of working quite well.

2. In an industrial community which entrusts half of its production to a mere handful of concerns, competition no longer closely circumscribes private power. The pleasant nineteenth-century image of the manufacturer whose prices, wages, even his investment in new machinery, are controlled by the actions of others unknown to him, can hardly be taken seriously except by those who are determined to do so. So we must concede that the individual businessman is the possessor of power of wide social consequence. The liberal had best begin to reconcile himself to a plain fact of life. The business-man, likewise, must come to expect social judgments on the social responsibility he has assumed. The trade union must expect to be similarly judged—although the fact will not come to most union leaders as a surprise.

3. The liberal may also take comfort from the fact that a much neglected but surprisingly effective process acts to curb power in the modern economy. One of the unfortunate conse-quences of the old orthodoxy was a myopic concentration on competition as the restraint on private power. As competition atrophied, it was easy to assume that private power was becom-ing increasingly absolute. The facts have probably been to the contrary. Competition—restraint from the same side of the market—has been replaced by restraint from the opposite side of the market. The spectacular case has been the labor market. No buyer of labor in the United States has power equivalent to that exercised by large corporations a half-

170

century ago. The reason is that the power of the buyer nourished the countervailing power of the trade union. Moreover, this process of checkmate is pervasive. The power of the steel industry as a seller required that the automobile companies be powerful as buyers and accorded advantages to those that were. The power of the canning industry as a buyer is matched by the farm cooperative on the one hand and by the chain stores on the other. There is nothing fortuitous about the tendency for power to beget countervailing power; it is organic. However it does not work evenly. The buttressing of weak bargaining positions has become, as a result, one of the most important of the functions of government.

4. In this system, the autonomous powers of those who guide the modern American corporation acquire their justification not in principle but in practice. They are defended by the theory of administration, not by the theory of economics. Some way must be found, in an economy that produces as many things for as many tastes as that of the United States, to effect a wide decentralization of the power of *final* decision. Nothing else is so important, and a goodly number of disadvantageous decisions is a modest price to pay for this decentralization. No one can say much in defense of the design (or price) of American motor-cars but no one can view with equanimity the problems which would arise were there an appeal from General Motors to higher authority. On decentralization of final decision depends much of the capacity of the economy for accommodation and for change. This is one of the important recent discoveries of the left. Even in avowedly socialist countries, capitalism, though defeated as an idea, survives because of the absence of administratively acceptable alternatives.

5. It would be hard to prove that the American economy selects its business decision-makers by merit, and rewards them in strict accordance with their contribution to the social welfare. But clearly it does recruit diligent men who are rarely accused of failing to take either themselves or their tasks seriously. Many die young. Management in the United States regularly accuses workers of low productivity; American labor, which is not restrained in its criticisms, rarely returns the charge. By contrast, most British and continental trade-unionists have long since ceased to suppose that the boss is useful. The personal earnings of management in the United States, even when adventitiously out of line with accomplishment, are not a subject of much concern mostly because envy, in this land, is almost exclusively confined to the contemplation of others of nearly equal income.

6. Just as the exercise of private economic power is justified on purely pragmatic grounds, so with public authority. There is no controlling principle governing the relation of American government either to the economy or to freedom. Each act of the government can safely be judged on its merits provided only that these are viewed comprehensively. Americans, as each election in recent times has made increasingly clear, do in fact, take a largely pragmatic view of the role of the state. Were others similarly persuaded that the role of government is a practical not a moral issue, they might be happier men.

7. On economic matters there are, in harmony with American capitalism as it is, three ways in which state power must be exercised. There are, first, the task for which the state has superior competence. The provision of education, economic security, a substantial amount of housing, indispensable medi-

cal services and, no doubt in the near future, a minimum standard of nutrition are all of this sort.

Second, the state must intervene to align the exercise of private power with the public welfare. This is an exceedingly complex affair and the ancient instinct of liberals, which is that the intervention should be such as to establish a predisposition toward the right decisions rather than to make the decisions, accords with the broad aim of decentralization of authority. The intervention is, however, far less narrowly confined to reducing the exercise of private power by developing competition than American liberals continue to suppose. It may consist in large measure in helping to establish countervailing power. By far the most durable accomplishments of the government in the last two decades have not been in regulation or in the re-establishment of competition. They have been in supporting trade unions to a point of bargaining equality with employers, in arming farmers with the bargaining alternative of being able to sell to the government, of placing the force of law behind the minimum-wage demands for unorganized workers. These are the measures, not the anti-trust laws, which have most effectively regulated the exercise of private power. It is also clear that they fit a good deal more logically into capitalism as it is.

Finally, and most important of all, it would appear certain that private decision will have to be supplemented by action that will ensure tolerably full use of the resources of the economy.

No one should suppose that this is an easy task—the day when New Dealers could pin their hopes on public works and public spending is past. The income which is subject to control by the government is small compared with the possible changes resulting from exercise of private decision. There are still only the most imperfect and limited designs for expressing the government's effect on income—for supporting consumption, expanding public investment and diminishing the appropriate taxes in the event of a slump. The problem may not be safely solved until some effective way is found of expressing the profound social interest in a high and stable level of private business expenditure, including, in particular, private investment.

The chances are favorable, nonetheless, that we shall find means of keeping the economy functioning at tolerably high levels. There are no physical barriers. We are greatly helped by the fact that there is no single path to salvation that must be found to the exclusion of all others. Nothing in the theory or practice of American government would justify complacency in our ability to select a single right course from among many plausible wrong ones were that the problem. Happily it is not.

The barriers to a solution of the central problem of the American economy are far more in the area of beliefs than in the area of fact. As this essay has sufficiently emphasized, the triumph of practical action over confining doctrine has, in modern America, been a substantial one. It is reasonable to suppose that it will rule in the future. This may not be a solvent for the present uneasiness but it is still a reassuring thought.

The grand conception of universal education as it took shape under the pen and deeds of Horace Mann was revolutionary and impressive. As many acquired learning, it was reasoned, a few would be developed to act as intellectual creators and leaders. With this ideal before them, Americans multiplied their schools and colleges, steadily increasing the years of education. For more than a century they built more buildings and widened the opportunities offered to students.

Have American educators, confronted by unusual conditions during the depression and the period following World War II, begun to doubt the ideal of maximum education for all? Are they trying to discover ways of limiting the opportunities which American youth has hitherto enjoyed?

7

Perry Miller

EDUCATION UNDER CROSS FIRE

I call therefore a complete and generous education, that which fits a man to perform justly, skilfully, and magnanimously all the offices, both private and public, of peace and war.

—MILTON

This education comes to us from nature, from men, or from things. The inner growth of our organs and faculties is the education of nature, the use we learn to make of this growth is the education of men, what we gain by our experience of our surroundings is the education of things.

—ROUSSEAU

I

If ever an ideal molded a society, it is the American belief that the more education a child can get, the better. If there is an American credo, this is its primary article. In 1837 Horace Mann, the prophet of the American system, declared that already time had ratified the soundness of "universal education through the establishment of free schools." Michigan's Chief Justice Thomas Cooley wrote in the Kalamazoo

177

decision, "We supposed it had always been understood in this state that education, not merely in the rudiments, but in an enlarged sense, was regarded as an important practical advantage to be supplied at their option to rich and poor alike." Education, he insisted, voicing what by mid-century was the axiomatic identification of school with democracy, is not something "pertaining merely to culture" which only the wealthy may enjoy, but something essential to American society.

The growth of an America that in Mann's day had barely entered upon the most massive material expansion of history can be charted in the mounting statistics of the "advantage." Nine million in the common schools of 1878, sixteen in 1898, twenty million in 1920. A hundred thousand in the high schools of 1878, seven hundred thousand in 1900, and then seven million in 1940. In 1914 one college student for every twenty-five persons of collegiate age; in 1940, one out of every seven on some sort of campus. Horace Mann, extravagant idealist, never dared dream of so stupendous a universality.

The America of the future will not be the America of the past without an educational graph that continues, both absolutely and relatively, to rise. "Not only," said the Biennial Survey of 1918, "should college education be open to everybody, but nearly everybody should have it." It is only since that date that this proposition has been widely questioned. Henry Adams, a disgruntled man, dying that year, declared the wonder of education to be that it did not ruin everybody, teachers as well as the taught; but John Dewey, who at the turn of the century attempted to assume the mantle of Horace Mann, said that a society for which stratification into separate classes would be fatal "must see to it that intellectual opportunities are accessible to all on equable and easy terms." If, then, by the middle of the twentieth century there is reason to scrutinize this historic affirmation, in the very existence of that doubt our Republic now faces a dislocation in a basic tradition.

It may help, therefore, if we can arrive at a definition, or at any rate a description, of what role education has in fact played in this democracy, at least since, under Andrew Jackson, the society began to call itself democratic. Leaving aside the explanations of a hundred supposedly definitive (although competing) textbooks of "educational sociology," I propose the blunt observation that there was early thrust upon the American educational system a dual obligation, and that the endeavor to satisfy simultaneously both these demands is now resulting in a state of tension best described as advanced schizophrenia. Two loyalties, heretofore considered compatible, have begun to diverge, and the antinomy amounts in effect to an epitome of the age.

On the one hand, American schools exist to service society. They replace the dying elders. This truism would hardly need comment did not the most widely used textbooks of teacher training—products of Schools of Education where the obvious is never left unaccounted for—begin their exposition of this social function with a preliminary demonstration of the appalling disadvantages of perpetual life—with which elementary calculation we must begin. But the question, which is not so obvious, is: for *what* society does the school train society's recruits? The present uneasiness over the plight of education arises from the fact that only in the last decade has this question been seriously thrust upon the American people.

In colonial New England, where our public school tradition

originated, service to society meant training ministers. A child
learned to read and write so that he could ultimately preach
sermons. Those not destined to such dignity went a limited
distance along the educational way, and upon reaching their
limit—as the majority quickly did—fell off into being farmers
or merchants. True, Puritan education, still medieval in form,
included John of Salisbury's ideal of the education of princes,
or at least of magistrates, within the more comprehensive aim
of forming priests. The New Haven Hopkins Grammar School
was dedicated in 1684 to preparing youth "for ye Colledge
and publique service of ye Country in Church and Commonwealth." Thus magistrates were students who had gone (or
should have gone) a good distance on the road, but who
stopped short of the final goal; nevertheless, they had not, in
order to become servants of the Commonwealth, been separately instructed. The educational hierarchy, from dame school
to Harvard College, was so constructed that those who per-
severed to the summit automatically became ministers. After
God had carried us to New England, said the founders of
Harvard, and we had obtained the necessaries of livelihood
and a civil government, "One of the next things we longed for,
and looked after was to advance Learning, and perpetuate it
to Posterity; dreading to leave an illiterate Ministery to the
Churches, when our present Ministers shall lie in the Dust."
To train ministers was thus the purpose of education. It was
not concerned, for example, with suggesting to young men
that they fly kites in a storm, to discover, by any act so ridiculous as knocking their knuckles against a key on a string,
whether there be a consanguinity between lightning and the
mysterious stuff of electricity.

In the nineteenth century the conception of a free society

pre-empted that of a literate ministry. New states beyond the Alleghanies wrote into their constitutions: "Knowledge and learning generally diffused through a community being essential to the preservation of free government, . . ." [1] Education must be universal, said Mann, because while it is good that the wise discover new truths, it is better that truths already discovered be spread among the masses. "Diffusion, then, rather than discovery, is the duty of our government." In its fine simplicity, this sentence is the classic statement of what for over a century has been the controlling aim of American education.

Of course, there was a philosophy behind it. Mann was close enough to Puritan sources—although a "liberal" in theology—to conceive the mission of universal diffusion upon the premise of original sin. Republican institutions, he argued, offer scope for the nobler propensities of mankind, but at the same time they stimulate the "lower order of faculties belonging to the human mind." Freedom, in short, excites appetites and arouses passions. If these are not tamed—Mann deeply impressed this doctrine upon our educational inheritance— then the very liberty which is our glory "will hurry us forward into regions populous with every form of evil." Only one institution restrains us from this looming disaster; Mann paid tribute to the clergy as checks upon depravity, but to him it was clear that in the nineteenth century education alone could save republican society. It alone could catch the child in his impressionable and innocent years, and mold him to the Republic's desire.

The shift of emphasis from Horace Mann to John Dewey indicates, no doubt, an immense intellectual revolution; yet

[1] The Constitution of Indiana (1816).

181

Mann, despite his theological idiom, is closer to Dewey than to the founders of Harvard. Both he and Dewey call upon the schools to make a kind of citizen who, because of his training, without any supernatural assistance, will behave in ways useful to society. Discarding the last vestiges of the notion of sin, Dewey in 1916 called education "a continuous reconstruction of experience"; in the psyche of the student, his theory and Mann's would work the same effect. The drying up of a sense of sin did not break the progression of American theory from Andrew Jackson to the present. Education serves society by equipping children to take a decent and efficient part in the national prosperity; if Dewey's version stresses the efficient more heavily than the decent, in either case the terms are interchangeable, and inefficiency merely becomes the new form of sin. In both conceptions, education is not preparation for a remote future, not a preliminary acquisition of tools to be used by the mature preacher, but a device through which society insures that freedom will not be abused. The student is not about to enter society; he has already been seized by it, and school days are already communal experience. Because the schools alone instill into impressionable youth the norms that hold the society together, that prevent the chaos which otherwise would be the consequence of freedom, education can—nay, absolutely must—be made universal.

So the drive behind the American ideal of a universally diffused education has not been just a fine sentiment; it has been a vital thrust of the whole community, an achievement of cohesion. Only in this perspective can we comprehend the otherwise miraculous growth in the last fifty years of the schools of pedagogy. The Normal School and the Teachers' College are manifestations of a deep-seated persuasion; they

owe their ready triumph over legislative committees and
school boards to the fact that these were already imbued with
it. So much fun has been made of the "educators" that it would
be impertinence to compound an impotent satire. What should
be emphasized is the promise they have given of making the
schools efficient, on the widest possible scale, in everything
from music appreciation to the cooking of cabbage. America
would indeed triumph over the defeatism of the past if class-
room activities might be so geared into actual life that the
graduate, furnished with a reconstruction of experience, could
enter smoothly upon the responsibilities of adult citizenship.
Without recognizing the depth and sincerity of this expecta-
tion, we cannot begin to understand contemporary America.
No doubt the Normal Schools have also maintained a skilful
lobby, and now hold so effective a monopoly that they constitute a major industry; but they could not have imposed a single
regulation requiring such and such a "course unit" as the
prerequisite to promotion, had there not already existed in
the minds of legislators a profoundly democratic conviction
that the schools should be so conducted as automatically to
produce exactly what America wants.

It is easy enough to construct a satire on educational sociol-
ogists merely by quoting their textbooks, their "blueprint,"
for example, of the "Optimum Citizen" and of the "Domestically Efficient Person." Burlesque itself can hardly improve
upon the latter: she should "be able to bathe, dress, and
otherwise care for the baby," and also "be able and disposed
to keep the home free from flies and vermin." What more
logical, therefore, than to give courses on these recondite
subjects, measure them in hours and credits, and offer M.A.'s
which in turn lead to raises in salary? It is important to re-

member that such forms of instruction carry out, in meticulous detail, the American conviction that education must qualify persons for real life; flies and vermin do not, after all, belong in the American home. Again, it was Horace Mann, struggling against the now inconceivable amateurishness of the Massachusetts schools, who delivered in 1838 a radical lecture, "Special Preparation, a Pre-Requisite to Teaching." Precisely because all children are not alike, he said, but differ according to "substructures of temperament and disposition," there is every reason why education must not become stereotyped, and consequently why teachers must have professional training. "Every teacher ought to know vastly more than he is required to teach." A hundred years later, the natural working out of this observation was legislation that imposes upon the teacher, before he or she be certified, so many units of "educational psychology."

Far-reaching though the effect—or the strangle-hold—of the Schools of Education has become, another development within the Schools themselves, especially within those of "higher" learning, offers a still greater exhibition of how they have been adapted, or adapted themselves, to the requirements of society. In ordinary parlance, this is called "specialization." It cannot be diagnosed only as an occupational disease. Not so much did the vast increase of knowledge produce this result as did the American conception of how knowledge can be made available to the democracy, of how it might, if the word is permissible, be packaged. The transformation at the end of the nineteenth century of the college into the university was a response of the American spirit to the over-ruling injunction of the age. When duty whispered low, Thou must, the colleges replied, I can, and articulated themselves into

134

Departments, and then into "fields" within Departments. The American record of proficiency in two World Wars, let alone in household appliances, is testimony to the success with which the educational system not only met, but even anticipated, the challenge of modernity. Its end-products were happily able to cope, well enough to wage successful war, with the paper work of bureaucracy, the logistics of steel, and (with some immigrant assistance) the fissionability of uranium.

By 1880 or 1890 the need was for skills. How strong was the pressure is illustrated less in the physical sciences, where specialties inevitably developed, than in the humanities. The old-fashioned course for the senior year on moral philosophy, taught by the college president, suddenly became the Department of Philosophy; for a brief period held together by a few magnetic personalities, it soon found itself parceling out its functions as though it were chemistry. Specialists in social psychology, intellectual history, anthropology, mathematical logic, semantics, and Basic English took over investigations that had languished under a too purely contemplative love of wisdom. In literature, the result was even more disastrous: dates, sources, influences, textual criticism became the subject-matter of modern language instruction, and a proficiency in philology was made the qualification for an ability to teach Shakespeare and Keats to American youth.

There were great teachers who resisted these tendencies, and who still spoke intelligibly to laymen, but they usually suffered from a paucity of students. The candidate for the Ph.D. chose to work under a professor who could recommend him for a specific job. There remained fewer and fewer on the faculty who felt, as Morris Cohen put it, "responsibility for the student's total view of the universe." The university became an assemblage of experts who respected each other's preserves. Hence the professors of Education had a mandate to bring order into the primary and secondary schools by planning the curriculum and telling teachers how to teach— though, of course, not *what* to teach! The democracy was pleased, because on the lower levels means were adapted to ends, and on the higher the desired professionalism was secured. To the extent that education in a democracy must service the immediate needs of democracy, the American schools up to World War I more than fulfilled their obligation. The record was something to be proud of; it had not been imposed by authority, as in Prussia, or been attained as in England by virtue of class distinctions. Jude the Obscure was inconceivable in America. Commencing even in the Puritan theocracy, where the rendering of scholars serviceable to the community as well as to God was first suggested, the ideal of diffusion ran through the centuries with an ever-increasing purpose, and the twentieth century promised to realize it to the full.

II

If this relationship to society were the sole dimension within which the problem of education were posed today, if the only criterion were "service", it could safely be entrusted to the experts. Most histories of American education conceive it within this single frame, and formal discussion concerns itself only with ways and means for "implementing" Horace Mann's diffusion. The ease with which the professionals take their mission for granted reveals what an immensely inarticulate major premise it has become. Even the revolt against specialization that has appeared in the last decade, the movement for

"General Education" or for the "common core of culture," justifies itself on the plea of social utility. Apologists explain that because the contemporary scene has become complex, there must now be found principles of unity, so that all Americans may converse. The Harvard report, *General Education in a Free Society*, argues that to counteract multiplicity we must pitch upon an island of unanimity in order to save our communal sanity. While the high school "reflects dimly like a clouded mirror the diversity of our society itself," it is also evident that democracy "depends equally on the binding ties of common standards." Hence the report recommends inserting into the curriculum an "organic strand" of General Education.

On the surface, all this seems no more than the swing of the pendulum in a direction opposite to that of a half-century ago. If the issue in education today were no more than a shifting of ballast, it could be comprehended in a merely historico-sociological context. American education would appear to be overhauling itself in order to render still more extensive services to society than it did in the past generation when it rushed into precipitous agreement with Professor Dewey that instruction should be a "reconstruction of experience."

But between the lines of these pronouncements there is to be detected another theme, which can hardly be dissociated from certain other phenomena in the realm of education that do not altogether accord with the story of ever-triumphant diffusion. The advocates of common purpose glance aside from their proposals to the low salaries of teachers, to crowded class-rooms and inadequate installations, and toward the indifference, the astonishing callousness, of the populace toward these deteriorations. They cannot argue their case

187

without at least skirting the undemocratic proposition that all students are not biologically capable of the utmost education. They do not sound the tocsin for universal diffusion; they lament the vulgarizing effects of the radio, films, television, the comics and the tabloids. Nor can the spokesmen for unity dissociate their campaign from the problem of "academic freedom." Their manifestoes are haunted by the memory of portentous cases, the array of which grows with the years, and their claims for the organic strand suddenly become confessions of a failure of accord between the schools and the people. In the background lurk the spectres of teachers' oath bills, legislative hearings, unrenewed contracts for non-conformist instructors, and reputed decisive actions of trustees. There is the distant echo of Veblen's growl that business men have replaced the clergy on governing boards. The movement toward unification of the cultural heritage cannot be interpreted simply as an intramural reform of the course offering; there is a suspicion of lines forming for a showdown. There is a broad hint that, possibly for the first time in the existence of the Republic, the pursuit of knowledge, far from being an obedient servant, may find itself at odds with the society that has supported it.

To understand the situation, we must look at the history of American education from a point of view different from that inculcated by the historic rationale. In this light, the school system has a different story to tell, one that is only incidentally related to its servicing of society. While it has indeed been occupied with the preparation of citizens, it has also devoted itself to an activity that might be best described as domesticating the disreputable. Or, if that seems too strong, as bestowing reputation upon unreputable ideas that it could not otherwise ignore. The schools have seldom performed this function well, and never gracefully, but however timorously or belatedly, they have done it. Yet—and here is the irony—this unplanned intrusion, rather than their success in attaining universality, constituted their inward being. They have experienced a constant renewal, a succession of new leases on life, or escapes from stultification. Again and again, confronted with a new doctrine, a shattering discovery, a shocking literary fashion, the schools have, after an interval of resistance, come to terms with it, and eventually undertaken to teach it.

The arch-example of what a quarantine against the fructifying contagion of the outside world does to education is undoubtedly the English universities of the eighteenth century:

> Feuds, factions, flatteries, enmity, and guile,
> Murmuring submission, and bald government,
> (The idol weak as the idolater,)
> And Decency and Custom starving Truth,
> And blind Authority beating with his staff
> The child that might have led him; Emptiness
> Followed as of good omen, and meek Worth
> Left to herself unheard of and unknown.[2]

The intellectual history of Britain in this era is a dynamic chapter, but it can be told with barely a mention of the colleges. Intelligence flowered in coffee houses and taverns, in salons, and in Grub Street. The Royal Society was a focus for science, but the schools ignored it. The universities in all conscience served a useful function and they also turned surplus younger sons into dull curates. But the life of the mind was something else. It required in the nineteenth century a

---

[2] Wordsworth, *The Prelude*.

reform imposed by a Royal Commission to turn the currents of discovery once more into the universities.

A republic, Horace Mann contended, cannot afford institutions with limited objectives. It has no place for schools that draw aside from the currents of life. There is not enough money, even in a rich democracy, to maintain a mandarin ritual, and there is no market for the product. For better or worse, American graduates must run the gauntlet of American life. This nation has not yet reached the stage—call it civilization or decadence—wherein it can waste education upon younger sons alone.

Thus, paradoxically, the American schools discovered, in the first place, that they were linked to a democratic society by the necessity of insuring freedom. In the second place, they found that they could not, even if they tried, circumscribe their notion of what constitutes freedom. The challenge has come to them from the outside, from quarters not academically respectable; often it has come from Europe, and their resistance has been fortified by xenophobia. That the American schools have proved, on the whole, receptive is possibly a contribution to our culture more important than their conquest of astronomical numbers. In every case, the impact forced an internal shake-up. It opened up new ranges of experiments or of courses—it even raised up new teachers. By this process American education has been invigorated, not by buildings, stadia, or even by increases in administrative staffs.

Periodically, the schools forget this, but they have never been allowed to vegetate in comfort. They have been obliged, often to their chagrin, to catch up. Whenever they have settled down with the satisfied certainty that they were manufacturing the optimum citizen, they have been rudely jolted from without. They have had to atone by incorporating into an expanding course program what at first they scorned. They have discovered that even while servicing the society, they were forced to explore topics which, at least when first broached, seemed by the official standards of that society to be simply scandalous.

The Harvard community of the 1830's may be taken as a miniature model of the American experience. Having stabilized an intellectual revolution, sloughed off Calvinism and converted itself to "liberal Christianity," the college was devoting itself to the service of society by raising up urbane scholars, of whom Holmes and Lowell were the paragons. Yet at the acme of its complacency a number of the undergraduates found themselves acquiring two separate educations—the one vended by the faculty, and the other surreptitiously acquired from their reading of imported books by Coleridge, Carlyle, Cousin, and the German romantics. This generation, one of them remembered, were never really interested in their college work, although their careers were determined by it, but were much more devoted to "pursuits outside the curriculum." Through the historic proclamations of Emerson this band became articulate, whereupon the great pundit of the Divinity School, Andrews Norton, excoriated them as "the latest form of infidelity." One of the infidels, who for years had been struggling to keep alive a church in the business district of Boston, replied in 1839 that he could no longer speak the language of his professors. His generation, he explained, having been brought "into contact with a great variety of minds," with "men of discernment and acuteness" outside the college, had there learned that the formal liberalism of Harvard was half-hearted and its metaphysics obsolete. They

191

beheld vistas to which Coleridge and Carlyle, considered by the faculty despicable and dangerous, were better guides than Professor Norton. Emerson delivered the sentence by which not only Harvard education of that time, but all American education since, must be judged (remember that he spoke of the "clergy" as the representatives of scholarship rather than of piety): "I have heard it said that the clergy are addressed as women; that the rough, spontaneous speech of men they do not hear, but only a mincing and diluted speech."

In the lexicon of 1949, Transcendental talk may not seem to have captured the rough conversation of men, but it came closer than that of the Harvard faculty. For thirty years after *The Divinity School Address,* Emerson was an outcast from Cambridge. By now the moral is clear: by excluding Emerson, Harvard injured only itself; hence it does sorry penance by naming the hall of philosophy after him and teaching him in "survey" courses. He is even read, if not understood, in the high schools, and students find it quaint that he was ever considered subversive. Today, of course, the pace is faster; the schools are not granted decades in which to accustom themselves to radical ideas, but must act within months. While educators draw up blueprints for the optimum citizen, students are bombarded with ideas which, from the point of view of the blueprint, excite a lower, or at any rate a different, order of faculties. If diffusion means the diffusion only of mincing and diluted speech, especially if it means only the jargon of professional educators, there will always be found channels outside the schools for making audible the spontaneous conversation of men.

In science, as in literature, the impetus to discovery came from outside the academy. The schools here responded with more alacrity, since the utilitarian appeal was stronger, but the process of accommodation was much the same. Again, the problem was not so much one of diffusion as of knowledge itself. "Hard hands," wrote Abbott Lawrence in 1847, while offering to endow Harvard with a scientific school, "are ready to work upon our hard materials; and where shall sagacious heads be taught to direct those hands?" By agreeing to furnish the heads, American education was again servicing society, and Lawrence was insistent: "Let theory be proved by practical results." Still, experience soon demonstrated the practical worth of theory, and pure science was fostered by applied. The democracy accustomed itself (not too easily) to indulging scientists in the disinterested, even if expensive, quest of discovery for its own sake, on the chance that they would turn up a profitable theorem. The astonishing hospitality of the schools to Darwinian evolution, as contrasted with the hesitations of the pulpit, and to evolution's progeny, sociology and anthropology, indicated the strengthening within the system of a conception of knowledge as something which might be pursued without always calculating the tangible benefits. Since the turn of the century, the efflorescence of this ideal has progressively been less and less inhibited by the elder one of a universal diffusion subserving a merely efficient citizenship.

The historian of the future will assuredly behold in the decade of the 1920's an explosive era in the history of the American mind. By continuing to call it the Age of Wonderful Nonsense or of bathtub gin, we willfully conceal from ourselves how drastically it severed modern America from the nineteenth century. The schools and colleges notoriously failed, at first, to grasp what was happening; Mencken's barrage against the pedagogues was altogether in order. But in the subsequent years, the profession has again done penance, and more vigorously than in the 1830's. Though this is over-simplification, it is still not quite extravagant to say that the multitudinous reforms of the last decades amount to a con-scientious effort of the academicians to systematize and to regularize the impact of the Jazz Age. Which is to say that once again they have been preoccupied with the secondary but persistent function of American education, of domesticating the disreputable. In a democracy, education feeds upon, or is fed by, the hurly-burly, the sprawling turmoil, of an ebullient culture.

III

On the very page where Horace Mann proclaimed that dif-fusion and not discovery is the duty of government in educa-tion, he also declared, "A love of truth—*a love of truth;* this is the pool of a moral Bethesda, whose waters have miraculous healing." It did not occur to him that the quest of truth would lead into those realms of appetite and passion against which it was the purpose of education to guard. In his mind there was no possibility that the regions populous with every form of evil would ever be confused by a republican society with the regions of scientific, economic, or literary investigation. Never-theless, in his formulation and in a myriad others after him, American education was serenely dedicated to the service of two masters: "the advancement and diffusion of knowledge." Down the years, diffusion—measured in numbers, buildings, laboratories—carried advancement on its back. Discovery floated on the tide of expansion. But today the spokesman for education does not hit upon Mann's confident accent; instead, he is more apt to sound as though bracing himself for a grim ordeal, and to say, with President Seymour of Yale, "We seek the truth and will endure the consequences."

What consequences must be "endured"? What is the implied threat? Were it only that conventional or received opinions must be upset, the past century assures us that such crises can be weathered. Is it that demagogues and investigating commissions raise the cry of subversion? There are strong bulwarks against such attacks. The obligation to be independent, said President Killian in his inaugural address at the Massachusetts Institute of Technology, lies upon all our institutions of higher learning. All educators know this, and know that the devotion to intellectual discovery is not only nothing to be ashamed of, but is rooted deep in the truly American tradition. Though newspaper headlines make much of this or that episode, periodic attacks upon academic freedom are nothing new, nor would the recent outbreak be anything more than a recurrence if it were not revelatory of forces at work beneath the surface, forces deeper and more pervasive than merely demagogic frenzy.

The real threat to education is the fact that America is entering upon a phase of social evolution different from any we have known. "In a period of armed truce," President Killian continues, "the fundamental principle of academic freedom is subject to stresses which we have not met before." Others more outspokenly call it "cold war." Cold or hot, war is war, and does not encourage heresy. Energies must not be dissipated. The prospect before American education is baldly this: the spontaneity of the environing society, which has hitherto provided the impetus toward the advance of knowledge, which has supplied the courage for adventure, may be stifled. A nation committed to static defence, to a dread of

195

innovation, to anxiety, may gird itself for global conflict, may gear its laboratories to industry and its class-rooms to the military, but will it do so by paralyzing the sources that hitherto have imparted the incentive to exploration? If the wind is no longer to blow where it listeth, will American education remain education in a free society? If Mann's innocent sentence, that the duty of government is diffusion and not discovery, is to mean that, under pressure, discovery must be curtailed, then diffusion, no matter how effectively it be preserved, ceases to be the diffusion of education. If the grinding of the wheels means that the ineffable qualities of discovery must be sacrificed for the brute quantities of diffusion, then the educational crisis is indeed more than a matter of programs and numbers. The illiteracy rate may be reduced to zero, but a diffusion that does not carry with it the excitement of discovery, though it may have clear prescriptions for the optimum citizen, will become an assembly line for the production of serviceable robots.

Apprehension deepens into trepidation when, along with such reflections, we consider what effect the economy itself appears to be working upon the educational establishment. Although it now seems that the total number of school children —which in the late '30's, for the first time in our history, declined—may for a while increase, the relative ratio as against the total population is going down. Obviously connected with this fact is the shortage of teachers. Benjamin Fine estimated in 1947 that over the previous seven years, 350,000 abandoned the profession. The reason might be supposed simply to be that they were not paid enough, but Professor Seymour Harris takes us to a deeper and more ominous level of explanation: as the rewards of those occupations which require educated employees have shrunk, we find ourselves with an over-supply of them, and we can no longer recompense them on a scale commensurate with that of tradesmen and laborers. Thus, by a logic which requires an economist to comprehend we seem to have too few teachers because we have too many.

Uneasiness on such purely economic grounds has been anything but quieted by the Government's post-World War II generosity to the veterans. That program is itself a supreme witness to the deep hold upon the American mind of the historic conception that a state's duty is to make education as widely available as possible; it incarnates the pervasive conviction that whoever has a claim upon society best receives recompense for lost time and the confronting of danger in the form of education. Thousands of youths who in 1941 would have been content with a high-school diploma, upon perceiving that a college education was a help toward acquiring the superior comforts of an officer, came home from the services resolved to get a college degree. In the four years since the V-Days, the economy has absorbed these graduates more easily than economists anticipated, but the rate of production continues. Who would dare to promise that in the next years all of those whom the democracy has rewarded according to its traditional lights will automatically step into the "advantages" they expected? In the midst of the Depression, out of the heart of Middletown, rose the cry recorded by the Lynds: "I think we've been kidding ourselves in breaking our backs to send our children to college. There just aren't enough good jobs to take care of all the college graduates." That in the America of Jefferson and Mann and Lincoln such a lament should so much as be whispered proclaims the end of an era. If this is a sign of the times, it amounts to sounding a retreat from the democratic ideal of education universally diffused. By a curious twist in history, democracy itself is brought to the point of suspecting that the ideal of diffusion, which for over a century was assumed to be synonymous with the very being of democracy, is no longer obvious, or is even admirable.

Within the schools themselves, this "retrograde" movement —if the word be not too strong—is being hastened by a corrosive conviction that education simply cannot be given to all in equal degree. The Schools of Education devise finer and more intricate, and possibly reliable, methods for measuring "primary mental abilities." Psychologists and "counsellors on careers" accentuate the withering doubt, that the masses are not universally educable. Few of them—as yet—say it too loudly, but out of their classifications the implication emerges. The noble old American faith appears riddled. The prospect is no longer for indefinite expansion, but for shrinkage and contraction, for reconciliation to the notion of an inferior training for the many, while guarding the superior for an elite who must be prevented from becoming so numerous as to force down the level of wages. By no stretch of the term can such a program be called democratic, and should the nation bring itself to proclaim this philosophy, it will have difficulty convincing even itself that it is any longer a democracy. "Restricting the body of knowledge," says Albert Einstein, "to a small group deadens the philosophical spirit of a people and leads to spiritual poverty."

It is, therefore, as a part of this pattern of constriction that assaults upon academic freedom take on their more serious meaning. These are not merely the results of a jitteryness among trustees, congressmen, and chambers of commerce;

they are steps toward the curtailing of the content of research and instruction. They announce that there are forces now at work in the American democracy which are far from assured, as was the age of Jackson and Lincoln, that education can do harm to nobody, and that the more of it anybody can get, the better citizen he will be. In the motto I have prefaced to this essay, John Milton spoke for the Puritan revolution of the seventeenth century; as that revolution became the industrial development of the nineteenth, the conception reached down from the middle classes to the populace in general, and so the doctrine of education for citizenship was extended to all. But as America is suddenly thrust into the position of a very great power—of *the* great power—fears arise lest the American way of life be endangered. Thereupon, the assumption that education prepares citizens is transformed into a demand that it prevent Americans from entertaining or even examining subversive ideas. The investigators undoubtedly are patriotic men, but the result of their investigations is certainly a limitation upon the free play of mind, an effort to confine education to certain limited, definable, and frankly nationalistic ends.

Hence the American educator in the year 1949 is caught in a tension of forces which play upon him with peculiar severity because upon the schools converge the issues of civilization. A shift has been insensibly wrought in the meaning of the traditions, and it is no wonder that educators are bewildered. On the one hand, the tradition of social service, which has hitherto been one with the belief in universal diffusion, is being transformed, before our eyes, into a program of restriction and limitation. But the tradition of a disinterested devotion to knowledge for its own sake, which originally had distinctly aristocratic connotations, contends for democratic freedom in the face of the democracy's hesitation. The conception of a complete receptivity to all ideas or fancies, no matter whence they come, which Rousseau opposed to the classical Miltonic conception of education for the offices of peace and war— this conception now insists that curtailment is death, that career must be open to talents, that everybody must be trained to the utmost of his capacity. And this conception now thrives, not alone upon some Rousseau-istic fervor, but upon the hard experience of the last century, which has persuaded the researcher and the teacher that a steady growth of knowledge is health, and that the slightest inhibition is fatal.

The predicament of the conscientious educator is indeed agonizing, the more so as he is convinced that it is an epitome of the whole civilization. He is the victim of historic forces that have altered their characters. Hitherto diffusion and discovery were pursued simultaneously, because they were entirely complementary: in fact, diffusion supplied the margin within which discovery could operate. But a reversal of diffusion will certainly bring the threat of a narrowing of the field for discovery. An economy of contraction—whether it be the result only of an over-production of scholars or also of the retrenchments imposed by an armed truce—is not compatible with a policy of intellectual expansion. Discovery is outgoing and improvident, and will risk any idea or experiment; retrenchment is not. Discovery requires ever-new materials to work upon; a nation frozen into a cold war will not readily supply them. America, above all nations in recorded history, has thus far embodied the reason working experimentally and experientially; it had a continent to exploit, and no limits to its wide-flung shores. So it builded schools and colleges. If it has suddenly become in effect an island economy, and the space between its coasts has violently shrunk, then the pressures will surely be exerted upon the educational system. It, along with the rest of the culture, may try to seek safety in rigidity.

If the history and experience of America mean anything, they mean that such a course foretells disaster. History is littered with the corpses of civilizations that reached the limit of expansion, dug in behind walls and moats, and there yielded to decay. There is still no evidence that America is irrevocably caught in a determined cycle of rise and decline. The instruments in our hands, the resources, the difficulties already surmounted, are immense. No society ever reached the end of its expansion with so much trained intelligence to command, with so many potentialities for understanding, and thus for transcending its predicament. American education has paid dividends so incalculable that the nation has not yet begun to tap them, and has accumulated the mightiest reservoirs of knowledge ever put at the disposal of a great power. It is not written in the stars that discovery must necessarily perish, even though it now seems possible that discoverers may have to fight for the right to discover.

In this situation, the educator, if he is to preserve his self-respect, has little or no choice. If the end of the era of indefinite expansion has indeed come, then he must stand, more firmly than ever he felt he would be called upon to stand, for the freedom of investigation, for the principle that nothing, not democracy itself, and not even the American way of life, is so sacred that it cannot be studied, analyzed, and criticized. Furthermore, the results of such criticism must continue to augment the content of education. The accumulation of knowledge cannot be arrested; the educator will be, it is assumed, loyal to his country, but he will manifest that loyalty by meticulously remaining faithful to the pursuit of learning, and to the transmission of learning to posterity, no matter how many conflicts this devotion may lead him into. Unless he is to surrender entirely his function, and to become merely an instrument of national policy, he must keep alive a passion for knowledge that is first and foremost its own excuse for being, and take the position that under present conditions, this insistence is his major responsibility to the future of democracy.

Of course, much depends on events, on the hazard of peace and war, but still more depends, in American education, upon the teachers themselves. Inside the schools, in the libraries and laboratories, in techniques and scholarship, in the hard-won freedom of speculation, in the American itch of curiosity, they have enough to draw upon, enough energies to maintain the pace of discovery. There is no guarantee that the powers making for constriction are invincible, and there is no assurance that a slackening of numerical diffusion must inevitably signify the end of innovation. It has not yet been conclusively demonstrated that this democracy is incapable of understanding what is happening to it, that it will abjectly submit to an undemocratic conception of education simply because economists argue that this is the only recourse. It may not accept the new definition of the socially useful, and it may not forever subject its teachers to hysterical tests of "loyalty." There is a kind of invigoration that comes with contending against society for the welfare of society, and of this paradoxical strength American education now stands in desperate need.

It is altogether possible that the great democratic God, to whom Herman Melville prayed in similar extremities of doubt, may disregard such seemingly incontrovertible facts as quantitatively accurate measurements of primary mental abilities. There may be—who knows?—enough average qualitative ability, along with a little give-and-take, to keep education going as a democratic venture. Or there may be, if only the educators will keep it alive. In the present posture of affairs, the future of American education—and so of the republic itself—hangs, above all other considerations, upon the courage, the devotion, and the vision of the teachers themselves.

The scientist does not consciously seek the role of destroyer. The theoretical scientist's goal has been concentrated upon the pursuit of laboratory truth. The technologist attempts to apply the findings of the laboratory to the practical needs of mankind. Each protests that he cannot foresee how his discoveries may be used or misused. To what extent can these experts—and to what extent should they—attempt to control the products of their genius?

Science can destroy man. New discoveries—planned or accidental—are almost daily occurrences. And always there is the human element of control and decision, usually exercised by men without technical training.

8

Harrison Brown

OF SCIENCE AND MAN

I

"If some higher power were to give you the opportunity of traveling to another time, what destination would you choose?"

I turned and looked into the gentle eyes of my professor. It was close to midnight but the firelight still cast fleeting images which lived, then died, never reappearing in the same form. Where would I go if given the opportunity?

"The present seems pleasant enough," I replied.

A favorite section from one of Bach's Cantatas silenced my professor for a few moments. I looked about the wonderful room with its cases stacked full of books, the round table in the corner covered with papers, the bulky leather chairs which to me seemed centuries old. For that matter, in my mind's eye my professor was an octogenarian, although he couldn't have been over fifty at that time.

"Surely you wouldn't stay in the present when so much could be learned by going elsewhere!" His voice brought my mind back to the topic at hand.

"Given the option of going forward or backward," I said,

207

"I suppose that I would go forward." I paused and groped for an expression of the reasons which had prompted my statement. "In a few centuries, mankind will have learned nearly everything that there is to be known concerning the operations of our universe. It would be exciting to learn the facts as they will be known by then."

My professor's expression indicated disagreement. "Given an infinite length of time, we will not even approach knowing everything," he said. "For that matter, I believe that as time goes on we are losing more than we are gaining. While we are increasing our knowledge of material things, we are losing the most precious possession of mankind—wisdom. No, I would not choose the future."

"Where would you travel in the past?" I asked. "In the period of Faraday? Maxwell? Newton? Galileo? Copernicus?"

"Those times were certainly as exciting as the present—in many respects even more exciting. But I do not believe that I would stop there. No, I would go far beyond that time, beyond ancient Rome, beyond Greece, to an era when wisdom and beauty were far more treasured than they are today." He closed his eyes as he spoke.

I did not ask to which time he referred, for by then I knew. Frequently on my visits to his home I had seen him scanning a huge volume of the Vedas in the original Sanskrit, laboriously writing translations of the sections which particularly appealed to him. I had known that he had, but a year previously, first started to study that exceptionally difficult language. Before twelve months had elapsed his translations of substantial sections had been acclaimed by Sanskrit scholars as among the best in existence. I had heard some of his colleagues say from time to time, "If he would only concentrate his full efforts on science, he would make remarkable achievements." And I had noticed that those of his colleagues who kept their noses more strictly to the scientific grindstone were frequently less kind in their comments.

My professor was oblivious to the thoughts of his fellow-scientists. He had done good work in science and he still loved science deeply, but his interests were as vast as his mind. The fact that he was a professor of physical sciences did not confine him to an academic pigeon-hole. He was a great man and the wisest that I have known.

My friend talked on. "The great ones of those days possessed a freshness, a deepness of insight, an understanding and an appreciation of life which is seldom if ever attained today. Compared to them, we moderns are robots—intellectual robots."

I did not know enough to permit me either to agree or to disagree with my friend. But since leaving his charge a number of years ago, I have thought often of my professor and of his statement. I have thought of the many evenings spent at his home with fellow-students in talking about science; of the occasions when he would read aloud from Gibbon, or *The Pickwick Papers* or *Alice in Wonderland*; of the times when we persuaded him to play his violin or read aloud from the Vedas or reminisce about his student days at Göttingen. But most frequently I have thought about his statement that evening concerning intellectual robots. It has taken long to appreciate what he meant.

As time has passed, an unhappy realization has gradually penetrated my consciousness. I have come to realize that my professor was a member of a rapidly vanishing species in

America and, for that matter, in the world—the species of man which can justly claim the broad knowledge and the broad interests which are so essential to the crystallization of wisdom. The principle of natural selection has operated to extinguish this species and to replace it with a species of man which possesses a greater short-range survival value within our society; a creature not dissimilar in behavior from certain forms of insect life—the specialist.

The growth of what Ortega y Gasset calls "barbarian specialization" has gone hand in hand with the plunge of our society towards the brink of destruction. As the operations of our society have grown more complex, involving the utilization of more difficult and specialized techniques, the compelling drive of circumstance has forced men to assimilate greater knowledge of subjects which have become continually more restricted in scope. All about us we see automobile salesmen who know little else than how to sell automobiles; we see chemists who know little outside of chemistry; we see economists who know little outside of economics; we see lawyers who know little outside of law; we see doctors who have ceased specializing in ear, nose and throat, and who now specialize in ears alone.

As time has passed, our specialization has increased to the point where communication between specialists in two different fields frequently comes close to being impossible. The scientist has difficulty communicating with the business man; neither can communicate satisfactorily with the politician. Under the circumstances the only thing they can do is trust each other, thus creating a situation analogous to a game of "follow-the-leader" where the leader travels most of the time with a blind-fold over his eyes. The end result may not be dissimilar to that encountered on occasion by the army-ants when they become ensnared in a "circular mill." Each ant follows the chemical trail laid down by the ants ahead of him. The ants at the head of the column, having no compulsion to lead, are pushed forward by the ants following. Occasionally the course of the leader ants, which is dictated by the terrain, is such as to cause them to come into contact with the rear stragglers of the column which is pushing them forward. They immediately become followers themselves, and the column marches solemnly around in a circle, no ant questioning the movements of the others. They march in this manner until all have perished.

We have, in effect, permitted a situation to develop where-by a society run by specialists requires the continued education of more specialists in order to provide yet more specialized techniques to permit the further intensification of specialization . . . *ad infinitum*. The fact that the right hand of our society does not know what the left hand is doing creates dangerous situations, particularly when both hands determine whether or not the body lives.

The world of science and technology and the world outside of science and technology can be used as concrete examples of the dangers in which we have become involved. The average intelligent non-scientist has little conception of the impact of modern science and technology upon society as a whole; he does not understand the motivating compulsions of scientists; nor does he comprehend what science can and cannot do. He tolerates science primarily for three reasons: science creates material comforts and profits; through medicine it permits people to live longer; through technology it aids in the winning of wars. Beyond that, the non-scientist does not look.

The average scientist, on the other hand, is not much concerned about the outside world. He has passed through a
specialized training of an extreme variety, during which he
has found it necessary to concentrate his full efforts on the
study of science. He knows a great deal about a particular
field of science, but little else.

It is appalling to see the numbers of scientist-Ph.D.'s being
turned out by our universities who can scarcely speak proper
English, whose knowledge of history, literature, and the arts is
infinitesimal, whose appreciation of their own responsibilities
to humanity is non-existent. These men, when they leave
school, often become obedient cogs in vast industrial-research
machines—and the last flicker of the flame of original thought
usually dies away. Others remain with universities and colleges, and, alas, are likely to perpetuate the robot-training
system. More than one state university provides curriculæ for
its chemistry and physics majors consisting of chemistry,
physics and mathematics for four years, one year of German,
two years of compulsory military training—and nothing else.
Those universities may produce capable scientists; but such
scientists are frequently intellectual pygmies in matters outside of their fields of science.

It is ironical that as scientific and technological considerations have entered more and more into major decisions of
industry, agriculture and government, the little communication
that exists between scientists and non-scientists has become
more and more unintelligible to both parties. It is all the more
ironical because technological expansion, stimulated and
guided by the trilogy of human desires—profits, longer living
and the winning of wars—but otherwise unguided, has molded
the modern physical world in which we live. Scientists and

non-scientists alike realize that to a large part of the world technological expansion has brought unprecedented comfort. But neither realizes in full measure that to an even larger part of the world it has brought unprecedented agony. Nor do they always fully appreciate that to the world of the future our technology may bring total catastrophe—or that it may aid in the molding of a balanced world in which men may have the opportunity to live in reasonable harmony with their environment and with each other.

From a short-range point of view, America has benefited more and has suffered less from technological materialism than has any other nation. Blessed with tremendous natural resources, unhampered by major problems of over-population and protected by extensive bodies of water, we have been permitted to create a standard of living which is one of the highest in the world. Our technology, developed under the impetus of industrial and agricultural expansion, and to a lesser degree under the impetus of the needs of national defense, but otherwise uncontrolled, has given us great health and comfort. Indeed, we in this country have benefited to such an extent from these uncontrolled, uncoordinated and nearly random developments that we are tempted to believe that the present *laissez-faire* pattern can be continued indefinitely. We hear such slogans as "Better Things for Better Living Through Chemistry," and "Horizons Unlimited," and we nod our heads in agreement. In our enthusiasm for the benefits of science, in our faith that science can provide answers to all questions and can remedy any and all material difficulties in which we may become involved, we have become blinded by half-truths. We have ignored the future, and we have misunderstood the past. Above all, we have not examined the opposite side of the ledger—the dangers involved in technological materialism uncontrolled and unintegrated with other features of our society.

Scientist and non-scientist alike recognize that applied science can be used, and has been used, for the benefit of society. But, unfortunately, they do not recognize in full measure that applied science, unwatched, improperly handled, and not understood by men generally, can become, if we are not careful, mankind's Nemesis. In their attitude toward technological materialism, both scientists and non-scientists have in a very real sense been saying: *video meliora proboque; deteriora sequor*—"I see the better and I approve; but the worse is what I pursue." To that might be added: "And I do not comprehend the consequence."

II

It required six years, working first as a scientist, then as a technologist on the development of the atomic bomb, before the realization came to me with full impact that technological materialism had created grave dangers for modern man—dangers with which he may be unable to cope in the limited time available. I was given the scientific education which has become traditional in this country. The combination of competitive necessity and interest caused me to ignore all else. In spite of the kindly admonitions and examples given by my wise professor-friend during my undergraduate days, I lived and cared only for science. I saw the world about me only as one of wondrous technological advances. Because science was good, the uses to which science was being put by non-scientists should likewise only be good.

The discovery of uranium fission, and with it the realization on the part of many scientists that an atomic bomb might be a possible end-result, jolted many of us into at least a half-world of reality. But it was by no means an irreversible effect we felt. After all—if the atomic bomb should prove to be as devastating a weapon as we thought it might be, would people not at last realize that wars must be a thing of the past?

But as year followed year, and as it appeared more certain that an atomic bomb could indeed be manufactured, I began to comprehend that even should an atomic bomb be exploded during the war, it would constitute but a small part of the whole technological picture—that all of the atomic bombs that could conceivably be manufactured could not possibly have as devastating effect upon our society as the sum total of misuses to which science and technology had unwittingly been put by mankind throughout our history.

The atomic bomb is a symbol of the way in which science and technology have converted wars into operations of unprecedented destructiveness, thus placing our civilization in immediate jeopardy. It is a symbol of the fact that the first half of the twentieth century will go down in history as the period within which technological developments occurred that converted destruction from a difficult operation into a fantastically easy one. I came to sense that as yet we have seen only the crude beginnings of what can be done, should circumstances dictate. Now that nations, each in the interest of its own military security, have mobilized science, we can expect developments in the technology of war to proceed at an accelerated pace.

But were there not other effects of science and technology that might be equally dangerous? Slowly I perceived that there were indeed other equally dangerous effects—effects which operate more slowly, but which must be reckoned with as seriously as we must reckon with atomic bombs.

Science and technology have placed in the hands of the rulers of nations tools of coercion and persuasion of unprecedented effectiveness. Modern implements of war make it relatively easy for small groups of men to enforce their rule over larger groups. In modern totalitarian states, the weapons in the hands of rulers make successful popular revolts impossible.

Improvements in transportation and communications have increased the effectiveness of police action. Revolutionary methods of mass communication provide powerful tools for persuasion. Today, when propaganda can be spread to millions of people, when the governed can be unknowingly fed with untruths and kept in ignorance of the truth by government control, the mass of the people becomes almost powerless.

It would be pleasant to believe that by creating new techniques in transportation and communication, thus making the world effectively smaller, some sort of dent might have been made in minimizing the concept of intense nationalism. But the reverse has been true. The establishment of vast industrial nations, competing with one another, and the creation of centralized national authorities of ever-increasing power, have more than overbalanced the possible good effect upon nationalism of increasing communication and education.

Even our best intentions have brought trouble. The spread of sanitation measures and the control of disease to ever-increasing bodies of humanity has brought about the problem of overpopulation. Increased populations and wars have, in turn, placed tremendous drains upon our natural resources, upon our power reserves, upon our arable land.

In short, I came to realize that science and technology, partly through greed, but largely through ignorance, have created a situation which threatens to destroy us. Many of my colleagues reached similar conclusions during the dark days of the war. Alamogordo, Hiroshima, and Nagasaki served to underline the conclusions and to create for the benefit of all mankind a deadly image of the possible shape of things to come.

In the face of these considerations, many persons *quite understandably* believe that technological materialism is inherently "evil"—that science and technology are in themselves "bad." It has even been urged that the world strip itself of its science and its technology and decree a "moratorium on science" so that mankind may "catch up" with modern technological developments.

Ruth Benedict has observed that heretofore man has survived because of his plasticity. She says: " . . . this plasticity has been the soil in which human progress began and in which it has maintained itself. In the ages of the mammoths, species after species without plasticity arose, overreached itself, and died out, undone by the development of the very traits it had biologically produced in order to cope with its environment. The beasts of prey and finally the higher apes came slowly to rely upon other than biological adaptations, and upon the consequent increased plasticity the foundations were laid, bit by bit, for the development of intelligence." [1]

Then Miss Benedict raises the question: "Perhaps, as is often suggested, man will destroy himself by this very development of intelligence."

Science and technology are important manifestations of the

[1] Ruth Benedict, *Patterns of Culture* (Boston: Houghton Mifflin Co., 1934).

217

intelligence and plasticity that have in the past permitted human beings to survive. The discovery of the usefulness of fire, the development of flint weapons and tools, of bronze and iron implements, the invention of the wheel—all of these were technological developments that permitted man to live and to multiply in his environment. Few persons would claim that those innovations were in themselves "evil" or "bad." Yet, those developments, coupled with innumerable subsequent developments of similar importance, have so modified our environment as to threaten seriously our existence. When looked at from the point of view of the events of the last few decades, it appears that the scientific and technological manifestations of our intelligence may indeed destroy us. And as a result, where science and technology were once considered "good" because they helped man to survive, they are now called "bad" by many persons because the accumulated knowledge appears to threaten our existence.

But to speak of abandoning our science and our technology is as reckless as to speak of abandoning our intelligence and abandoning the very plasticity that has permitted us to survive thus far. Man can no more abandon his intelligence than could the dinosaur his size. Our intelligence, and with it our science and technology, will exist as long as man exists. But, fortunately our predicament is somewhat different from that of the dinosaur whose size, which once permitted him to survive, destroyed him when his environment changed. The dinosaur did not create the environment that eventually destroyed him. Man has created his. The dinosaur had no control over his environment. Man, if he wishes and if he is willing to apply his plasticity, may have control over his.

Science and technology offer man important tools that may

enable him better to control his environment and as a result enable him to control his destiny. Man must learn how to use those tools properly and he must apply his plasticity to the task of devising the social and political institutions that will permit him to utilize the tools with maximum effectiveness. Science and technology in themselves are not the causative factors of our present grave position. The ignorant way in which science and technology have been applied by man in the absence of balancing measures, *in vacuo,* constitutes the chief danger. As we have not thought sufficiently far into the future, the net result of our haphazard and unplanned use of science and technology has been almost disastrous to society. Now, realizing the danger that confronts us, we should study the future, plan accordingly, and utilize those aspects of science that can aid us in molding a more hopeful destiny. But before this can be done, the scientist and the non-scientist must understand each other.

III

One of the most unhappy moments of my life occurred on the day shortly after the war when I journeyed with several of my colleagues to Washington for the purpose of discussing with some Congressmen and Senators an important piece of legislation concerning atomic energy. The experience was unhappy because for the first time I appreciated the appalling difficulties of achieving understanding between two such diversified groups of reasonably intelligent men. Clearly, as far as the Congressmen and Senators were concerned, we were from a different world—a world in which a different language was spoken, a world in which the customs of life were as different as if we had just journeyed for the first time from a remote region of Central Africa. Even our appearance startled them; they apparently had visualized atomic scientists as being old and bearded men possessed of pointed yellowing teeth and diabolic laughs. Instead, they were confronted by young men of ordinary appearance, undistinguishable from millions of others throughout the country.

We attempted to explain to the eminent legislators certain features of the nature of science and scientists, and something about the manner in which scientific research and development functions. But it was soon clear that we were attempting to explain things that either could not or would not be understood. Science to these men was solely a world of mysterious "atomic bomb secrets" and other weapons of war. We left Washington bewildered and disillusioned. How could we give to such men any conception of the scope of science—some knowledge of its significance? Unfortunately, an impression of the scope of science, like that of art or religion, cannot be conveyed in a few words. "Somehow," a friend of mine said as we left, "they must be made to understand."

We had attempted to tell the legislators that the scope of science embraces all things in our universe, past, present, or future, which are subject to direct or indirect observation, calculation or deduction. The scientist studies and attempts to understand the nature and behavior of animate bodies ranging from bacteria to elephants, of chemical elements from hydrogen to americium, of chemical compounds from water to proteins, of complex phenomena from the interaction of nuclear particles to the behavior of the human brain, to the behavior of large groups of people.

The pure scientist is solely concerned with measuring, correlating, integrating and understanding. He attempts to reduce

220

the innumerable phenomena of nature to lowest common denominators. He does these things because, to him, an understanding of how nature works is the most absorbing, soul-satisfying experience in the world. His actions are governed by his curiosity and by his scientific attitude. Seldom are his experiments or his theorizing knowingly governed by questions of applicability. The great pure-scientists have considered science an end in itself—like literature, art, or music. In correlating, in understanding, in finding order where chaos once existed, the scientist finds beauty and personal inner satisfaction. Thomas Huxley expressed the inarticulate feelings of many scientists when he wrote that the research worker is inspired by "the supreme delight of extending the realm of law and order ever farther towards the unattainable goals of the infinitely great and the infinitely small, between which our little race of life is run."

Year by year, the measurements, the correlations, the theories and the explanations are slowly accumulated in scientific publications. These bits of knowledge add up to a vast reservoir of knowledge—a reservoir which contains much knowledge which is of little "practical" value to society at present, and yet which contains much knowledge of immense "practical" importance to the future. It is from this reservoir that our physical technologists must draw in solving the problems of the design, production, and distribution of our material goods. It is from this reservoir that our medical technologists must draw in curing diseases and physical disorders. It is from this reservoir that our agricultural technologists must draw in solving the problems of crop production.

Technology is the application of the findings of science to the attainment of useful ends. In general, the technologist does not discover new principles of nature's operations—he utilizes principles that have been previously discovered and catalogued. The technologist draws upon the available reservoir of scientific knowledge, and designs machines and processes which will accomplish designated tasks. In this sense, inventors are technologists, as are electrical, chemical, and mechanical engineers, as are many chemists and physicists employed in our modern industries.

The technologist usually possesses a type of mind different from that of the pure scientist. Where the scientist is interested in discovering "how" something works, the technologist takes for granted the fact that it works, and applies the information to the solution of his practical problem. While the scientist is interested in studying the operations of nature as an end in themselves, the technologist is interested in studying nature as a means to a specific end.

A typical example of the line of demarcation between pure science and pure technology is again provided by the development of the atomic bomb. The bomb was made possible by a long series of discoveries and scientific developments in nuclear physics, notably the discovery of radium by the Curies, of the neutron by Chadwick, of artificial radioactivity by the Curie-Joliots, studies of neutron-induced radioactivity by Fermi and by Seaborg, the discovery of heavy-hydrogen by Urey, the development of the cyclotron by Lawrence, and finally the discovery of uranium fission by Hahn. It is important to remember that not one of these developments or discoveries was prompted by the desire to make an atomic bomb, or by thought that atomic energy might eventually be released in usable quantities. Indeed, it was not until some time after Hahn's discovery of uranium fission that it occurred to some scientists that an atomic bomb might be an actual possibility.

Once it was grasped that an atomic bomb was a possibility, the problem of producing a bomb then became a problem of technology. Physicists and chemists, utilizing principles that were in the main already known, developed processes for production; engineers designed flow-sheets and plants; pilot plants were built and studied; full-scale plants were constructed and put into operation. From the time when an atomic bomb became a theoretical possibility, its evolution, although on a larger scale than most modern technical developments, followed the same pattern as the production of nylon, or the production of fluorescent lighting.

During the war, the large numbers of physicists and chemists who worked on the development of atomic bombs acted generally not as scientists but as technologists. They were not particularly interested in discovering new principles of the operations of nature—they drew from our reservoir of basic scientific knowledge and applied that knowledge to the achievement of a concrete and preconceived objective. Indeed, during the course of the development of the atomic bomb, the reservoir of basic scientific knowledge was not enlarged to any great extent. During that period few discoveries were made that are judged today as having first-rate scientific importance.

Any technological development depends for its success upon the pieces of fundamental information accumulated bit by bit through the years by scientists the world over. No technological problem can be solved, whether it be to build a new bridge, to build an atomic energy plant, to cure cancer, to create a special new alloy of unprecedented strength, or to grow more crops per acre on a sustained basis, without adequate reservoirs of fundamental knowledge. The size of the reservoir of fundamental scientific information is perhaps the most important single feature that determines the extent to which man can control his environment.

New scientific discoveries make possible new technological developments. As it is impossible to predict the nature of new scientific discoveries, it is impossible to predict with accuracy the extent to which science and technology, properly applied, can help in solving some of the more urgent problems now facing the world. It is possible, however, to make one important generalization: the major technological problems that now confront the world—producing enough food to feed the hungry, producing enough goods to clothe people and permit them to live in reasonable comfort, raising the cultural standards of living—these problems will not be solved in a satisfactory manner in the absence of vigorous quests for new knowledge in *all* fields of science, ranging from nuclear physics to astronomy, from bacteriology to zoology, from anthropology to mass psychology, from bio-chemistry to psychiatry. Contrary to the belief held by many people, man has suffered and is suffering under the handicap—not of too much knowledge—but of far too little knowledge. This is nearly as true in the physical and biological sciences as it is true in politics, government, and the broad fields of human relationships.

If science and technology are to be brought into proper perspective in the world of tomorrow, three tasks of prime importance confront the people of the world, and in particular the people of the United States. First, broad research and development programs should be started, aimed in part at solving our more immediate technical problems, but also aimed in larger measure at no goal in particular other than increasing our store of fundamental basic knowledge. Second, there should be a complete renovation of basic scientific education so that scientists are familiarized with the broader aspects of our culture, are stimulated to awareness of the many perilous problems that face the world, and are made conscious of their responsibilities with respect to those problems. Third, the general public, the non-scientists, must in turn be exposed to sufficient science through education so that they understand not so much dry fact, but rather the spirit, the potentialities, and the intent of science. If strong efforts are made in these three directions, much will be accomplished toward absorbing a strong science and technology into our social structure so that mankind can receive maximum benefit, not only materially, but aesthetically as well.

Perhaps the reader will feel that too much emphasis has been placed on the atomic bomb, both as a grim fact and as a symbol, but we scientists who aided in the creation of the atomic bomb were perhaps the first large concerted group which attempted to break the bondage of specialization and assume responsibility for educating non-scientists concerning the implications of a major new development. The task was not an easy one, partly because of the limitations in the scope of our knowledge, and partly because of the limitations in knowledge and imagination possessed by those to whom we were attempting to convey our viewpoints.

The first major step in that direction occurred a month before the first atomic bomb was exploded at Alamogordo. A committee of seven reputable scientists, appointed by the Director of the Plutonium Project, submitted to the Secretary of War a significant report urging that the United States make immediate plans for the international control of atomic energy. After warning that atomic bombs cannot possibly remain a "secret weapon" at the exclusive disposal of this country for more than a relatively few years, and that in a war to which an atomic armaments race might lead, the United States might some day be at a disadvantage, the Chicago committee of scientists stated:

"We believe that these considerations make the use of nuclear bombs for an early unannounced attack against Japan inadvisable. If the United States were to be the first to release this new means of indiscriminate destruction upon mankind, she would sacrifice public support throughout the world, precipitate the race for armaments, and prejudice the possibility of reaching an international agreement on the future control of such weapons.

"Much more favorable conditions for the eventual achievement of such an agreement could be created if nuclear bombs were first revealed to the world by a demonstration in an appropriately selected uninhabited area."

In spite of the hopes that many of us placed in the Chicago report, by early summer it was generally recognized that the final decision as to the dropping of the bomb would probably be made essentially on the basis of expediency. In view of that possibility, and in order to make the record as clear as possible, a petition was drafted, signed by sixty-seven scientists, and sent through proper channels to the President of the United States. The petition urged that this country not resort to the use of atomic bombs in the war unless the terms to be imposed upon Japan were made public in detail, and Japan, knowing these terms, refused to surrender. To this day I do not know whether or not the petition reached the President.

Certainly the military, perhaps not understanding the scientists, had seemed to place every obstacle in our path.

The policy of our government became clear, however, when Hiroshima was destroyed and President Truman stated " . . . We are now prepared to obliterate more rapidly and completely every productive enterprise the Japanese have above ground in any city. Let there be no mistake; we shall completely destroy Japan's power to make war. . . ."

A few days later Nagasaki was demolished, an event which seemed to many of us an inexcusable tragedy.

In retrospect, the naive hope held by most atomic scientists immediately following the destruction of Nagasaki was indeed of colossal size. We thought that the time for "the great awakening" had arrived; that peoples everywhere and leaders everywhere would immediately understand that war must be a thing of the past. We assumed that the people, together with their leaders, would certainly do everything within their power in order to prevent another conflict. It all seemed so obvious!

But, to the contrary, the first evidence of our nation's course of action manifested itself when numerous government and military officials solemnly stated that atomic bombs were so difficult to make that no other nation would possess them in our lifetime. And then a General announced that we had found a defense against the atomic bomb. This was followed in rapid order by declarations by Admirals, other Generals, Congressmen and Senators, to the same effect. And, finally, officials of our government made statements to the effect that we would always maintain the lead in atomic warfare; that we would always be supreme in atomic warfare; that our stock of bombs would remain bigger and better than that belonging to any other nation. A greater hoax, a more devastating illusion, had never before been perpetrated upon the American people.

For the first few weeks following the Japanese defeat, we scientists, though dumbfounded and amazed by the official statements being uttered, could say nothing. By a combination of security regulations and psychological constraint, we were put into a position wherein we were effectively silenced. We were told by presumably responsible persons that "everything was under control"; that "certain delicate negotiations might be disturbed" if we should speak our minds; that "an excellent piece of legislation for domestic control of atomic energy had been prepared and its passage through Congress might be jeopardized should we speak out of turn." What turn? The hoax gradually became apparent.

In late September, unable to remain silent any longer, we scientists spoke out. We spoke out with the truth as we felt it in our hearts. But I fear that it was too late. Already minds were closed. Already, the people's imaginations had been saturated with dreams that seemed real because the people wanted them to be real. And thus it was that such ridiculous issues as "the secret of the atomic bomb" became national issues, beclouding the real issues, and tragically confusing the populace to the point where apathy, in its worst possible manifestation, has resulted.

The difficulties experienced by scientists during our attempts to express our viewpoint constitute one of the strongest condemnations of the educational policies and general national fetishisms which exist within the United States. If we, ourselves, had possessed broader viewpoints, perhaps we could have succeeded. If our military men, our government officials, our Congressmen and Senators, our President had possessed more understanding of the operations of science and technology, perhaps the results would have turned out for the better. It is tragic that because of lack of understanding, and lack of communication—in short, because of *specialization*, we Americans now find ourselves swimming in syrup.

Homer Lea once wrote: "As an individual can form no conception of personal death, so neither can nations." Yet, the great nations of the world, which if united in friendship could create a world set free, are deadlocked, each nation fearful for its own security, no nation fully realizing the proximity of personal death. Clearly the people and the leaders of the world have fallen asleep and are dreaming dreams that cannot be. They are dreaming the dreams of men who have cast off the world of reality, and have replaced it with a vision of a world that may have existed once, but will never exist again.

There can be—indeed there *must* be—a way out. But the way will not be shown by those who dream of the past as perfection. It will be shown by those who ponder this problem in the world of reality in which we live. Let each of us thirst and struggle for knowledge in the desert of his own loneliness. Let each reach his own conclusions and merge them with those of other thinking Americans. Let each of us be unafraid to act. But, above all, let each of us attempt to attain an attitude such as that to which Lanfrey's classic description of the historian applies:

"His patriotism is simply love of the truth. He is not a man of any particular race or of any particular country. He is a citizen of all countries and he speaks in the name of all civilization."

Propaganda has made recent history—for the democracies, much of it bitter. Hitler's words swept the German people into Nazism and war; Communist propaganda has played a strong role since 1946 in enslaving Eastern Europe and spreading doubt and dissension in lands toward the West, and in the Orient. Today the United States and her friends must meet such challenges with measures of their own.

In privately operated news, radio, motion picture and magazine services we are relatively rich. These agencies are established, experienced, proficient in their way. Primarily they are designed to bring information to the American people. That is to the good: to inform ourselves is of high importance.

Our talent for informing others has been less impressive. Our private news services are limited in this field and consequently the government must carry the heaviest load. Today we must reach both hostile and friendly peoples. But first we must know what we want to tell them.

News and ideas to America—American news and ideas to others: both are vital. How well are we meeting the challenge they represent?

9

Erwin D. Canham

AMERICANS AND THE WAR
OF IDEAS

I

The great decisions of our time must be taken in the hearts and minds of mankind. To a major degree, these decisions will be taken by and about Americans. Thus it is imperative that Americans should be adequately informed of the events of the world, in order that they may reach judgments and adopt policies which are necessary to a stable international society. It is equally imperative that other nations and peoples should know adequately the facts about Americans. So the problem of a two-way flow of information has become one of the urgent challenges of the time. This chapter can be only a brief report from the battlefront in the war of ideas.

First it needs to be said that though Americans are probably better informed than the people of any other large nation in the world, they are at the same time not nearly well-enough informed. Despite the massive machinery of information, there are great gaps in knowledge and serious distortions in interpretations. The stentorian voices they have called into being—the voices of press, radio, and films—suffer from the

233

intrinsic evils of bigness. They magnify error as well as truth, and circulate misinformation as efficiently as they disseminate fact. They need internal self-regulation. They need self-imposed responsibility. And somehow they need to preserve diversity, as the tendency toward concentration continues as a result of economic pressure.

Alongside the familiar press, radio and film media for the purveying of information, other channels have multiplied in recent years. Organizations of trade unions, churches, service clubs, women's clubs, educational groups, have attained immense spread and considerable penetration. They play a large part in guiding people's thinking and even in providing them with information. And of course the periodical press and books are significant, along with the newspaper press.

For a major examination of this subject, I will concentrate on the newspaper press, because it is my own particular field. Much that has happened in the American press has been paralleled in somewhat similar fashion in radio and films. And the newspaper press remains the basic news-gatherer for all three media. So it is perhaps not disproportionate to devote our attention first to the newspaper press.

The hard core of news, from the local neighborhood to the ends of the earth, is gathered for Americans very largely by three great organizations: the Associated Press, the United Press, and the International News Service. A handful of individual newspapers maintain skeletonized news-gathering systems throughout the world. Radio networks have a few correspondents abroad, but depend in large measure on the newspaper services. American news weeklies, in their present prosperity, maintain substantial news-gathering staffs abroad. Exchange arrangements exist between these basic newsgatherers and other far-flung news systems, such as Reuters, and various national news agencies.

General information for Americans, therefore, reaches them through relatively few hands. It may well take more people and a larger payroll to bring Americans bananas from Central America than it does to bring them news from the whole world. Nevertheless, the news that is presented to Americans is more extensive and more adequate than the news presented to any other people. It is also more substantial than that ever presented to Americans before. It is fair to conclude that Americans should be the best-informed people in the world. But that conclusion is not the whole story.

Analysts in the United States of public opinion down through the years have established to their own satisfaction the following conclusions:

That about 30 per cent of the electorate, on the average, is *unaware* of almost any given event in American foreign affairs.

That about 45 per cent of the electorate is *aware* of important current events but cannot be considered *informed*. These people retain little information. Although they may follow discussions of the issues of foreign policy, they cannot frame intelligent judgments about them.

That only 25 per cent of the electorate consistently shows knowledge of foreign problems.[1]

These percentages of information are relatively high. They drop considerably on issues which are not considered "big news" at the moment. In a great number of surveys, Dr. Gallup's "American Institute of Public Opinion" has found

[1] *Public Opinion and Foreign Policy*, edited by Lester Markel (New York: Harper and Brothers, 1949).

that less than one-fourth of the voters showed enough knowledge to rate as informed in foreign affairs, and on domestic issues about one-third could be said to be informed. The degree of information varies with income. In one survey, 88 per cent of voters with less-than-average incomes, compared with 82 per cent with above-average incomes, were totally unable to cite the purpose of the Marshall Plan.

And yet more than 80 per cent of the voters are reached by both radio and newspaper. In 1947, approximately forty million homes in the United States, more than 94 per cent of all homes, had radio sets. Two-thirds of the people listen to radio newscasts regularly. Newspapers also have an enormous audience: 80 per cent of the people read a daily or weekly newspaper regularly. About 50 per cent of the people read magazines. More than one-half of the American people belong to organized religious bodies and attend their services; fifteen million persons belong to trade unions; five million to veterans' organizations; several million more to women's clubs and other fraternal or group societies.

These combined sources represent extraordinarily diffused channels for information. But the information which flows along these channels is just as strikingly constricted as the channels are broad. The news that reaches Americans from China, for example, will come through the eyes and ears of a very few correspondents on the spot. They may well be cooperating in friendly competition, but their ideas and training will probably be identical. The dispatches they send will be remarkably similar. This applies particularly to the three big news agencies, and in a lesser degree to the individual newspapers.

Correspondents overseas for the news agencies work under

conditions of high pressure. On the one hand, they are in most cases intensely competitive. A matter of seconds is vital in rushing an important bulletin to the United States ahead of the rival agency. This competitive speed, which of course has its good side, also tends to produce haste, inaccuracy, over-simplification and superficiality. On a different level, many correspondents for news agencies must bear heavy business responsibilities. Often they are obliged to try to obtain new customers for their own news agency in the areas where they work, and they must at the same time pay special attention to the particular needs of old customers. Sometimes the commercial side of this work seems to overshadow their news-gathering, to the ultimate detriment of the American reader. This is, of course, not the intent of the agency. It is a result of the desire to spread the agency's dissemination of news throughout the world, and thus to put it in a strong economic (and news-gathering) position. Agencies that lose money cannot stay long in business. And it is important, as will be emphasized later in this chapter, for American news to flow freely to other parts of the world. The big channel for this flow is the very American agencies now being described.

Thus, the dual pressures of time-competition and commercial interest may prevent the correspondents of American news agencies from doing the job of which they are capable. Their difficulties are myriad, and I have not attempted to mention all of them. Often they must face the foreign language barrier, which is difficult to hurdle. There may be censorships, controls, and intimidations of endless variety. Governments and special interests in areas where they work may actively seek to conceal or distort the news. The assignments they have to cover are likely to be complicated, involving deep roots in national and racial history. Sometimes, as in China, the correspondent is perched on the edge of a continent, coping with official communiqués which have little relation to the truth, seeking to discern the true situation through a turgid alien cloud. At other times the American correspondent will be a newcomer, who, while almost certain to be an able reporter, may have had little opportunity to understand the intricacies of the problem he is trying to report.

But the correspondent out in the field is by no means the weakest link in the information production line. He is able to do a far better job than his cable editor will allow him to do, or than most editors will print. The plain fact is that newspapers are printed for people to read, and the great majority of readers are not interested in profound or carefully qualified accounts of events in faraway places. The news must be made interesting and impelling to them. That means that simplification and dramatizing are imperative. Sometimes the result is that the news is "suped-up" on the cable desk, and the language of the sports pages finds its way into events that are far too grave to be considered in such terms. And yet the editor has the problem of getting this news into people's minds—into the maximum number of people's minds. He has to compromise between sobriety and reader interest. On the whole, he does his job with great skill. But many abuses may creep in. And there are various other places all along the production line where mistakes may occur. The skill and sense of responsibility of the ultimate headline writer is not the least of the variables.

For the most part, the news-gathering system for radio is identical with that for newspapers. The same bottle-necks apply. But when the news is finally disseminated, radio often comes out with an even more truncated version than that which finds its way into newspapers. If newspapers have scare headlines, newscasters have scare voices, and commentators understandably have opinions and prejudices.

It may well be that news editors underestimate the tastes of their readers, or their interest in constructive affairs. But this supposition is not conspicuously proved by direct newspaper experience. The newspaper of which I am editor, *The Christian Science Monitor*, limits itself to news it believes will be of constructive value to the citizen—even when it is news of crime or melodrama. But ours is a very special case. Most newspapers are under the imperious mandate of commercial success, and must lay stress upon what they believe will most interest their readers. In very few cases indeed does this result in the kind of news coverage of the world which would satisfy a minimum standard of genuine adequacy. If the choice is between a little girl who has fallen down a well and the balancing of the budget in Italy, there is no question which will get the headline in the average newspaper. And yet the balancing of the Italian budget may be the decisive point in the preservation of a free world!

All this may seem to make for a gloomy picture. Yet that is only relatively so. For half a century, the tradition and practice of news objectivity has been growing within American newspapers and news agencies. Throughout the nineteenth century, a great deal of the news that reached Americans was presented with definite slanting of some sort. Particularly, the news of domestic affairs was subject to the hand of political or economic control. A major event would be presented strictly from the viewpoint of the individual newspaper. Furthermore, in the field of foreign affairs in those days, the American news agencies had not yet established their own networks around the world. They were almost entirely dependent upon arrangements with foreign agencies: Reuter, Havas, Wolff, etc. Dispatches from these sources were generally written from a nationalistic viewpoint.

But steadily during the present century, and with increasing force during the past decades, an effective news objectivity has become more dominant in American newspapers and agencies. There still remain a few newspapers more typical of the nineteenth century than of the mid-twentieth. And there are substantial areas to which American newspapers do not as yet give adequate attention. But the change, viewed dispassionately, has been impressive.

The news-column reporting of recent presidential campaigns (exclusive of the editorials and the columnists), is a good illustration. The news agencies, which furnish the bulk of national political news to American newspapers, usually provide cool and competent accounts of the activities of the candidates. Indeed, the dynamic and newsworthy characteristics of President Truman's campaign in 1948 gave him an undeniable advantage on most American newspaper front pages. It is true that on their editorial pages the great majority of such newspapers supported Governor Dewey, just as they had in most cases supported President Roosevelt's various opponents. But the election was not decided to any perceptible degree on the editorial pages, and the attention of readers was focused on the front pages perhaps ten times more than it was on the editorials and columnists. President Truman, like President Roosevelt before him, won the battle of newspaper headlines.

Another example of increased objectivity in American news

coverage is found in the reporting of labor affairs. Here the change has been particularly notable in the last decade. Ten years ago, many major strikes were meagerly reported. Today, although there may be serious gaps as viewed from the eyes of the labor partisan or of the employer, there is a widespread and careful effort to tell both sides. Today, the union press agents are often more skillful than management in getting their story to the public. Both sides, however, are newly conscious of the critical importance of full publicity. Few suspicious doors are slammed in reporters' faces these days.

No one will seriously claim that the millennium has been reached in American news reporting, but the fact remains that each decade of recent history has seen an evident improvement in the American press. In this field of newspaper activity there is no reason to assume that progress will stop.

The urgent need today is for the editorial viewpoint of American newspapers, and of the syndicated columnists, to assume the same responsibility that has been observed steadily increasing in the news columns. The greatest recklessness in the American press today, as in the radio, is not in news reporting, but in the unbridled presentation of pseudo-news, of so-called backstage secrets, and of the most violently conceived bias presented in the guise of fact. Character assassinations and slanderous attacks are still manifest in the newspapers and over the air waves. Irresponsible conduct in newspapers and other fields is nothing new and we do not today begin to match the violence of eighteenth-century and nineteenth-century attacks upon public men. But our contemporary keyhole columnists and opinionated pundits still pursue their careening way.

Such irresponsibility produces two effects. On the one hand,

241

many people accept statements from these sources as fact, and consequently become hopelessly confused. Their thinking boxes the compass along with the recklessness of their informants, or they select and accept the statements that most nearly fit their preconceived judgments. On the other hand, perhaps even more people lose confidence in newspapers, or in radio commentators, and sink into an attitude of skeptical cynicism. Either result is deplorable. Either condition makes people ineffective citizens, and tends to undermine their confidence in their institutions.

Temporarily, newspapers or radio may reap the rich fruits of sensationalism. The Hooper ratings of the most reckless commentators is the highest, and the most violent newspapers achieve the largest circulation figures. But these are only specious gains, if they are at the expense of a stable society, believing in its institutions. In the long run, the results of lack of confidence are failure—but sometimes it takes a very long run to reach that point.

It is also well to remember that readers and listeners build up considerable resistance to sensationalism. People are more case-hardened to sensation, they have adjusted themselves to it, and they discount it. Despite the irresponsibility of many columnists and commentators, objectivity is penetrating more and more into the decisions of publishers and editors. News-objectivity, which is already a relative fact, is being paralleled by the beginnings of opinion-objectivity.

What does this rather clumsy phrase mean? It is employed to represent the obligation that rests on the editor or publisher to reach his policy decisions with the best interest of the community as a paramount consideration. This sounds like cant, but it is a very practical thing. Recent newspaper history teems with examples. Perhaps the best one is that of the *Denver Post*. For many years, under the notorious Bonfils-Tammen ownership, the *Denver Post* was wildly sensational in its news and opinions alike. Indeed, it would have been difficult to tell the difference between news and opinion, since news stories and headlines were continuously colored with prejudice and bias. The old ownership died out, and the current heir installed E. Palmer Hoyt as publisher. Mr. Hoyt had a record of high and objective standards of community service. He transformed the *Denver Post* almost overnight. Today, in reaching a decision on policy, the paper thinks first of the welfare of the community and of the public interest. Another good illustration is the complete remolding of the *Washington Post* under the ownership of Eugene Meyer.

There is a further matter to be considered in this brief investigation: it is obvious that American newspapers are in a transitional stage. They are ceasing to be competitive representatives of particular and clear-cut viewpoints, as in the days when the average medium-sized city had six to ten newspapers. There are today only 117 American cities with daily local newspaper competition, in contrast to 1277 cities which possess only one newspaper. There are twelve daily newspapers per million population today, compared to twenty-three per million in 1920, and twenty-nine per million in 1900. The number grows less each year.

Throughout the nineteenth century, and rather consistently until 1920, the major groups in American thinking had representation through the newspapers. The citizen in a typical city had his choice of the newspaper which came closest to his views. He did not ask for editorial objectivity, and he rarely enjoyed news objectivity. He wanted the editor, and the reporter, to pour on the fuel in keeping with his own conceptions—usually his prejudices. As long as he agreed with what was being said, he was perfectly happy. It is a wonder that news coverage improved at all under these circumstances, because in every controversial matter readers tended to want to read what they believed, and they wanted to hear no good of the opposition.

But very soon the numbers and diversity of newspapers began to shrink. The primary cause of the disappearing newspaper was economic. It is not a sound business policy to maintain two expensive newspaper plants in a single city when each is dark for twelve hours of the twenty-four. Thus morning and afternoon newspapers began to be combined. This process alone almost halved the total number of separate ownerships—and, therefore, viewpoints.

Meantime, the cost of publishing newspapers had been mounting swiftly. Trade unions in the mechanical side of newspaper production are old and powerful. They have set up tight standards of apprenticeship, and have been able to maintain relatively high wage scales. This fact, combined with certain mechanical conservatism among publishers, has delayed technological change. It should be possible to set the type that goes into American newspapers for a fraction of what it now costs, by using practicable and well-proven new devices. Type can now be set swiftly by stenographers punching tape, as in a telegraphic transmitter, rather than by highly skilled linotype-operators. Printing, photo-engraving, and other processes could equally be much less expensive. Thus, union standards are one great barrier; the capital investment involved in change is another.

Many of the same factors which produce bigness and mass production in American industry at large have impelled consolidations and chain ownership of newspapers. And always in the background is the natural desire of advertisers not to support too many and too expensive advertising media. They shun the least effective of the newspapers in a given community, and their disfavor intensifies that paper's economic troubles and speeds its downfall.

Everything conspires—to date—to reduce the number of American newspapers. Economically, this is an inevitable and defensible event. Ideologically, it is too soon to prophesy whether the consequences will be all to the bad or all to the good—or perhaps in between. But dwindling diversity is certainly the major fact concerning American newspapers and their service to the people in mid-twentieth century.

We are faced by many paradoxes. Some of the most conscientious and responsible newspapers in the United States are published in so-called monopoly communities. Some of the worst newspapers are published where the competition is most intense.

It is also well to remember that no news "monopoly" is ever absolute, even if a single newspaper is the only daily publication in its community, and even if the publisher owns the only radio station. There is no community where important regional newspapers from the nearest big city do not penetrate. Radio coverage from other stations or other networks freely and vigorously enter the territory. The newsmagazines are widely circulated.

Moreover, the "monopoly" publisher knows that the ultimate fate of any monopoly in our society is likely to be some form of public regulation in the general interest. As newspapers approach the status of public utilities or common carriers, they run into dangers of governmental controls which are graver than anything they have faced for a century in this country. The only alternative to such controls is a quickened sense of self-regulation and a voluntary acceptance of responsibility. Such an acceptance has visibly begun. But at this moment, American newspapers are in a race between their own growing sense of objectivity and responsibility, and the dangers of regulation and loss of public confidence which have come with sharply dwindling competition. Only if American newspapers—and the same observation applies to radio and news-reels—show an increasingly adequate sense of objective responsibility to the news—and to the needs of the community —can they hope to escape the controls which apply to all public utilities. For the disseminators of ideas, such control may well be fatal.

At the mid-point of the century, the particular problems facing radio and films are more acute than the immediate position of newspapers. Newspapers emerged from World War II more prosperous and solid than anyone could have foreseen in 1940. In 1930, many prophets said that after a decade or two radio would undermine newspapers, both in commercial revenues and as a disseminator of news. In 1930, the prophets of doom were numerous and sounded realistic.

But by 1949, the situation was reversed. While many newspapers were not particularly well equipped to face a possible depression, and casualties might be expected to be high, radio and films were much worse off. Television had upset many of their calculations. The expenses of gearing-up for and producing through this challenging new medium were swallowing up the earnings of radio stations—and they were only in the early stages of their reconversion problems. The films, too, were just beginning to feel the pinch of television stay-at-home entertainment.

Radio itself has put heavy emphasis on entertainment in its post-war programming. The number of its news commentators and reporters was cut down. There was no longer the former financial margin for sustaining programs, since television was eating up accustomed surpluses. It was too early to tell whether the use of frequency modulation would break up or modify the old networks, re-introducing more individualism and local flavor on the air.

Thus, at the moment, uncertainty darkens the future of radio and television, threatens the financial stability of the industry—and renders it foolhardy to guess exactly what role these immensely potent media will play in the informing of Americans. But these problems will certainly be solved and it can be assumed that the informative role of these instruments will necessarily be large. Here, too, the tendency will inevitably be toward consolidation and bigness. There may well be three or four great networks, as there are three news-gathering agencies, but they may well be colossi of a considerable similarity. They will involve immense capital investments, conditioned as newspapers are by the heavy stake they have in this game.

It must be repeated that the only safe and democratic answer to bigness, in radio and films as in newspapers, is the voluntary acceptance of responsibility. There is already considerable governmental enforcement of responsibility in radio, for good or ill. The licensing power, unavoidable though it is in connection with an industry dependent upon a limited

247

number of frequencies, could be gravely abused if it sought
to control the editorial or news policies of radio networks or
stations. Sometimes the licensing power has fringed upon such
abuse. Such potential abuse can best be avoided by a voluntary
response to the challenge of public service.

The greatest blot in this field of communication media is
glaringly evident in our films. This medium remains, so far,
technically the most potent of all the methods of conveying
information to people. It hits people harder, penetrates deeper.
And yet news-reels are the most limited, inadequate, and in-
complete of all media. Documentaries are relatively few.
Whenever a real effort is made to convey news events in an
adequate fashion by film, the result is likely to be magnificent.
The educational advantages of films are also large, as the
armed services proved during World War II. Many efforts
have hopefully been begun to use this great new tool in postwar education. Yet the surface is barely scratched. The vast
resources of the film industry remain predominantly shackled
to its entertainment deities. And so films, which might well be
in first place of modern "propaganda," remain in a bad third
position as disseminators of factual information to Americans.

Such, then, is the bare framework of the information system
by which Americans are informed of the doings of their world.
How is it operating? Who is winning the war for the minds
of Americans? The answer, surely, is that the facts are winning. Americans have had to face many grave decisions since
the end of hostilities in 1945. Their response has been that
of a fallible human group: it has not been as foresighted and
prescient as some had hoped, *but it has been evolutionary.*
This apparent fact strikes many Americans as one of deep

significance: first, because it would be unique in our turbulent history; second, because of its augury for the future.

There was, first of all, the period of good will and Great-Power unity. Responding to the sweeping events of the last year of the war, Americans tried to be friendly and co-operative with the Soviet Union. They agreed to large concessions, ranging from deep Russian penetration in the occupation of Germany to the possession of the Kuriles.

Slowly and steadily disillusionment set in. It was accompanied, for the first year or so, by the natural and inevitable reaction to four years of intensive war participation. Americans in uniform wanted to come home and to stay at home. Those who had remained about the domestic hearth shared this desire even more fervently. Demobilization and reconversion were imperious goals. It is a wonder that our original participation in the peace machinery survived as integrally as it did. But the steady flow of fact accenting the United States' world responsibilities prevented Americans from tossing aside their global burdens as they had in 1920.

Soon, under the impact of disillusionment with Soviet policies—and perhaps because of it, the clear evidence that a still troubled world was upon us—the traditional trend toward physical withdrawal was reversed. American force became revitalized. More significantly, under the Marshall Plan, we undertook the immense task of restoring economic health to Western Europe, at once a vital barrier area and the repository of so much that is stable and valuable in western civilization. Soon Western Europe began the first steps toward its own unification, and finally the North Atlantic Defense Pact was readied to add its guarantees for peace. Under the circumstances, these were all long strides for the American people to take. They could not possibly have been made had not the channels of information been full. Americans saw and understood that another aggressive force was at large in the world. They put aside their faith in immediate conciliation and slowly began to set up physical safeguards.

At the same time, Americans retained and perhaps enlarged their confidence in the free system of which they found themselves the major heirs in the contemporary world. Their domestic policy followed a middle path. They found little to recommend itself in socialism, but at the same time they indicated their willingness to respond quickly to domestic problems, when and as they became acute.

The only ultimate test of the thinking of Americans is in their actions. That is why I believe the facts are winning, for national policy has continued to move steadily forward. Our confidence in the importance of freedom has not been shaken. The seductive propagandas of the extreme left and the extreme right have equally failed. We refuse to go over to the police state or to revert to the big-business state. We refuse to turn back the hands of the clock—or at least very far. From time to time various elements of reaction have seemed to return. But on the whole these have been balancing factors. When the people re-elected President Truman in 1948, they indicated plainly that they rejected laissez-faire reaction. To carry out their apparent mandate is another matter, for the coalition Congressional majority remains relatively conservative. And so, while domestic policy remains in a state of balance, we are steadily accepting and implementing in the international scene our heavy responsibilities to a free world. This is better, perhaps much better, than might have been expected of Americans in 1949.

250

II

If it is important for Americans to know certain facts, then it is equally important for the facts about Americans to be known. The position of world leadership which we have reluctantly come to occupy is vulnerable and dangerous if it is not based upon an understanding of our motives and acts. Today that knowledge is fragmentary, distorted, and opposed by a flood of defamatory propaganda.

There are various levels of misunderstanding and misrepresentation. There is apathy and unawareness. Many of our best friends, little susceptible to Communist propaganda, are nevertheless enormously ignorant of the United States. There is resentment. Every act of a great power treads on somebody's toes. Latin America suffers under old sensitivities, and remembers the days when this country was bitterly called "the Colossus of the North." The Arab world has burned with resentment over U. S. policy in Palestine. There is an unavoidable "have" and "have-not" relationship between the United States and most of the rest of the world. The role of benefactor is a delicate one in private life, how much more so is it between nations!

Thus we face an uphill job in making America known to the rest of the world. Again, it is perhaps surprising that we have not done far worse. For we have only just begun to become aware of the significance of this new verbal warfare. Congress in 1948 appropriated for the first time since the end of the war what might be considered an adequate opening budget to carry out the official phases of the international information job. What private media did was dependent upon the vagaries of the economic system, was limited by the dollar shortage, and was continuously hampered by the relative lack of responsibility of those who directed the media.

The grim reality of Communism's challenge to free people everywhere—despite the ubiquity and effectiveness of Communist propaganda—works for us in reverse. Wherever people have seen what Communism actually does in operation, we are winning the propaganda war. Elsewhere the results are in doubt. It is quite as important for us to tell people in the "gray" areas and the "white" areas the facts about Communism as it is to tell them about ourselves. They need to know both systems in order to judge between them.

The load of telling people about America falls upon government and private enterprise alike. Manifestly, under our system, government is called upon to do only what private enterprise cannot perform. Thus the first task is to clear the way for private enterprise. Here the three press associations, Associated Press, United Press, and the International News Service, are of prime importance, and so, obviously, is the motion picture. In Western Europe and Latin America, the ideas people have of the United States are derived very largely from what they read or see. The three press services supply news to hundreds of newspapers overseas. Most of these newspapers are under political domination, and many of them still suffer from a severe newsprint shortage. Hence they do not publish a great deal about the United States. Much that they do print is sensational, rather than important or serious. The news agencies follow a rule of reader interest in their export of copy, just as they do in supplying domestic newspapers. The result may well be an unbalanced picture of America, with a heavy proportion of disaster, crime, the bizarre and the fantastic.

Precisely the same situation prevails in the export of motion pictures. Whether we like it or not, American films have undoubtedly created more lasting impressions abroad about the United States than has any other single influence. They comprise about 75 per cent of the total motion-picture coverage of Europe. They penetrate to the remotest places, almost everywhere in the non-Communist world, and even to some slight degree into the Soviet Union and its satellites. The average foreigner, seeing an American film, naturally assumes that he is seeing a typical and representative picture of American life. He takes the average product of Hollywood to be a sort of documentary of the United States and its folkways, as Lester Markel points out.[2]

But along with all the distortion and one-sidedness of the press coverage, the films, and the other products of private enterprise that go abroad, there is a powerful counterbalancing factor. It is the fact that these are *private* voices. They are not contrived as propaganda. The hand of government does not lie upon them. Along with all their froth and trivia, there is also a sound basis of fact and true interpretation. In an alternative choice between completely free production of these media and governmental control, there would be no doubt that free men would choose free production. There is moreover a vigor, a competitive zeal, a creative power in the free way—with all its faults—which would be largely lost in the alternative.

At the same time, all who produce these immensely powerful voices of America should soberly weigh their responsibilities. They should remember that they are more effective propagandists than anything Congress can set up and pay

[2] *Public Opinion and Foreign Policy, op. cit.*

for with taxes. And along with their altogether proper effort
to do a job that will interest people and penetrate into their
minds, they must always keep a sense of balance. For every
neurotic social drama or musical extravaganza, there should
be a film showing American life in all its integrity and
decency. There are such films. There might be more of them.

However, there are many obvious shortcomings in private
enterprise, and a supplemental government program has now
become indispensable. Since the passage of the Smith-Mundt
Act in 1948, this job has been much improved. Long-term and
short-term techniques are used. For the longer period, these
methods include information libraries, films, mobile units,
exchange of editors, professors and students, pamphlets and
documentary materials, and various cultural approaches.
These methods have been widely appreciated in many parts
of the world. Their penetration may be slow, but it is steady.

Short-term instruments include primarily the Voice of
America radio programs, and the distribution of news and
textual material to newspapers, radio stations, and leaders
of public opinion. The radio impact is at its most effective
behind the iron curtain. There, especially in the Eastern
European satellite countries, large numbers of people are
eager and hopeful listeners. They are awaiting the day of
liberation. Inside the Soviet Union there are also many listeners, when the American sending stations are not "jammed,"
for some five million radio sets have short-wave facilities.
The Russian audience, in the words of former Ambassador
Walter Bedell Smith, is confused. "The average Russian,"
said Ambassador Smith,[3] "believes what he reads and what
he hears. He believes what he reads in the Russian paper and

[3] Report of "United States Advisory Committee on Information," 1949, p. 22.

he also believes what he reads in the *Amerika* magazine; he believes what he hears over the Russian radio and what he hears over the Voice of America. And since those are in a state of conflict, he is in a confused mental state."

The magazine *Amerika,* incidentally, is an illustration of one of the most effective propaganda operations the United States has ever undertaken. By an early postwar agreement with Soviet authorities, fifty thousand copies of this profusely illustrated, handsome magazine may be sold inside the U.S.S.R. All the material has to be non-political and non-controversial. This stipulation was a great blessing, for it has made the magazine much more effective as a mirror of American life. Devoid of self-conscious propaganda, it can tell the story of American fundamentals. One recent article, on snow-removal, was typical. Four-color pictures showed vast scarlet machines blowing the snow off a transcontinental highway smooth as a billiard table. Such highways, such technology, constituted propaganda without words, although an accompanying article told an interesting story of our transportation network and the problem of snow—a problem that also exists in the Soviet Union.

With continued appropriations from Congress, with a carefully recruited staff—which needs strengthening in numbers and talent—and with a steadily clearer concept of what U.S. policy really is, the official Voice of America has become reasonably effective. But a long time remains before the information arm of a three-part policy—the other two are military and economic—will be in proper balance with the other two. When the United States really gears up to do an informational job, as it did during the Italian elections in 1948, it can achieve tremendous results. But the plain fact is that neither private enterprise nor government is more than halfway implementing its responsibilities.

What is needed, beyond any question, is an awakening to crisis. This modern propaganda war for the minds of men, at home and abroad, is only half-understood by many Americans. Too many people think that it is a war of diplomatic jockeying and of atomic stockpiles. The truly effective bomb, the genuinely atomic idea, is, of course, the concept of freedom. When once Americans, privately and publicly, domestically and internationally, realize and act upon the realization that their heritage of individual freedom is an idea capable of conquering—and liberating—a world, we can say that the war of ideas is being won.

We have created fairly effective channels upon which ideas can flow. The channels are less effective abroad than they are at home, but they exist. Now the problem is to articulate the ideas which we will send along these channels. The competing voices are loud. But through it all is a still, small voice. It is the truth about man—the significance of man and his birthright of freedom. Out of the din of the multiple presses and the loudspeakers there still rises this cry of truth.

I believe man himself can and will win—with truth—this battle for men's minds. I do not believe man has shrunk because his voice is louder. For man is an absolute, and the individual is his expression. I believe some of us have become bemused by the complexity of modern institutions, and have imagined a golden age of earlier simplicity and lucidity that never existed. Bigness is bewildering, but it is not necessarily false.

It is true that these are days of vulgarization. But the content of mass information of today should not be compared with the luminous word of Plato or of Bacon. The comparison is between today's mass information and the black ignorance of the masses of old.

We have superlative tools of communication. But the key to man's relationship to his society lies in an understanding of the truth about man. In the United States, without being fully aware of it, we have achieved a new dignity for man. We have applied our basic concepts to the betterment of the common lot. We have a technology, and we have a spirit. Both must be understood by ourselves, and communicated to others. We have made a beginning. Awakening—and action —can take us the rest of the way.

When a nation swings from a peacetime strength of 170,000 men under arms in the 1930s to one of 1,600,000 today, both the military and the citizenry must recognize new obligations —and new dangers.

What protections against militarism lie in the methods by which we have developed our armed forces?

This and other questions must be answered. It is important to understand the revolution in military training which began in World War II and is now being carried forward year by year with new groups of young Americans. This type of training is the fulfillment of an obligation of the military to the country.

There is also an obligation of the country to the military— one that all Americans today should keep in mind in times of peace as well as in war.

10

C. T. Lanham

OUR ARMED FORCES:
Threat or Guarantee

We Americans have always been inclined to regard the professional military man with distaste—often with suspicion. Our Constitution bristles with provisions to insure his effective subordination and control. The Congress and the press have been vigilant to detect any indication of a developing military caste or the emergence of a potential man-on-horseback. With the broad oceans to protect us and no powerful or ill-disposed neighbors on our borders, we could afford, or thought we could afford, to indulge this traditional antipathy. Accordingly, in previous times of peace, we eliminated this source of fear by reducing our Army to a state of impotence, walling it up in isolated and forgotten garrisons, and then wiping it from our minds and from our consciences. This negative policy nearly lost us our independence in 1812 and came perilously close to costing us the free world in 1917 and in 1941.

As a people we are aware of this today, but basically our new alertness is fiscal. The moral, social, and political implications of the Armed Forces of 1949 largely elude us. Our personal responsibilities as citizens in the grave problems presented by a professional military establishment that now exceeds 1,600,000 men trouble us but little. Therefore, we are reasonably content to appropriate some sixteen billions of dollars for our fighting forces this year and then wash our hands of the business.

The matter is not so easily disposed of. Our billions will not automatically protect us from the evil forces that walk the world. Our billions will not provide us with assurance that the fearful concentration of military power we have been forced to create will not become an all-dominating influence in our national life. Power such as this begets power. It is felt in every nook and cranny of our existence. It lends strength and reality to our foreign policy and, almost unavoidably, a measure of direction. It touches on almost every department of our domestic political life. It has profound and far-reaching effects on our economy. It becomes, by its very size and its inherent controls, the most formidable educational force in our land. These matters stand out in bold relief. And yet the American people pay little more attention to their military establishment today than they did to their moribund force of 170,000 between the last two wars.

For the most part, our military leaders are aware of the heavy civic responsibility implicit in the size, the character, and the quality of our fighting forces, and are rising to it. But the problem is of such paramount concern to a free people that they should not divorce themselves from its solution, for quite obviously the wrong solution can be even more disastrous to them than no solution at all. I propose, therefore, to set forth certain trends in the national military establishment which by their very nature merit the attention of the thoughtful citizen.

Traditionally, armies are instruments of political oppression. The tale of man's groping toward the light is told to the rhythmic tramp of marching armies. That he has loosened to some degree his ancient bondage, has come about in large measure through his occasional triumphs over organized military force deliberately designed to keep him in subjection. Our own birth as a nation sprang from such a triumph. The implications of that struggle are still deep in our national consciousness, but the once clearly etched lines tend to blur. If we love our freedom, we should never forget that an army by its very structure and by the enormous physical power at its disposal provides the one sure means whereby that freedom may be struck down.

The Constitutional subordination of the military to the civil is not the complete answer to this danger that we believe it to be. What civil authority, what civil controls could stand for a day against a well-trained, well-organized, responsive military force bent on its destruction? Indeed, what one ever has? Nor does it require a high degree of imagination to visualize the situation that would result should atomic or biological warfare be directed against us. The very magnitude of the disaster would rocket the military into positions of unprecedented power. To quell panic, to restore law and order, to prevent sabotage, to succor the civilian populace, and to perform comparable tasks requiring organized force, the military would necessarily be called upon to take over many critical centers of civil authority, as well as those police powers which control and order our lives. In such circum-

YEARS OF THE MODERN

stances, a few key men of evil intent and evil ambition, backed by a politically inert army, could strike us a mortal blow.

Clearly, then, in peace or in war, our surest guarantee against the military lies in the military itself—in the quality of mind and heart of those whom we select as our military leaders, in their moral rectitude, in their spiritual solvency, in their civic consciousness. Similarly, for our armed forces as a whole, our safety lies in their understanding of the freedoms they have engaged themselves to defend and in the fundamental concept that they are citizens of the United States first and soldiers, sailors, and airmen after. Nothing less than this can assure us that our own creation will not turn at some critical juncture in our national existence and destroy us. And, indeed, nothing less than this will provide that moral purpose which is decisive in battle.

Before all else, then, we should consider our military leaders, for in their hands rests the over-all power we instinctively and correctly fear. Since ancient times governments have sustained themselves by organizing and staffing armies with leaders of like mind and like interests. Thus, in nations other than our own, the corps of officers has usually been drawn from the aristocracy, the economically privileged, and the politically reliable. Armies so created were used and are used with fine indiscrimination against their own people and against neighboring states.

Our own bitter experience as colonials led us to draw our corps of officers from the broad base of the people, and to take special care that it did not evolve into a rampant military caste either by accident or by design. We have been and still are unwise in many of our transactions with the military, but in this respect we have been wise beyond our knowing. It has

264

been the basic source of our internal security against the military since first we set an army in the field.

To insure a broad, democratic selection of potential military leaders, we established two service academies and placed the selection of candidates in the hands of Congress. Almost without exception, all candidates for West Point and Annapolis are selected on the basis of competitive examinations, thus assuring equal opportunity for the rich and the poor. Throughout our history, these two institutions have provided our Army and our Navy with the nucleus of their corps of officers. As a group, their loyalty has never been questioned, nor their devotion to the democratic faith. From their ranks have come our greatest battle leaders and many of our most able statesmen. In spite of the popular canard, few of these men have evinced either lack of vision or rigidity of mind. Again and again they have been called upon to shoulder the intolerable burdens of an unprepared country fighting for its life. Again and again, with inconceivable power placed in their hands, they have demonstrated those virtues we hold highest in American life—competence, humility, integrity, devotion to the public good, instant response to civil authority, and a profound belief in our institutions and in the democratic process.

Since the war's end, there has been a determined attack on the two academies that have produced so many men of this caliber. It is difficult to determine the basis for the attack, since the charges are misty and lacking in documentation. There is no charge of failure. There appears to be, at bottom, only the indictment that West Point and Annapolis produce men with a "military mind." No one, to my knowledge, has ever defined just what a "military mind" might be, or a legal mind, or an academic mind, or a medical mind, or whether they are good or bad. If, however, the great American military leaders whom our country has heretofore honored were endowed with "military minds," we might be well advised to try to increase their number against our day of need.

While we toy with the idea of scrapping our two military academies or drastically altering them, we have allowed the quality of our officer corps to deteriorate by sheer economic neglect. For forty-one years there has been no systematic revision of the pay structure of the military establishment. Today the situation for the bulk of our officers has reached a point not too far removed from desperation. What was a generous wage in 1908 has sunk to the marginal area in 1949. Housing is now available to fewer than 15 per cent of our people who are entitled to it. In common with those of our fellow citizens, our taxes have pyramided (contrary to popular belief, there is no distinction made in this respect between the civilian and the serviceman). In many other areas, our economic life has shrunk to a not-too-genteel poverty. The Congress is now aware of this intolerable situation but the price already paid is heavy. Since the war's end, there has been an exodus, reluctant but steady, of some of our most gifted officers, those whom we can least afford to lose. Neither love of country nor devotion to a profession can blind a man forever to his obvious responsibilities to his family.

As ominous as this is, its corollary is even more ominous. No longer do the applications for the two service academies pile up in astronomical numbers. Of late there have even been disturbing numbers of vacancies. Many of the young cadets and midshipmen are dubious about careers in the service. There is fairly good evidence that many intend to resign as soon as they have served the minimum number of years following graduation. This, too, should be cause for alarm, but the evil chain of cause and effect does not stop here.

The two academies can supply only a fraction of the officers required for the military establishment. This in itself is healthy, for it brings freshness and vigor to the services and precludes the possibility of intellectual and professional inbreeding. Formerly, the competition for these positions among college graduates was enormous. Thousands competed for a few vacancies. The figures today imply a different story. Every American should ponder them. *Sixty-two per cent of our Air officers, 43 per cent of our Army officers, and 38 per cent of our Navy officers have not completed the second year of college.* True, these are battle-tested leaders for the most part and can be relied upon to acquit themselves well. But the fundamental fact remains: the broad educational background vital to high command in modern war is missing. The range of selection is narrowing at a dangerous rate. The law of supply and demand cannot be flouted indefinitely without dire consequences, and this is one of the consequences. Quality merchandise is seldom found in the bargain basement. It is well to think of this when we think of our possible involvement in a climactic war, for there is no reward for finishing second. There is no bargain rate for victory. And to date, there is no price tag on freedom.

A third reason why we are losing a substantial number of our more able leaders, and failing to attract the top-flight young men we must have, lies in the public abuse to which the officer, and in particular, the regular, has been subjected for the last four years. The professional pacifist, the cloudy-minded and the party-liner have all played their parts. But the great majority of the American people and our former servicemen have played theirs, too. To each, the officer was the symbol of the thing he hated—of war, of authority, of subordination, of fear, of sacrifice, of frustration, of heartache. They forget that the leader was subject to the same authority, the same subordination, the same fears, the same frustrations, the same sacrifice, the same heartaches, and his own particular brand of misery compounded by the soul-trying responsibility he carried.

To the officer, this treatment at the hands of his fellow citizens is incomprehensible. He has nothing to be ashamed of, nothing to apologize for. Whatever his faults—and in common with all the rest of humanity, he had his share—they sprang from the head and very seldom from the heart. That this is the truth is best evidenced by the national sensation which results when a rare professional fails to live up to the high code that the services and the American people expect of him. Yet all falls from virtue were almost automatically attributed to the regular in the public mind. Few realize that our armies were staffed by some 900,000 officers; still fewer realize that of these, less than 15,000 were regulars.

The world we know still stands. True, it is shaken, bewildered and fearful of the dark tides rising about it, but nonetheless, it still lives and hopes. Ultimately, the fact that it does may be credited in substantial part to the professional ability, the deep civic convictions, the integrity, and the unstinted devotion of this little handful of talented American military leaders. Our people would do well to review their history and remember it.

Between our two great wars, the American serviceman probably hit an all-time low in public esteem. Parents wept when a wayward son ran away from home and enlisted. A girl seen with a man in uniform found her reputation gone. In some sections of the country, better-class restaurants and amusement establishments displayed signs reading "No soldiers, sailors, or dogs allowed." Brothels and dives flourished wherever the military took root. Unhappily, there were reasons for this state of affairs.

The basic pay of the enlisted man was $21 a month. His uniform was shoddy and ill-fitting; his diet heavy, monotonous, unappetizing. His barracks were drab and depressing. Opportunities for self-improvement were non-existent, libraries scarcely known. Except for two or three weekly movies of the lowest B variety, there were no post diversions. Even the most indefatigable chaplains stood before nearly empty chapels. Venereal rates and disciplinary rates kept company far up the graphs.

Units were painfully skeletonized. A company of infantry, which at war strength stands at some two hundred men, considered itself fortunate when fourteen or fifteen men could be mustered for training. Training itself was stylized, perfunctory, soul-killing in its monotony. In essence it was largely meaningless, even under the most gifted leaders, for no one could systematically overcome the absence of men and equipment.

Given such circumstances, the quality and the character of the great bulk of men attracted to the service of their country could be predicted to a nicety. Some criminal courts assisted the recruiters by offering their clients the choice of jail or enlistment. Thus, in time, the United States serviceman became generally unacceptable to all save the most vicious elements of the civil community. The uniform became a badge of social inferiority and a mark of failure, rather than the prideful thing it should and must be. The serviceman himself, whether good or bad (and there were many fine men who endured even these conditions for love of their task), became by a combination of financial and social pressure an outcast in his native land.

His lot vis-à-vis the officer was little better, for, even with all the good will in the world, the mental, moral, and cultural gap between the peacetime officer and the average peacetime serviceman was unbridgeable. There was no single point of contact. Accordingly, the run-of-the-mill officer tended to command rather than to lead. He dealt out justice with an even hand and exercised a species of benevolent paternalism. Nearly always he was respected; often he was held in genuine affection.

Scarcely one aspect of this day-to-day, on-the-ground training bore any resemblance to the bewildering array of problems, human and tactical, that would automatically appear when the drums began the long roll—and the drums were in fact, being readied. Thus, the wealthiest nation in the world, and potentially the most powerful, collected in the name of the national defense the broken, the defeated, the morally maimed, dressed them in the uniform of their country and labeled them "our regulars." And to our young, aspiring officers we said, "Work with these men. Lead them. Train them. Ready them for war in order that you, and they, may learn your infinitely complex trade and the secrets of leading great national armies wisely, humanely, justly." Thus America from 1920 to 1940!

It is not my intent to try to tally the bloody price exacted for this crime against ourselves and against free men every-where. Perhaps no one can. Those transactions are over and done. Today we stand at a point where we may yet controvert the cynical platitude that "we learn from history that we do not learn from history." If we aspire to this, we should address ourselves forthwith to the moral, social and civic problems presented by 1,600,000 young Americans under arms.

We could ignore 170,000 men in uniform before the war without material consequence to our society. We could allow our armed forces to become almost an asylum for the derelict and the unemployable without serious danger to our institutions. We could erect a social barrier between the serviceman and the rest of the country without undue concern for what occurred on the military side of that barrier. But when that number of uniformed men is increased by 1000 per cent, we will do any of these things at our peril.

Each year upwards of 400,000 young men are being returned to civil life after a substantial period of military service. Whether we like it or not, one fact is clear: the national military establishment has become the greatest single educational force in our society. We dare not ignore it. Our high command is generally alive to the significance of this fact and to the obligation it imposes, but the American people seem to be looking the other way. Surely, let it be repeated, it is high time we took a long, hard look at the fighting forces we have created.

Never before in our history, whether at peace or at war, has the quality of our armed forces been so high. The educational level is above the national average. The moral tone is even higher. In terms of physical and mental well-being our men stand pre-eminent. Careerwise there is no ceiling. Pay for the basic serviceman has increased nearly 400 per cent. His food in quality and in preparation compares easily with better-class restaurants in our large cities. His uniform has been smartened and is now tailor-fitted. He is proud of himself and proud of that uniform and proud of his service.

By and large, he is a young chap—more than 600,000 are under twenty-one, many seventeen and eighteen. He presents a constant challenge to our military leadership, for he is alert, vigorous, ambitious, questioning, and quick to detect the phony and the inadequate. He is a youngster for every citizen to be proud of, to glory in; and he should be their constant, high-priority concern.

Our military leaders are determined that these men shall not re-live the bitter experience of the regulars in the twenties and thirties. They are determined to return them to their homes not merely as master journeymen in the deadly trade of war, but as mature citizens, strengthened by self-discipline and fortified in the democratic faith. Thus our Army, our Navy, our Air Force seek not only to develop a better fighting man from the magnificent human material at hand, but a better citizen. Ultimately the quality of our citizenship determines the effectiveness of our arms.

Too many of us forget this. Too many of us are bemused by our fabulous war potential—our stock pile of atom bombs, our fearful weapons, our fantastic ingenuity, our pyramided wealth. We forget that man is still the fundamental instrument of war. We forget that the effectiveness of the tank, the bomber, the fighting ship is measured by the effectiveness of its crew. Our furious concentration on material power to the complete exclusion of moral considerations can ultimately destroy us. The centuries have underscored this truth with blood and ruin

272

for those leaders, both civilian and military, who have ignored it. Repeatedly, gigantic concentrations of physical power have gone down in defeat before a lesser strength propelled by conviction; it is platitudinous to observe how often the Goliaths have perished at the hands of the Davids.

Even those countries which are the most barren politically and the most insolvent morally strive endlessly to create the illusion of civic virtue and moral rectitude. For they, better than we perhaps, realize that neither a nation nor its army is any stronger than its convictions. Therefore, our people as well as the military should be increasingly vigilant lest we come to evaluate our strength exclusively in terms of military might. Our true strength resides in the philosophy upon which our country stands and the degree of understanding and acceptance of that philosophy by all of us, in uniform or out. Here lies our fundamental security, whether the threat be external or internal, by ideology or by force. It is around this concept of civic virtue that we must build and maintain our military strength. To do otherwise is to build a colossus of straw.

Until the eve of World War II this basic consideration played no really significant part in our military thinking. Until that time we had taken for granted the ancient virtues of our people—a deep knowledge of our freedoms, an almost instinctive awareness of dangers that threatened those freedoms, a broad fund of factual information from our amazing press and radio, and a public school system that had always been the source of our civic strength and unity. In mid-1941, these complacent assumptions crumbled. For in that year we suddenly discovered that the young men in our expanding Army were often sullen, divided, confused. We found that

great numbers of them were literally ignorant of the catas-
trophic events in Europe and the dark portents in Asia. And
since they saw no danger, they saw no compelling reason why
they should be called upon to serve in the fighting forces, the
creation they had been taught to despise.

In common with millions of their fellow citizens, they appeared to be unaware or indifferent to the human values at
stake in a collapsing civilization—values which they would
soon be called upon to preserve at the final price of their lives.

A perverted philosophy had found its way into our national
blood stream; a philosophy which placed peace before freedom, comfort before sacrifice, personal privilege before the
common good, and rights devoid of their companion obligations. It was summed up nicely in the argot of the day, "What's
in it for me, Mac?" It is not likely that any nation which
clings to such principles will long endure; and it is certain
that any military force so motivated will collapse at the first
shock of battle.

The Japanese at Pearl Harbor did for us what we could not
do for ourselves; they united us. Nevertheless, the great gaps
in the moral armor of our young fighting men had been made
clear. Anger and indignation at Japanese treachery had served
to unite us, but anger and indignation were not substitutes for
an understanding of the freedoms we were committed to preserve or the moral issues involved or the nature of the dark
forces that were loose in the world. Therefore, the Armed
Forces, and in particular the Army, undertook to repair these
shocking failures as best they could.

This was indeed a strange and an unfamiliar mission; and
since it was strange and unfamiliar, mistakes were made and
acceptance was slow and difficult. It took us some time to real-

ize what Spinoza meant when he observed that "men fight better with ideas on the ends of their bayonets." It came as a shock to many of us to be reminded that even with the crystal-clear issues presented by our own War of Independence, General Washington had found it necessary to engage Tom Paine to do a similar job for his army. Yet constantly we had heard the great captains of history testify that the critical factor in war lies in the moral domain, in the will to win. That ineluctable power is derived from the spiritual and moral roots of our country.

Thus were our traditional patterns of military thought shaken. Since then we have been groping toward a set of moral standards that will dignify the fighting man. Today our concepts are beginning to take form. We realize, for example, that we can no longer live in our former military isolation, divided spiritually and intellectually from the civil community. We realize, too, that in the very name of national defense itself, the man in uniform, no matter how humble or exalted his position, must regard himself above all else as a citizen and that his primary loyalty must be to the free society he represents. Thus, bit by bit, a new philosophy is beginning to take on form and substance. At the moment, we see it shaping up toward four broad objectives.

At the head of the list we set as our goal the preservation of the dignity and the identity of the individual serviceman. Man can suffer no greater indignity than the loss of his identity. He can sustain no heavier spiritual blow than the thought that his life or his death is of no consequence. Too often has the conviction that he as an individual is of no importance led the serviceman to the conclusion that his effort is of no importance either. If that thought be generated in enough men in our fighting forces, the end result in battle is clear. Moreover, men who are spiritually unfulfilled, men who are scarred by the savage anonymity of traditional military practices, are prey for the demagogue, tinder for the incendiary, and potential followers of our friend, the dramatic figure on horseback.

Therefore, we strive to build an officer corps that will recognize, honor, and preserve the dignity and the identity of the humblest serviceman. The American people bear an equal obligation in this task, for it is their duty to convince the fighting man that his aspirations, his well-being, his service are all matters of prime importance to his country. In no other way can we fulfill the desire that lives in every human heart to count for something, to be "needed."

Our second aim is to provide an answer to the inevitable question, *"Why?"* The American can be led but not driven; and if he is to be led, he must have an adequate and an intelligent explanation of the things he is called upon to perform. This, of course, does considerable damage to that ancient school of thought which contended "Their's not to question why." Enlightened leaders have always done their best to answer this ever-present question, whether spoken or unspoken. Now, as it should be in the army of any free people, it is a fundamental requirement of command.

As might be expected, this policy has been questioned by certain of our military men, but strangely enough, it has also been challenged by some of our civilian critics. This, in common with much of the philosophy I have been describing, has been indicted as "mollycoddling." It has been categorically charged by some that such procedures will destroy the discipline without which a military organization cannot exist. In my judgment, the critics of these policies are mistaking the shadow for the substance. Quite apparently they are advocates of that brittle counterfeit of discipline which is based on fear. We seek the tougher, more enduring discipline that is rooted in understanding. This, the true discipline, by its very definition renders a fighting force propaganda-proof and subversion-proof. The cold truth is that nothing short of this has ever produced a first-class American fighting unit and nothing ever will.

Our third goal is to bring to our young men an understanding of the American ideal; to nourish that ideal; and to build an abiding belief in the future of our country and the democratic process. Here lies the very bed-rock of motivation. Nevertheless, it is occasionally contended that this is none of our business. For our part, we contend that such an understanding must live in the heart of every fighting man and that anything we can do to strengthen it, we should do. No group should have a monopoly on civic education; it is a job for all of the people all of the time.

Our fourth objective is to keep our men aware of the great national and international issues that confront us from day to day, in order that each may understand the vital interest these matters hold for him both as a citizen and as a serviceman. The military man, as well as the civilian, is entitled to a free, uncensored flow of information. We believe, however, that these matters are of such vital import to the serviceman that we cannot leave the question of his current knowledge entirely to chance or inclination. To do so might well mean that at some critical juncture in our national life we would again discover to our dismay that our servicemen know everything about Dick Tracy and nothing about Yugoslavia; everything about the current plight of Little Orphan Annie, but nothing of the

North Atlantic Pact; all of the troubles of Li'l Abner, but nothing of the deadly transactions in China. Therefore, in addition to providing our fighting men with broad access to the press and radio, we make positive provision to bring them objective presentations of the more important matters occurring in their country and in their world, and then encourage organized discussion and examination of the issues on a duty-time basis. There is no attempt to influence the serviceman's thinking. On the contrary, every effort is made to encourage him to think for himself and, in the democratic tradition, to discuss his views with his brothers-in-arms. The virtues of this process both from the civic and the military points of view are too obvious to warrant elaboration.

These four goals are fundamental in respect to the human side of our armed forces. There are many derivative objectives, but I believe these four are sufficient to make the point that the philosophy of our fighting forces has traveled far and fast since 1941.

None of this activity means that our Armed Forces are being "democratized" in the sense in which that word has been bandied about in the last four years. No military organization can exist under such a concept. Although it is not generally known, our own history is studded with abortive attempts to "democratize" our Army. The favorite device was the election of officers. All of our wars, from the Revolution to World War I, began with substantial numbers of militia and volunteer units operating under an elective system. In every war it failed quickly and completely and had to be abandoned. Variations on the "democratization" theme fared no better. Leaders cannot be selected on the basis of personal charm and popular appeal.

278

Armies cannot operate by vote. There is no surer and no quicker way to destroy a fighting force than by such procedures. Lenin and Trotsky knew this full well when, with icy deliberation, they destroyed the Imperial Russian Armies in a matter of days by their famous General Order No. 1. This order, among other things, wiped out all distinctions of rank and established Soldier Councils. It is significant that the Soviets wasted no time in building a new army and in building it on classical lines. Parenthetically, it might be noted that the officer corps of the Red Army at once became the new aristocracy of ancient Russia and that the power vested in it is in keeping with the rest of the terror that lives in that dark land.

But let us not lose sight of the point. We can destroy our Armed Forces tomorrow, or reduce them to a level of impotence, by legislation for reasons that appear adequate, or for no reason at all. We can destroy our fighting strength with equal ease by requiring the armed forces to adopt any one of a dozen "democratization" schemes. Of the two methods, the first is infinitely preferable, for at least the country will know precisely what its strength is. By the second method, the surface illusion of a non-existent strength might well be preserved. Should we ever decide to wreck our military establishment, let's do it quickly and cleanly and with full awareness of what we are doing.

The above considerations return us to our point of departure. Are our Armed Forces a threat or a guarantee? In our effort to preserve a free world, have we created a monster that will destroy the very thing we seek to preserve?

My answer is a not too surprising "no." A military organization bent on circumventing, subverting, or overthrowing the civil government would not assiduously instruct its troops in the processes of that government and in its virtues. No power-drunk high command would insist on placing citizenship and its concomitant loyalties before soldiership and its loyalties. No military hierarchy seeking to extend its power and influence would repeatedly petition the civil government to relieve it of the burden of governing the conquered Axis countries. All of this is true beyond cavil. In essence it has always been true. And it always will be true unless the American people, through indifference or ignorance, allow their officer corps to degenerate into an assembly of amoral opportunists and the armed forces themselves to become a "skid row" on the grand scale.

Unfortunately, our chronic distaste for the military impels us in both directions. As a people we have contributed little to the good ends the national military establishment is seeking. We have been content to pay the heavy price of admission to the big military game in order to throw bottles at the players and chant the favorite American refrain, "Kill the umpire."

We are in danger of destroying the morale of our officer corps by our ceaseless and senseless attacks. Our military leaders are the villains of the postwar novels, the scoundrels of the magazine pieces, and the favorite stereotype of the cartoonist. Whether the intent be premeditated or not, the end result is the same: vicious wedges are being driven between our military leaders and our men and between our military leaders and the civil community. That way lies disaster for any country.

Our soldiers, our sailors, our airmen find themselves in little better circumstance. Nearly a year ago President Truman appointed a national committee to study the moral aspects of this vast problem and to assist him in bringing to the people a realization of their responsibility for its satisfactory solution. That committee has seen at first-hand some of the ancient troubles of the military vis-à-vis the civil communities. It has observed the old barriers going up again between civilian and serviceman. It has heard the question "Are you a volunteer or a selectee?" and heard the snort of derision when the answer was "volunteer." It has heard the testimony of youngsters with fine educational backgrounds and of impeccable behavior who cannot understand why they are generously received when in civilian clothes and snubbed when in the uniform of their country. The committee has learned without difficulty that the serviceman is considered legitimate prey in many of the communities adjoining military installations. The rent gouger, the clip-joint operator, the madame, the professional gambler, are coming out of hiding and operating with increasing brashness in the face of community indifference. The committee has had adequate opportunity to watch the military struggle with these evils, but knows that they will never be eliminated without the help of an aroused and indignant citizenry.

Over weekends, virtually every city in the United States is host to hundreds of young servicemen, but few of these cities are very good hosts. The preoccupied civilian hurrying to his comfortable home scarcely notices the eighteen-year-old soldier leaning against a lamp post, wondering where to go, what to do. Our country is swarming today with youngsters in uniform who are away from home for the first time. Many are lonely, homesick, a bit bewildered by this vast land of ours and the strange people in it who ignore a young fighting man in these troubled times. He has a right to be puzzled, a right to be a bit stricken in his pride, for our debt to these young men who have volunteered for service at the outermost frontiers of the free world is already considerable and may some day be beyond the price of any of us to pay. We are a cruel and callous people to our professional military men.

Every day this is evidenced in hundreds of ways. Whether we realize it or not, we are creating patterns in the minds of these men. We are creating a picture of the thing that we call democracy and that we profess to cherish. It may well be that on some evil day these young men will be called upon to walk with death so that this democracy may live. In some remote area of the sky, on some strange sea, on some fear-ridden foreign field, the fate of the free world may depend upon the image of that world carried in the minds of our fighters. Men fight, if fight they must, and die, if die they have to, for a living, breathing thing that commands their devotion and their allegiance. They do not fight for a slogan from a propaganda mill—not free men. Thus, every American citizen is contributing subtly and perhaps decisively to the fighting heart and the fighting spirit of the men who are sworn to defend his life and his freedoms. He may well be spelling out his own destiny.

In the late 1890s a child in New York City, lying abed on a winter night, could listen to the thud of hoofs on the snowy street outside and have a sense of a secure world. It was a feeling of safety which men and women throughout America also shared.

Fifty years later the sense of security had been supplanted by fear: the fear of economic disaster, of Communism, of atrocious weapons of modern war.

Once again Americans face the challenge of peace. They have faced it before, with no great success. Today's peace is disturbing, uneasy. In 1946 we unwittingly aided the Communist drive by demobilizing too quickly. We discovered that an ill-armed victor lacks power at the peace table. We are stronger now; but thanks to our shortsightedness, so are other powers.

Yet we still have peace, and with it, an opportunity.

11

Sumner Welles

PEACE: OUR GREATEST CHALLENGE

What will be the shape of the future? If humanity can be dissuaded from suicide, what lies ahead for the generations to come?

We at least perceive the new and shadowy forces that loom about us. Their outline is as yet indistinct. But they are no longer so dim that we can fail to realize we are witnessing the inauguration of a new era in the history of man.

What kind of world is it going to be? Will it confirm the predictions of the prophets of doom that the new Dark Ages have commenced? Will there be a period of recurrent devastation during which the very nature of the human race and the very surface of this ancient planet will be transformed? Or will the civilization now being born justify those optimists who tell us that a ready-made world government is now imminent and that this will solve all of those ills which now beset this tragic world? Or are we going to see a long-continued contest between two titanic forces that will last until at length the volcanic tremors that now convulse civilization gradually diminish; and there is eventually evolved a new political, social, and economic system which assimilates what human experience has shown to be worth preserving in the ideologies that now contend—until humanity finally enters an age wherein wars have ceased, the dignity of the individual is universally recognized, and men and women are free to pursue happiness?

We have acquired the habit of speaking glibly of world revolution. But it is only now that we are beginning to understand the implications of the term: how directly the world revolution that is in progress may affect our lives, and how radically the world into which we were born will be changed before the present generation has concluded its normal span.

When the United States entered World War I, most Americans believed that their country's entry would give rise to a world that would be "safe for democracy." They refused to see that such a world could not be brought into being by a mere military victory, but only through the subsequent sacrifices and the persistent and concerted efforts of all peoples.

When the United States was forced into World War II, an equally large majority of the American people believed that the victory of the United Nations implied the automatic establishment of a world order by which peace would be guaranteed and through which peoples would obtain the Four Freedoms. Once more, although the American people no longer believe that the ends for which they fought can be attained without an American assumption of responsibility, their illusions have been dispelled. There is no existing prospect of peace. And the light of freedom is being extinguished in an ever-increasing number of the nations of the earth.

Even here in the United States, for the first time since the American people won their independence, there is no longer freedom from fear. There is, on the contrary, fear of Communism, fear of the imminence of an atomic war, fear lest the

American standard of living vanish under a tidal wave of economic chaos.

I was born in that last decade of the nineteenth century in a New York brownstone house opposite the old Brick Presbyterian Church at the corner of Fifth Avenue and Thirty-seventh Street. As a child, as I lay in bed on a winter night listening to the sound of the muffled hoofbeats from horse-drawn carriages in the snowy streets, the sense of a secure world was absolute. That childish assurance that "All's well with the world" typifies the age. That delusion so influenced my adolescence and the earlier years of my maturity that it seemed inconceivable that even World War I could so afflict humanity as to engender the revolutionary forces from whose culminating ferment there is now no escape.

In the history of civilization no human beings had ever so fully enjoyed the sense of security from foreign aggression as the English-speaking peoples at the turn of the century.

Here in the United States scientific discoveries and the development of the machine had not yet diminished our geographic isolation. The Victorian Era was ending in a world in which all but localized hostilities appeared to have become obsolete. Civilization had brought about the consecration of enlightened principles of international law. Notwithstanding the uncertainties inherent in the nature of the German, the Russian and the Austro-Hungarian Empires, the Hague Conferences of 1899 and of 1907 seemed to presage a community of nations among whom justice and the pacific settlement of international controversies would become the rule rather than the exception.

That social maladjustments and inequities were universal,

and that economic security was enjoyed only by the privileged few and not by the underprivileged many, is wholly true. But there existed only the first glimmering of any political consciousness of the eventual disasters which the persistence of such evils must bring about. The American philosophy of the last decade of the nineteenth century was based upon the assumption that this country could safely take it as a matter of course that all major wars had become a thing of the past, and that American safety from any threat of aggression or invasion was axiomatic.

It is not strange, as we of the older generation look back, that isolationism has maintained so firm a grasp on American thought. It was not only that the conscience of the American people was revolted by the obliteration of all of their bright illusions. It was far more a "fear of fear itself." It was a very human unwillingness to accept a destiny in which physical security would no longer be of the essence of American life.

Yet, outside of the British Isles, such a sense of security has never existed in Europe; much less in Asia and in the Middle East. It is today precisely that kind of security for which the peoples of the world clamor.

Even in Europe, war long seemed to mean little more than brief and localized hostilities at the close of which victor and vanquished, like prize fighters in the ring, would shake hands and, after a brief interim, resume normal relations.

To their cost, the Western democracies learned better after 1914. Even the best-informed Americans held, after Hitler's violation of the Versailles Treaty and the occupation of Austria, that totalitarian dictatorships would refrain from outright war because they realized that wars of aggression could not be financed and must ruin the economic structure of

Europe. Only two weeks before Hitler's blitzkrieg in Poland, a group of New York businessmen, supposedly conversant with international affairs, told me in my office in the State Department that Hitler would never go to war because Dr. Schacht knew that the German economy could not stand the strain; they were confident that the military preparations and the general mobilization already decreed by the Nazis were nothing more than a dangerous bluff.

It was this form of wishful thinking that caused so large a segment of American public opinion to prefer to accept the isolationist propaganda of the Lindberghs and of the America Firsters. If by some mischance war broke out, it could be no more than localized hostilities in Europe's millennial tradition. And if the still more improbable occurred, and widespread hostilities did, in fact, ensue, the Western Hemisphere would ever remain immune—provided the United States maintained a course of isolation, of blind neutrality, and supported that bland rejection of any sense of national responsibility which Calvin Coolidge had made so popular.

Yet once this kind of wishful thinking had been shown up by the blitzkrieg for what it was, and the simple lessons taught by World War I had again been learned, Fate once more placed in the hands of the American people the opportunity to make of this new war "a war to end all wars."

With the destruction of the Fascist and Nazi dictatorships and Japan's surrender, the United States enjoyed a position of actual supremacy unrivaled since the decline of the Roman Empire. It possessed a Navy and an Air Force equal in strength to the forces of all other powers. In sheer numbers the American armies were, of course, inferior to those of the Soviet Union, but in their mechanization and in their striking power they were far superior. In its material strength, in its natural resources, and in its industrial capacity, the United States would for many years be far more powerful than any combination of other states. It possessed the confidence of the liberated peoples. The free democracies were joined together in support of the principles which Franklin Roosevelt had so eloquently voiced. The faith of countless men and women was centered on Washington. They believed that under the banner of American leadership humanity could at last secure its salvation.

The following words, which one of Canada's most eminent sons, Leonard Brackington, not long ago addressed to the members of the American Bar Association, are in no sense an exaggerated interpretation of this world-wide aspiration:

"Today and for many days the leadership of the free world is yours, not for the asking, or the taking, but for the giving. It is the gift of men, not because of the things you have, but for the things you are. It is a gift which you cannot renounce for it is given not in patronage by princes, but in gratitude and hope by millions of simple, decent, home-loving, God-fearing, peace-seeking men and women who cherish freedom throughout the earth."

How have we Americans as a nation met our challenge?

How have we availed ourselves of this unparalleled opportunity to shape a free, a peaceful and a decent world-order that can realize the highest aspirations of all peoples?

How have we discharged the trust that Providence has conferred upon us?

Of the many lessons that the American people should have learned from the history of the past thirty-five years, the following are surely outstanding:

Unless collective security can be procured through a universal international organization like the League of Nations or the United Nations, there can be no assurance of world peace.

The appropriate moment for the establishment of such an organization, and for an agreement by the victorious powers upon the major territorial, economic and strategic adjustments to be comprised in the final peace settlements, is not the postwar period when selfish rivalries are once more uppermost, but on the contrary, the time before the victory is won, when the allied powers know that cooperation is essential to victory.

The last eighty years have, unfortunately, shown that without a conversion of the hearts and minds of the German people, the peace of Europe and the peace of the world depend upon the continued disarmament of Germany, and upon a form of German Government which can foster true democracy and effectively prevent the Pan-Germans and the German militarists from regimenting the German masses into war.

The final lesson is that any major power which demobilizes its armies immediately after a victory in which it has shared is thereby not only precluded from imposing peace terms upon such defeated powers as may prove recalcitrant, but is equally precluded from making its own views prevail with its allies in the implementation of the peace settlements.

It would almost seem as if the United States had deliberately spurned every one of these lessons that had been spelled out at so tragic a cost of human life and of human endeavor.

Franklin Roosevelt told me as early as the summer of 1943 that he felt it was imperative that an interallied agreement be concluded, without further delay, upon the international organization that must function in the postwar years. There are only a few who fully realize how much of his waning strength was expended during the last year of his life in making it possible for the Charter of the United Nations to be signed at San Francisco by June, 1945. It was not only that he was compelled to contend with a suspicious and ever more ambitious Kremlin. He was further compelled to override the obstacles interposed by a timorous Department of State and by spokesmen for the armed services, who insisted that all inter-allied discussions that might cause disagreements were *ipso facto* dangerous impediments to the successful prosecution of the war, and that no international organization could conceivably justify the military hazards to which its consideration during the war years must give rise.

Such steps as were considered at Teheran, Cairo and Yalta to further an understanding between the major powers on postwar political settlements were taken in the face of bitter opposition from the same sources—an opposition which secured no little support from many elements in the Congress.

The moment the victory had finally been won, there arose from the floor of the House of Representatives a raucous clamor for headlong demobilization. A majority of the members of the Congress responsible for this clamor could not have been ignorant of those pages in the history of the years after World War I, years during which the provisions of the peace treaties of 1919 were violated with increasing impunity in every part of the world. They were first rejected by Turkey and soon thereafter by victors and vanquished. They were infringed by the "Succession States." They were persistently flouted by Germany. They were ignored by Japan. The reasons were only too obvious. The primary reason was that, notwithstanding the American rejection of the Versailles Treaty and of all further American responsibility for policing the peace, the British politicians and the British press had compelled the British Government to undertake so rapid and so extensive a military demobilization as to destroy Britain's ability to back up her words with acts, should the need arise.

British demobilization during the years 1919 and 1920 and the increasing divergencies between British and French policies were directly responsible for this persistent violation of treaty engagements. Yet he who reads the pages of the Congressional Record for 1945 and 1946 will find that they are filled with demands for an immediate American demobilization; with appeals from American mothers for their boys to be brought home; and with pleas that the Congress oppose even a semblance of American military power. It is today a singular anomaly that many of the very Congressmen who were then loudest in their insistence that the United States immediately become a disarmed nation are today also the loudest in their demands that the United States "do something" to resist the onward march of Soviet Communism.

When we ask ourselves today for some indication to demonstrate that the perils to world peace and to our own security inherent in Germany have been realistically appraised by our own Government, and that the lessons of 1939 have been adequately grasped, we will be forced to admit that the dangers to be perceived in the reconstruction of a unified, powerful and highly industrialized Germany, and in the return of an unregenerated German people to the family of nations, are again being ignored. Moscow's policies have brought about a division of Germany of a kind that had never been anticipated,

293

but such a division has inevitably intensified, rather than diminished, the psychopathic nationalism to which the German is naturally prone.

Only the cynic or the congenital skeptic would attempt to deny that there has been no greater disaster in our times than the rapid disappearance of any general recognition of the existence of a natural moral law. Yet I often wonder if, here in the United States, our lack of a better sense of proportion and a more realistic estimate of our own enlightened self-interest may not be equally disastrous.

One of the strangest phenomena to be found in the course of our national history made itself apparent during the winter and spring of 1942.

The attack upon Pearl Harbor had crippled our Pacific fleet. Any interruption of transit through the Panama Canal would have made it highly improbable that the coasts of California, Oregon and Washington could have been safeguarded. The thousands of miles of the Pacific coastline of South America were largely defenseless, and had an invading force been able to establish itself in Ecuador, Peru or Chile, air bases for an attack upon the Canal and upon the territorial United States could rapidly have been developed.

Whether the British Isles could hold out against an intensified German air assault was still conjectural. The progress made by the German and Italian armies in North Africa gave little ground for hope that the Suez Canal might not soon fall into Axis hands. In that event, not only would the whole of the Mediterranean have been closed to the Western Powers, but the Germans and Italians would then have been able speedily to join hands with the Japanese in the Red Sea; the Near East would have passed under German domination; and Russia's oil resources could not have been protected from Nazi attack.

Yet during those months of unparalleled danger to the United States, when the security and perhaps the very survival of the American nation hung in the balance, it is no exaggeration to say that most Americans appeared to be far more preoccupied with the problems arising in their daily lives because of meat and gasoline rationing than with a war which was threatening utterly to destroy them and their country.

It must today be apparent to every thinking American that the United States is confronted with a world crisis in which its survival is even more gravely threatened. The policies of the Soviet Union make it clear that the objective of the Soviet dictatorship is world domination and that it will seek to attain that objective by all available means, whether by deliberate promotion of human suffering; by subversion and civil strife in other countries; by the kind of coup d'etat that was successfully consummated in Czechoslovakia; or even, should all other methods fail, by a war of aggression. The use of atomic weapons and the possibilities inherent in biological and chemical warfare make it only too clear what the nature of any new war must inevitably be. The issue before the American people —even more than in 1942—is the stark issue of self-preservation.

At this very moment—the spring of 1949—although American foreign policy has ceased to be determined by purely partisan considerations, through the efforts of a few statesmen like Senators Vandenberg and Connally—the great majority of Americans are once more preoccupied with a host of questions which, important as the issues that these involve may occasionally be, are in any event less important and less pressing than the international dangers that are darkening the skies over America.

Even those two measures in which the United States Government has demonstrated vision and initiative—the European Recovery Program and the North Atlantic Defense Pact—have been sullenly opposed by a considerable segment of public opinion, on the ground that in the first case the expenditure thereby involved should rather be made at home, or, in the latter case, because such a departure from traditional American policy must result in future catastrophe. Yet had the leaders of public opinion in every American community merely taken the trouble to familiarize themselves with developments in world affairs that threaten the individual existence of every one of them, the national demand would have been for greater safeguards rather than for the lesser safeguards that so many propose.

Even if it sounds trite, we must remember that the United States today stands at the crossroads. The future of the world depends on the direction that the American people now choose.

The following seem to me to be our principal choices:

The American people and the other democratic peoples can by default or by submission permit Soviet Communism to gain control of the world.

The United States and its allies can force a preventive war upon the Soviet Union without further delay.

The American people can continue with greater understanding, with greater vigor, and with greater skill consistently to follow the policy of containment upon which they have now tentatively embarked; and can continue also to persist, within the limits of the Charter of the United Nations, in opposing further Soviet expansion, no matter how long the struggle may be and no matter how great the sacrifices incurred thereby.

There is a fourth alternative. This springs from the possibility that the oligarchy dictating the destinies of the Russian people may be replaced by other leaders who realize that Russia's present policies are doomed to failure and that they imply disaster for the Russian people—and who, in consequence, will agree to cooperate in an international policy of live-and-let-live and thereby, at length, permit the creation of that kind of world order contemplated in the United Nations Charter.

I believe that three of these four alternatives may be rapidly dismissed.

No democracy like the United States has ever waged a "preventive" war of aggression, and it is equally certain that neither persuasion, temptation, nor fear could persuade the peoples of Western Europe or of Latin America to join with the United States in such an endeavor.

We would, I fear, be more than ingenuous were we to believe that there are at present any signs upon the horizon which would justify the hope that the existing Russian dictatorship might in any near future be replaced, or that its present policies of world revolution and of world domination would soon be supplanted by more cooperative long-range policies.

The Soviet tyranny has been well consolidated during the years of Stalin's control. Only a breach between the Politburo and the leaders of the Red Armies could presage the overturn of the existing oligarchy. The masses of the Russian people know only what their masters permit them to know. To them the terror exercised by a ruthless police power has become a mere matter of routine. There is little scope for general popular discontent, let alone any concerted popular uprising. We would be oversanguine, indeed, if we anticipated any solution of the fundamental cleavage between Soviet imperialism and Western democracy other than that achieved by an eventual recognition on the part of Russia's dictators that Communist revolutions in the Western democracies are not going to succeed, and that the power the Western democracies can wield is greater than that which Soviet Communism can manifest in aggression.

Nor does it seem conceivable that the Western democracies will ever submit to the domination of Soviet Communism. What, in all seriousness, is the Communist fanaticism that free men and women in the Western democracies are being urged to accept? It stems from the Marxist fallacy that uniform methods of production will fashion the "one world" which so many of us seek. Even in its original Marxist concept, such a "one world" would only be achieved after a prolonged and bitter class conflict. In its Soviet adaptation, it implies ruth· less disruption, aligning class against class, neighbor against neighbor, and parents against children, until the so-called triumph of the proletariat has dawned. The industrial age has tolerated social injustices that are both tragic and shocking. But it is too often forgotten that Karl Marx himself regarded this very proletariat, which he was urging to break the chains that bound it, as nothing more than a mass of "stupid" human beings to be regimented by a select few who, like Marx himself, were capable of using the proletariat as the means for constructing the grim world they envisaged.

So far it is only in that one country, whose people have been traditionally the most degraded and whose living standards have been the lowest in all Europe, that Communism has proved successful and has afforded an example of how in practice it may work. We know by what a fluke the Communist system was imposed by Lenin and Trotsky in 1917. We also know that the small number of conspirators the two communist leaders spearheaded at that time could never have succeeded in their revolutionary attempt without the connivance of the German General Staff. Yet its dubious origins should never blind us to the fact that, for all of its crimes and for all of the suffering and oppression for which the Soviet regime has been responsible during the past thirty-two years, Soviet Communism has succeeded in unifying an inchoate mass of two hundred millions of human beings of diverse origins and culture, and has effected an economic system which offers men and women material security so long as they are submissive slaves to a police power. Nor can we be blind to the fact that Soviet Communism is making a mighty and aggressive state out of the largest and potentially the richest nation of the world.

At the same time, there are other facts of fundamental significance. Until now Communism has only succeeded among the Slavic peoples. Where it has been imposed upon the Western and Southern Slavs, such as the Poles, the Czechs and the Serbs, all of whom have progressed far along the road of modern civilization and all of whom have made a not too inconsiderable contribution to modern culture, there is little evidence of any truly popular support, or even of popular toleration, for a system that is inherently alien to the fundamental principles of the subjugated peoples. It has only made headway among Eastern Slavs, who throughout the course of history had made little contribution to the development of self-government and but scant contribution to European culture. Nothing could be more significant than the inferiority

299

complex demonstrated in this regard by the present rulers of the Soviet Union who day in, day out, proclaim to the Russian people that every scientific invention in the modern world and every cultural advance have been first achieved by Russian scientists and Russian artists alone.

In its Soviet manifestation, Marxism has become a doctrine that is merely precisely what the Politburo says it is. During the brief span of its existence, Soviet Communism has reversed itself from day to day. Lenin's condemnation of imperialism and of aggressive warfare is now forgotten or tacitly ignored. In only one aspect has Soviet Communism remained unaltered—Lenin's dictum: "Everything is moral which is necessary for the annihilation of the old exploiting social order."

As we peruse the course of history of civilized man, we are forced to the conclusion that only those waves of civilization have prospered which have been founded upon the recognition of the existence of a natural moral law. The civilizations of the Christian era have prospered because the Christian faith has emphasized morality and the value and dignity of the individual. In all of its essential aspects Communism, whether that of the Marxist doctrinaire or that applied in Soviet practice, represents the great antithesis—amorality and the subordination of the individual to a man-made state.

No, there is no likelihood that peoples whose culture and whose political convictions stem from an insistence upon the freedom and dignity of man, to whom the natural moral law is a reality, and whose polities are derived from Magna Charta, the Declaration of Independence, and the principle of "liberty, equality and fraternity," will ever subject themselves to dogmas that would deprive them of everything which had made life worth the living.

The remaining alternative proffers, at best, a protracted and profoundly troubled period of transition before we can hope to begin to shape a world in which men and women can again have a sense of physical security and constant progress toward the goal of ordered freedom.

Tragically enough, such a protracted transition period—a long-drawn-out cold war which may at any moment flame into a hot war—implies an experience without precedent to the American people, an experience for which their history, their traditions, their manner of being, and their previous geographical security have not prepared them.

Should we and the peoples of the other Western democracies successfully emerge from the uncertain years that loom ahead, we will all be compelled to demonstrate a degree of realism and of patience, a capacity for sacrifice, and a willingness to subordinate the unessential to the essential—namely, survival—that we have never previously been called upon to exhibit.

And after we survive this transition period, what can we hope to make of that new world that will then come into being?

The best has often proved to be the enemy of the better. Now again, because the contest between Soviet Communism and Western democracy has made it impossible for the United Nations as yet to function effectively, an increasing number of able and sincere citizens of the Western democracies are urging that the proper solution is to be found in an immediate abandonment of the United Nations, and the attempt to replace it with some form of a world government. There are those who question the expediency of concentrating upon this objective at a moment when the Soviet Government has refused to agree to the modification of any of the powers granted it under the United Nations Charter, and has repeatedly spurned all thought of a world government. To them the reply is made that, if the Soviet dictatorship rejects world government, then the sooner we all know it, the better, so that the remaining nations of the world may join in an out-and-out alliance against the Soviet Union. This is tantamount to the assertion that, since war between the Soviet Union and the West has become inevitable, the sooner it is brought on, the better for the Western peoples.

The implications inherent in this contention seem to me to be so desperate and so utterly sterile, with its tacit admission that the most terrible of calamities that the human race has known can no longer be averted, that the pleas of the various advocates for immediate World Government could normally be expected to fall upon deaf ears. But when we remember that only a few short years ago a vast number of Americans sincerely believed that the outlawing of war by the Kellogg-Briand Pact forever removed the curse of war, it should not be astonishing that perhaps an equal number of Americans may now think that, because the constitution of a world government has been elaborated in a form which is theoretically unassailable, the mere formulation of so worthy and desirable an ideal means that it will soon become a reality. What we Americans too often forget is that there is a vast difference between the mere formulation of an ideal and the attainment of that ideal. It is in the practical implementation of ideals that humanity has hitherto so frequently failed.

There will be few to deny that the surest means of procuring an international order under which peace can be maintained, human liberties guaranteed, and human progress advanced is through the establishment of a world government under which national sovereignties can be merged and under which world destinies will be determined by the freely expressed voice of all peoples.

It is strange, however, that so many Americans believe that the precedent offered by our own Constitutional Convention is a precedent for the remedies required today. The original thirteen colonies were inhabited by those who were preponderantly of the same racial origin, who spoke the same language, who had enjoyed the same experience in self-government, and who possessed educational and living standards that were very similar. There were no insurmountable obstacles to the integration of their respective economies.

But are we justified in assuming that the peoples of the United States and of the other Western democracies are today willing to subordinate the determination of their own destinies to a form of world government in which the four hundred millions of inhabitants of India and Pakistan, the seven hundred millions of China and of Southeastern Asia, and the hundreds of millions of the Soviet Union and of the Near East would be equal members? Are these persons, who are wholly uneducated in the experience of Western self-government, whose living standards are infinitely lower, and whose traditions and cultures—admirable as these in many cases may be—are altogether distinct, who outnumber the peoples of the Western democracies by three to one—are these persons yet ready to wield the potent influence they would necessarily possess? Would such a course taken at this moment in world history not be bound inevitably to lower, rather than to raise, our hopes of fashioning order and liberty out of mounting chaos?

World government in its truest sense is surely the best hope that can be held out to suffering humanity, but if we wish ever to obtain a world order under which men can live in peace and happiness, surely the right road for us to follow is the road upon which, however hesitatingly, we have already placed our feet. To what human experience can we point which would justify an attempt to take a short cut? Can we expect that a true world government will ever be brought into being save after the expenditure of an infinitely greater measure of "blood and sweat and tears" than that promised the British people in 1940?

The United Nations, like the League of Nations, is an association of sovereign states. Our national objective and the objective of all of the Western democracies should be to seize each opportunity afforded by time and circumstance gradually to improve and to strengthen that association, so that with the passage of the years the impediments to international collaboration now interposed by the exaggeration of national sovereignties may be eliminated. In the phrase of St. Augustine, the difference between a mob and a people lies in the fact that a people is "an association of rational men, united in the pursuit of common interests." The United Nations provides the means by which the existing mob of nations can be transformed into "an association of rational peoples united in the pursuit of common interests." In this endeavor, first things must come first. And so far as the United States is concerned, what should come first is an unremitting effort on the part of the American people so to exercise the influence and the power presently granted them that every function of the United Nations may be strengthened to the utmost possible extent.

The failure of the Security Council to operate effectively because of the Soviet veto, the inability of the major powers to agree upon an international control of atomic force because of Soviet opposition, and the stubborn refusal of the Soviet Union to permit the establishment of the international police force for which the Charter provides, constitute no justification for any refusal on the part of the Western democracies to try to increase the authority of the United Nations and to enhance the scope and efficiency of its functional activities. Can there, for example, in a world in which the population is rapidly outstripping available food supplies, be any greater deterrent to the international struggles that make for wars than a successful form of international collaboration in the conservation, production and distribution of the world's food resources, the task for which the Food and Agricultural Organization was created?

We Americans are wont to extol our national prosperity. It is high time that we grasped the fact that, even without unparalleled natural resources, that prosperity could never have been achieved except for the size of our internal domestic market. What right have we to assume that Europe could not achieve the same measure of prosperity if the thirty-odd tariff walls with which she is afflicted were obliterated? Here again, by strengthening, rather than undermining, the International Trade Organization established under the United Nations, the United States not only could help to remove some of the basic causes which engender war, but also help to assist the European peoples themselves in preparing the way for that European Federation upon which their hopes for the future

305

so greatly depend. Yet here again monopolies and vested interests in the United States are doing their utmost to emasculate the International Trade Organization and are bitterly opposing the extension of the American Trade Agreements Act on the ground that "a revival of European industry will cut into existing American markets."

Winston Churchill is, I think, everlastingly right in his repeated insistence that under existing world conditions, the best way to insure the ultimate success of the United Nations is to develop real regional organizations such as that which has been established in the Western Hemisphere. It is through such regional organizations that the peoples of the world can gain experience and knowledge of the most practicable methods by which the merging of sovereignties and the resultant compromise of selfish and purely local interests may inure to the general interest, and to the highest welfare of all peoples.

There could be no greater delusion than that held by those Americans who think that the world of the future will be a world created in the image of what our reactionaries so mistakenly call the "free enterprise system." They shake with terror at the very sound of the term "managed economy." If these Americans are going to determine our national policies, the Marxist prophecy that Western capitalism is now doomed to destruction may well be realized. The majority of mankind will not again accept a system which permits the regime of "boom and bust" or the gross social and economic inequalities which have disgraced the Western democracies and which have proved to be Soviet Communism's greatest propaganda weapon in appealing for the support of Western peoples.

Should Western democracy permit social injustices to persist in its own midst, it can never be that positive, vital force which it must become if it is to persuade hungry or under-privileged men and women of its advantages over Soviet Communism. With all of the confusion resulting from an initial period of trial and error, with all of the mistakes in kind and in degree for which they have been responsible, the postwar governments of Western Europe, such as the present Government of the United Kingdom, are seeking to fashion a new political and economic order under which social inequalities cannot again exist, but under which human liberties will continue to be fully guaranteed.

Science has already developed the means through which human toil can be reduced, human suffering alleviated, and human life extended. Is it conceivable that the peoples of the world will ever return in any guise to a political, economic and social system under which a few are granted unlimited privileges and the many are deprived of even the rudimentary essentials that are needed for security and happiness? Perhaps it would be well for all of us today to remember these prophetic words that Woodrow Wilson wrote a few months before his death:

"Our civilization cannot survive materially unless it be redeemed spiritually. It can be saved only by becoming permeated with the spirit of Christ and being made free and happy by the practices which spring out of that spirit. Only thus can discontent be driven out and all the shadows lifted from the road ahead."

In a world in which force, greed, fanaticism and injustice are still predominant, armed strength remains essential to the survival of even the most peace-loving of peoples. The advance toward collective security that is represented by such international agreements for self-defense as the Inter-American

Defense Treaty and the North Atlantic Defense Pact is of epochal significance. Such treaties afford the one means now available by which aggression can be contained. But if the American people are in the long run to succeed in persuading the minds and hearts of other peoples of the benefits of democracy, that warning of Woodrow Wilson must become a determining factor in the formulation of their own national policy.

In the poem from which this book derives its title, Walt Whitman long since foresaw the question that we Americans strive to answer:

"Years prophetical! The space ahead as I walk, as I vainly try to pierce it, is full of phantoms,
Unborn deeds, things soon to be, project their shapes around me. . . .
The perform'd America and Europe grow dim, retiring in shadow behind me,
The unperform'd more gigantic than ever, advance, advance upon me."

The declaration of faith made by the first President of the United States as he took office in 1789 is even more profoundly true today than it was a century and a half ago:

"The preservation of the sacred fire of liberty and the destiny of the republican model of government are justly considered as *deeply*, as *finally*, staked on the experiment entrusted to the hands of the American people."

Is not the answer for which we now so anxiously seek to be found in those very words?

The last quarter century has been a period of mass action in which the individual has often felt lost. In some cases he has surrendered himself to destructive ideologies. American youth in the early 1930s felt spiritually paralyzed by the impact of confusing events. Often there came an instinctive withdrawal from the surrounding life.

This life was crowded with excitement, but the excitement seemed unreal to them.

One young American first came to self-discovery in reading a book on Gandhi written by Romain Rolland. As he read he perceived that the individual could assert himself against seemingly overwhelming forces.

Re-reading, re-thinking, he found that every aspect of his world held a personal importance for him: America struggling out of the Depression was important; the War which soon engulfed the world had a clearer meaning; the San Francisco conference which brought the United Nations to birth had an even greater significance.

Two months after San Francisco came Hiroshima. A new and appalling sense of urgency had arisen, calling for swift action within and without the United States.

Only the individual joined in close concert for peace with other individuals of similar mind throughout the world, can take the bold action required. We must not only try to insure peace but to save mankind from self-destruction.

12

Norman Cousins

AN ADVENTURE IN IDEALS

To the extent that thought can fashion its own mirror, this is the story of a mind peering and prying into itself in an effort to observe the impact upon it of the world of ideas and action of the past twenty-five years. In short, these notes are largely autobiographical.

My reason for using the first person singular is that I am by age a direct product of the years under review in this book. No man can, or perhaps should, attempt to climb far enough outside his own skin and psyche to know whether he is typical of his times. And yet, typical or otherwise, two-thirds of my chronological existence coincides squarely with the period that historians may refer to as that of the Protest Generation that became the Violent Generation before it was through.

From the moment we were born, history laid siege to our times and our affairs. Our earliest memories were of World War I, of brothers or fathers or uncles who said goodbye and who never came back, of lowered voices in the other rooms reading and re-reading letters until they were leveled into rote. When we were old enough to think creatively about politics and philosophy, the depression laid strong hands on our ideas, and the old and accepted systems of thought and politics seemed feeble and irrelevant, fit for museums or textbooks but not for the throbbing issues of the day. By the time we got out of school, the word career had become a painful anachronism, and we grimly counted the physical and moral casualties among our friends. We were being propelled into a world which was as reluctant and unprepared to receive us as we were to become a part of it. We groped for economic footing and for intellectual anchorage. When the New Deal came along, the more conservative among us took hope and root in it, for which we were damned as timid experimentalists by our more politically adventurous contemporaries, and as irresponsible revolutionaries by our elders.

The books we read and the plays we saw and the things we talked about added up to a sort of philosophy of orphanism; to paraphrase Mr. Housman and Mr. Farrell, we were in a world we never made and there was nothing to indicate that it would ever be any different. We didn't belong, nor was there anything we really felt we wanted to belong to. When we surveyed the future, it was like looking out over a frozen tundra; if the thaw ever came, we were certain it would be in some far-off age. To be sure, there was excitement over the Oxford pledge and over Marxism and over the economic interpretation of history and over the debunking of the hero. But all these were flurries and not the real thing. For the fact was that we were going through the motions of being interested and being part of something when actually we ourselves lacked any real adhering surface to which ideas might stick: Archibald MacLeish some years later summed it up in the word, "Irresponsibles." It was the irresponsibility of default rather than of design. How did you go about being responsible when you weren't quite sure what there was to be responsible about?

The paradox, of course, was that we were being intellectually static in a politically dynamic world. This is not to say that we were unaware of, or uninterested in, the bulging and threatening shape of things to come. But these were things without impact; we could see them and take note of them, but they were outside us. It was like blinking at the size and speed of an oncoming locomotive while standing on the track.

Such was the curious sense of unreality and wasted motion, the sense of separation from our times, that was the dominant mood in our college years and through most of the 'thirties.

It didn't last—it couldn't. But the circumstances of the awakening weren't the same in every case. Some of us emerged out of it gradually, moved along by the momentum of events; others had to be blasted out of it by the war; still others by the continuing crisis following the war. And some of us, apparently, haven't come out of it yet.

In my own case, at least, the winds that blew from the East helped to ventilate my thinking and to clear off the foggy negativism that was the fashion of the time. I remember reading in 1937 about Gandhi for the first time in a form more substantial than scattered newspaper accounts. It was a book by Romain Rolland. It combined a short, highlight biography of Gandhi with an account of his spiritual and political development. The final chapters contrasted the ideas of Gandhi with those of Tagore, dramatizing the importance of this dualism in awakening India. In some respects it was like the Hamilton-Jefferson controversy, with important elements of the philosophy of each coming together to create a vital blend. Gandhi approached mankind through India; Tagore approached India through mankind.

What impressed me most about Gandhi was not only his philosophy, impressive though it was under the special conditions in India, or the effectiveness of non-violence, for the technique was frequently at odds with the philosophy behind it. What impressed me most was the dramatic proof that the individual need not be helpless against massed power—that he need not be overwhelmed by any supposed inexorabilism or fatalism, that there was scope for free will and conviction in the shaping of society, that history could be fluid, not fixed, if men were willing to transcend their egos in order to merge themselves with the larger body of mankind.

It is difficult to describe adequately my sense of wonder at all this, for an idea that until then seemed beyond debate or even speculation was the utter domination of individual man by his times. Since you never had questioned it, you never had to think about it. History was the ocean—alternately calm and turbulent—and the individual was the rudderless vessel. As for the great leaders and commanding figures of history, you had been in the habit of seeing them as products rather than as architects of their times. But Gandhi didn't fit into the conventional role of the historical leader. He was in no position of power, nor did he seek power. He exercised leadership without being an official leader. He was a person, Anyman, demonstrating the practical value of ethics as applied to political problems.

In reading Rolland, it was clear that Gandhi's teaching and his non-cooperation movement were enriched and invigorated as the result of Tagore's ceaseless prodding in behalf of universalism. Tagore recognized the danger to the world of yet another purely nationalist movement. He could see that the Gandhi movement might get beyond Gandhi; that the heat generated by noncooperation could become the fever of a national authoritarianism. India's problem, as Tagore saw it, was inseparable from the world problem. "No nation can find its own salvation by breaking away from others. The awakening of India is bound up in the awakening of the world." I can recall now the thrill I felt in reading Tagore's poetic definition of universalism:

Where the mind is without fear and the head is held high;
Where knowledge is free;
Where the world has not been broken up into fragments by narrow
    domestic walls;
Where words come out from the depth of truth;
Where tireless striving stretches its arms toward perfection;
Where the clear stream of reason has not lost its way into the dreary
    desert sand of dead habit;
Where the mind is led forward by thee into ever-widening thought
    and action—
Into that heaven of freedom, my Father, let my country awake.

Little wonder that I felt foolish for having been mired so long in the futility that was the fashion of my generation. Compared to India's, our problems were as wisps of smoke alongside a thunderhead. And yet, India was moving towards freedom precisely because a philosophy compounded of affirmation, action, compassion, and universalism was giving inspiration and direction to countless millions who were learning to think about the idea of freedom for the first time.

It was natural that the momentum generated by Gandhi and Tagore should carry me back to a re-appraisal of the American philosophers, and even more natural perhaps that I should begin with Emerson, with whom the Indian thinkers seemed to have such a rich affinity. What formerly had seemed to me in Emerson to be a collection of bland philosophical truisms somewhat in the lavender tradition now came alive with force and distinction. As in Gandhi and Tagore, there was the rigorous assertion of individual integrity and purpose as a foundation for service to the general welfare. There was the Gandhi-ian disdain in Emerson for conformity and convention: "Every true man is a cause, a country, and an age; requires infinite spaces and numbers and time fully to accomplish his design; and posterity seems to follow his steps as a train of clients." Then, in a one-line distillation of the Gandhi philosophy, Emerson wrote: "Nothing can bring you peace but the triumph of principles." Dozens of others had said it before Emerson; he brought it into rich focus.

It was Emerson's discussion of political philosophy that drove the final nail into the coffin for my disillusion; he defined both the power and responsibility of the individual in a complex society. He saw a wide and fertile field for individual action in advancing the general welfare. He didn't believe that man, collectively or individually, need feel he was incarcerated by history. The individual did belong. No state, no custom, no convention, could alter or destroy that fact. Then, almost as though he were anticipating one of the great debates of the twentieth century—the debate over inevitability and the "wave of the future"—Emerson wrote that we were not at the "mercy of any waves of chance. . . . In dealing with the state, we ought to remember that its institutions are not aboriginal, that they are not superior to the citizen, that one of them was once the act of a single man, that every law and usage

316

was a man's expedient to meet a particular case, that they are all limitable, all alterable."

Apart from the impact of such ideas after almost a decade of saturating cynicism, the re-reading of Emerson had an important by-effect; it convinced me that what I had read up until then had largely been mis-read or under-read. Why, I asked myself, should there have been such a gap between the Emerson I read at eighteen and the Emerson I read at twenty-four? The answer was simple but not pleasant: I had never really learned how to read. What had happened was that the books I had read had become ends in themselves, instead of means to ends beyond the books. I had read the things young people were supposed to have read by the time they got out of school. It was survey-course stuff—titles to check off on a long list that by actual measurements took up five feet or so on a bookshelf. To be sure, as I thought back about these books, each title called forth certain standardized associations, and I knew that with a little brushing up I could probably get by on an examination. And yet, how much of it had I really read? How much of it bristled with meaning? How much of it had given me vital insight into the author's purpose—insight essential to truly creative reading?

This led to an even more disturbing, although related, series of questions. If my reading had wound up in literary bankruptcy, what about my education in general? What, after all, was education without the understanding of books? How much of my formal education truly met my essential needs? Hadn't I been as uncreative in absorbing and making use of knowledge as I had in my general reading?

Before you could attempt to ponder the answers to these questions, or even be sure you had the right questions, you must first define what it was you had expected education to do. As you thought about it, you realized that no single definition could possibly have enough elasticity to be all-inclusive. Basically, you knew that you could expect education to narrow the gap between the individual and society, bringing individual capacity as close as possible to collective needs. You could expect it to produce the rounded man. You could expect it to enlarge the ability to think and the capacity for thought. You could expect it to be helpful in creating constructive attitudes —both on an individual and on a group level. You could expect it to impart basic and essential general knowledge for balanced living, and basic and essential specialized knowledge for specific careers. You could expect it to develop ethical values. You could expect it to furnish the individual with the necessary intellectual, moral and technical clothing for a presentable appearance in the world community.

But when I surveyed myself, I could see that the clothing didn't fit; indeed, that it was thin and embarrassingly scanty. I was over-exposed and under-developed. How much did I know about the most important science of all—the science of interrelationships—that critical area beyond compartmentalization where knowledge must be integrated in order to have proper meaning? Nothing. Did I have sufficient knowledge and understanding for vital participation in the world community? Hardly. Did I have any vital understanding of or feeling for cultures other than my own? Not enough to show. Was I able to see events against the broad historical flow? Only vaguely.

My feeling of inadequacy was not softened by the knowledge that I was not unique, nor by the fact that I was but a single unit among countless thousands turned out by the obso-

lescent assembly-belt of "modern" education. "Higher education" had indeed become a misnomer in the light of the new
needs. What seemed adequate at the turn of the century for
the purposes of top-level education now fulfilled only an inter-
mediate function at best. The danger described so well by
Whitehead—that events might outrun man and leave him a
panting and helpless anachronism—was rapidly becoming
more than a figure of speech. We were surrounding and con-
founding ourselves with gaps—gaps between cosmic gadgets
and human wisdom, between intellect and conscience, between
history and historical interpretation. The clash between knowledge and the uses of knowledge predicted more than a century
ago by Buckle had reached at least the skirmish stage.

On the level of educational techniques, as apart from purposes, what had been missing, at least in my case, now seemed
clear: reasons. I had been educated in everything except the
meaning and purpose of education itself. It was like a wheel
with beautiful spokes but no rim. If there was real direction
or destination, it was never convincingly explained. If there
was real integration to all the educational compartments in
which the various studies were located and isolated, I was
never apprised of it.

I had no reason to suppose that I could ever catch up with,
or even remotely approach, any of the definitions I tried to
rough out as to what constituted an educated person in our
time. But at least I had found the motive power for re-
examining and re-appraising my knowledge of history and
philosophy. Every book I re-read was as though I had never
come across it before. Every idea I explored had its own chain
reaction. What I was doing, of course, was attempting to seek
the vital connections between ideas instead of viewing ideas

319

as sovereign entities, which was the direction my formal reading had taken. You might call it the difference between the vertical and the lateral approach to history. The vertical, or conventional, approach, was to begin at a designated place and time in history, and then climb the chronological ladder until you reached the present. For example, if you were studying American history, you would start either with Columbus or with the Pilgrims or with the background of the Revolution, and then climb up in a straight line, event by event, until you arrived at, let us say, the New Deal. The same was true of the approach to French history or English history or European history in general. What ever the philosophy behind it, the effect of this method was to emphasize the nationalistic interpretation of history at the expense of a rounded view of the general development of man—politically, socially, culturally.

The lateral method however, could break down this compartmentalization and enable you to observe the interaction of events and ideas. You would use time as your principal frame of reference, selecting a certain period and then searching in many lands for common elements of common problems, and, most importantly, the inter-connections that affected mankind as a whole. If, for example, you took periods surrounding such key years as 400 B.C. or A.D. 350 or 1492 or 1789 or 1873 or 1914 or 1945, and used those years as arenas for the study of *world* history, with your emphasis on peoples rather than on nations, you could discover surprising mutualities—mutualities of experience, of philosophies and attitudes, of aspirations. You would discover, too, cross-fertilization of ideas among peoples that were otherwise obscured in the national or vertical study and interpretation of history.

320

In terms of a working philosophy, out of this expedition in ideas and morals came the confirmation and enlargement of the doctrine not only of natural liberty but of natural scope in creating liberty. I had come a long way from the cynicism and disillusion which had soured so much of my earlier thinking. And little by little, I could see the evidence growing all around me that many others of my generation were re-examining their beliefs against the background of an accelerating history. Nazism and nihilism were joined and mobilized and people were being killed; it dawned on many of us that notions of futility were an intellectual luxury, that the threat was alive and real, and that decisions might have to be made that we had thought need never be made again.

It was at this point that the second step or challenge in the general design of my re-education asserted itself. Admitting that there was no retreat for the individual and that he could find no refuge in fatalism or determinism, what kind of world was he trying to build—assuming the world could be saved for the rebuilding? T. S. Eliot said it for many of us when he wrote about Munich:

". . . The feeling which was new and unexpected was a feeling of humiliation, which seemed to demand an act of personal contrition, of humility, repentance and amendment; what had happened was something in which one was deeply implicated and responsible. . . . Was our society, which had always been so assured of its superiority and rectitude, so confident of its unexamined premises, assembled round anything more permanent than a congerie of banks, insurance companies and industries, and had it any beliefs more essential than a belief in compound interest and the maintenance of dividends? . . ." [1]

[1] From *The Idea of a Christian Society*, copyright, 1940, by T. S. Eliot. Reprinted by permission of Harcourt, Brace and Company, Inc.

321

Once again, our society was in the process of calling upon the individual to offer himself in sacrifice in order to perpetuate the group; but the individual didn't always define the bond that connected him to the group in the same terms that society did. If the individual, like Eliot, believed that society, no less than the individual, was obligated to live the life of virtue, could he justly say that virtue was at stake? The evil and the power of Nazism were quite clear; and there could be no doubt that the threat would have to be turned back. But was it enough just to fight *against* something? Why couldn't we fight *for* something?

Just as earlier you re-examined your own place in society, and the potentiality of the individual for effective ethical action, so now you re-examined your ideas on the nature of society, on the potentialities within the group for ethical ideas and action, and, in general, on government as an organism with a metabolism rate of its own, a conscience of its own, and a life cycle of its own. Unlike the previous search, which began with Gandhi and went weaving in and out, with no fixed pattern and stretching over the entire history of ideas, this search came to rest in two areas: classical Greece and late eighteenth-century America.

Greece offered the example of a civilization that, on the basis of the evidence, seemed to you to have passed into decay not because it had become moribund, but primarily because of sheer human error. In the case of America, you had a nation designed on a drawing board, the architects of which understood error in government as did no other group assembled before or since. With Greece, you had a golden age that was abruptly terminated precisely because the city-states themselves, in their dealings with one another, lacked a mechanism for dealing with error and so became its victims. With America, the concept of the inevitability of error, and the specific means provided to deal with it, represented one of the chief building blocks of the new government.

In each case, what I was interested in primarily was the anatomy of error. I use the word "error" not only in the familiar sense of blunder or mistake, but in the broader sense of avoidable failure. For history can be viewed as an accumulation of error; the nature of the error and the thought proceeding out of error often determine the rate of progress and the type of progress. Indeed, the story of men and nations is largely the story of their attitude towards error. The less democratic a society, the smaller the margin for error of its subjects and the greater the margin of its rulers. The more arbitrary the definition of error, the less important the machinery of justice. The more protection error receives in high places, the less scope for public opinion and an ungoverned press.

Apart from the errors committed by the highly privileged citizens of Greece under the double standard of virtue and morality that existed between themselves and their slaves, there was the endless series of errors in the dealings among the Greek city-states themselves. The great similarities among the peoples were no bar to war; indeed, it almost seemed as though their mutualities lubricated their antagonisms. What was missing was the means of bringing order into their collective life—the life of the city-states in their relations with each other. They made the mistake of attempting to seek national security through military coalitions or balance-of-power arrangements, or through conspiracy with sympathetic elements in the other countries. They made the error of not facing up

323

to the need of federation among themselves and the need for a rule of law which federation alone might have provided. Their leaders were unwilling to effect a larger junction except on their own terms, which is to say, domination of all others. Besides, as Madison later observed, the last place in the world to look for the basic motive power of federation is to official-dom, for it is unreasonable to expect rulers voluntarily to turn in their seals of office and accept a lesser role; the psychology of power and leadership has little margin for subordination. The motive power for larger law would have to be supplied by the people themselves. But this, too, was lacking.

Generally speaking, the frictions between the Athenian coalition in the north of Greece and the Spartan coalition in the South fell into two broad categories. In the first category, there were the ideological differences growing out of the contrast between an outgoing, culturally vibrant, liberal-aristocratic Athens, and an ingrown, inbred, militaristic, oligarchic Sparta. Along with this was the inevitable commercial rivalry between the two leading powers in Greece—one a maritime empire, the other a land power.

In the second and more important category were the frictions that grew out of the competition for physical security. For the ideological and economic differences, great as they were, did not figure as prominently in the causes of war as the fact that neither state had any real basis for confidence in the short-range or long-range intentions of the other. Each state felt insecure in the absence of any higher agency with power to protect it against attack. Thus, each prepared against the other—and the preparation took the form not only of military measures, but of jockeying for position and power in building up influence in other states that were needed as possible allies.

It was the old story—old even 2400 years ago—of the lack of specific machinery of law and law-enforcement to eliminate at least that aspect of the danger that grew out of the need to be secure. And law machinery in this case meant federation. Federation might not have resolved all the ideological and economic differences, but at least it might have made unnecessary and impossible the measures leading to war that each state took as the only means of protecting itself.

This failure made a profound impression on the American federalists. The function of the Constitution makers, as Hamilton and Madison saw it, was to build "monuments" to experience. Again, the key to good government was in the approach to error. There were two broad groups of error. The first grew out of the neglect or violation of principles. The second type was on the operational or functional level and proceeded out of the fallibility of man. As they saw it, then, theirs was a dual responsibility. They had to establish a framework of principle within which states could live side by side on a fairly rational basis. Next, they had to provide the people with the means of coping with error—inevitable error—by their elected and appointed officials.

On the level of principle, this meant that states within a geographic unit must have binding obligations among themselves for the greater safety of all. But these obligations were to be limited only to those matters affecting the common security and welfare. In all matters pertaining to the relationships of the states to each other, particularly when and where there were disputes, the central government was to have jurisdiction.

On the operational level, error was to be taken for granted. For no man was deemed wise enough to be free of error. The important thing was to limit the effect of those errors by depriving their makers of the natural secrecy in which errors breed and multiply. The dictator enjoys the privilege of enshrouding his errors; a democracy's chance for progress exists in direct proportion to its ability to keep errors out in the open. If one branch of the government makes the error of attempting to arrogate too much power to itself, another branch of the government should be able to correct it or at least to call public attention to it. The head of the government, for example, must remain within reach of free and open criticism. If the Department of the Army acts too arbitrarily, even though the action may seem natural according to military lights, it must subject itself to public scrutiny and judgment. The general term for all this was checks and balances; more accurately, perhaps, it is the error theory of government. In short, there must not only be an accounting *of* error, but an accounting *for* error.

In terms of my "re-education," the history of early Greece and the Constitutional period of American history had a profound effect on my thinking. It gave a deeper sense of purpose and usefulness to my fast-developing interest in and concern with the philosophy of universalism, for it added political form to ideological substance, and served to translate important aspects of universalism into their direct political expression. Another important result of the Greek-American juxtaposition was that it deepened and reinforced my conviction against historical determinism. Greek civilization died not because of any natural laws or life cycles affecting nations, but because the Greek peoples were unable to deal with the final error of war. It was inevitable that they would fight the one war from which they could not recover. Nor did historical determinism operate in the founding of the United States. Here was a magnificent example of the scope and power of free will and decision in the affairs of man. Here was the bold validation of the long-challenged theory of human progress. And here, finally, was the specific application of historical experience and principle to the deliberate creation of a structure of government possessing the form of law and the substance of justice.

It was natural that I should attempt to apply these lessons of federalism to my own time. In observing the decline and fall of the League of Nations, it seemed clear that the failure to invest it with a sovereignty of its own and with effective powers had doomed it from the start, in precisely the way that the Articles of Confederation were doomed and the Amphitryonic League in early Greece was doomed. This was not to say that there was any strict historical analogy between the League and the American states under the Articles. The process of federation would have been immeasurably more difficult for all the states of the world in 1938 than it was for the states of the east coast of America in 1787. But the basic principle was precisely the same; states within a geographic unit must unite or fight. Such differences and difficulties as existed in the way of federation actually defined the challenge. For these were the differences that spelled out the threat of conflict and made it critically essential to find some way to keep them from breaking out in open war.

But when you thought about federalism in 1938, you did so against the background of impending war. There was no doubt that the nations were now part of a single geographic

327

unit. The only real doubts concerned the auspices under which the attempt to coordinate the unit would be made—whether it would be done under democratic or totalitarian leadership. In short, whose world government would it be? Would it be brought about through organization or subjugation?

By the summer of 1939, these questions had a razor edge, for Germany seemed well on the way to hammering out a world unity according to her own design. Even without open warfare, Germany was bringing the entire continent of Europe under her dominion; indeed, the attempt was being made to have the entire world revolve on the Rome-Berlin-Tokyo axis. The effect of all this was to give a cold chill to world government enthusiasts, who now knew the absurdity and the danger of talking about world government without also defining exactly what such a world government was to be, and how it was to operate, if it was to deserve the support of the world's peoples who would have to establish it. In any event, we had a long way to go before we would be prepared to advance ideas for a world organization with enforceable powers. At the moment, the critical problem was staying alive.

When the war did break out, we were even less prepared to face it intellectually and politically than we were physically. There was a good deal we had to unlearn; we had been brought up on the vested-interest theory of war. Wars happened, we had been taught—in and out of school—because armament manufacturers had to keep their factories going. The common people were the innocent dupes, according to this theory; therefore, the way to deal with war was to spurn the call. The only trouble with the theory, of course, is that it didn't tell you what to do if the common peoples of the enemy, far from spurning the call, actually seemed to relish the kill and the conquest.

The curious air of unreality that existed during the first winter of war, when very little happened, and when there was talk of "certain accommodations" being made between the opposing governments at the expense of the peoples, did little to bring about the necessary intellectual reconditioning for what was in truth a fight for sheer survival. Indeed, it was not until Dunkirk that things began to snap into place. The change was as quick as it was deep. In just a few weeks or so, we had learned more about what we wanted to do, and where we were going, and what there was worth saving, than we had once thought it was within our ken to learn in a lifetime. We had come of age almost overnight; we weren't afraid to think or talk about values. We were facing T. S. Eliot's questions, many of us, and the answer seemed clear; if there were any values we really believed in, and if those values were lacking in our society, then we had to keep alive the *chance* to make those values real. For society was nothing outside us, like a distant mountain, but an organism of which we were a part; it was for us to say what we wanted that society to be, and it was for us to make sure that we could keep the right to change it in our own hands.

There was something vibrant and clean about the sense of conviction and affirmation that was rising within us as the challenge crystallized. It was something you didn't want to forget and were afraid to forget. You were afraid to lose what I believe William James once called "crisis clarity." You wondered whether, in the happy event that the challenge was successfully met and the threat destroyed, you could avoid the same cynicism that followed the previous war.

This didn't mean we were losing our critical faculties. In fact, we asked a great many questions—questions about democracy's internal record in America, about mistakes and weaknesses which have set up important debits on the balance sheet of the nation.

We knew that those debits told a story of abuse—abuse of the land, of democratic institutions, even of the people themselves. Only the seemingly inexhaustible richness of the ground we stood on prevented America from becoming a wasteland; few places in history had seen so much neglect, so much reckless exploitation. As for free institutions, time and again they were allowed to fall into jeopardy as the forms of democracy degenerated into corrupt politics—almost automatic by-products of an indifferent people. Indifference or unconcern or apathy—whatever you may call it—not only toward local and national politics, but also toward the long-range national welfare—these were the dead weights for long periods of time on the hopes for a vital, dynamic democracy.

No, we weren't blind to the weak points in our democratic make-up, nor were we fooled into thinking that we were defending a perfect democracy. What, then, were we fighting for?

The answer, of course, is that we were fighting not because of democracy's weaknesses, but because of its strengths, because of what it had offered in the past, and because of our hopes for what it might offer in the future. We were fighting because all history had yielded no better way for a people to make evolution and progress a reality, because the alternatives had proved themselves false.

We were fighting because democracy was a chance. And soft and sentimental as it may sound to a cynic, we were fighting because we wanted the chance to eliminate past weaknesses. We were fighting not for the reward of a perfect democracy but to make the most of that chance.

We were fighting because we wanted to keep decisions in our own hands. We were fighting for the sacred privilege of making mistakes and for the even greater privilege of attempting to set them right. We were fighting not only for the right to think, but for time to think.

We were fighting because of two words, "interrelationship" and "interdependency"—perhaps the two most important words of the twentieth century. For interrelationship and interdependence wound through every aspect of the lives of nations and those of their peoples. Whether in respect to government, culture, economics, or even daily living, the close connections and interconnections, new and old, seen and unseen, linked the entire human race in a great planetary unit.

But shining above all these considerations—economic, political, cultural, and everything else—like a beacon so bright, so powerful that it dominated every issue, every question, was one rock-bottom fact:

We were fighting because we had no choice in the matter. We were fighting because an ugly backwash of the past that some preferred to see as the wave of the future had tried to engulf us. It had carried with it forces that pressed a decision upon us that many of us had believed only we ourselves could make.

So much for the second challenge—the challenge to define values worth preserving and enlarging, as well as to define the conditions which might make those values possible.

The third challenge or phase of my re-education had the

sudden impact of an explosion. When the news broke about Hiroshima, I couldn't have been hit harder than if a report had just been flashed that the planet Jupiter had broken free of her orbit and that an interstellar collision involving the earth was possible and likely. For it seemed to me that man overnight had come face to face with the problems of human destiny, that he had conquered nature only to discover that forces inside him were more powerful and terrifying than any that existed outside himself. He had beaten back every natural challenge thrown his way: heat, cold, water, ice, sun, sand, and wind; but he had yet to comprehend that far more menacing was the environment he had created for himself. All at once, the planet became too small for his competitive urge and his quarrelsomeness. A sword was fixed with the point over his heart, and he was stumbling around in a darkened arena full of pits, holes, and knee-high obstacles.

All my life I had been a gradualist; in my thoughts on universalism and world government, I had been concerned primarily with the requirements of a world community organized under law and justice, and it had seemed self-evident that it might take several generations at least before such a community could be brought into being. But with Hiroshima, it became clear that a long-range ideal had become an immediate necessity, and that no amount of talk about the difficulties in the way of this universalism could dispose of the danger of trying to survive without it. The question was not whether we needed it, but only how we would have to go about getting it within the required time.

That night—the night after the day that man revealed the great design of his own destruction—I tried to sort my fears and hopes in an editorial for the *Saturday Review*. The gist of that editorial was that "modern" man had become obsolete, a self-made anachronism becoming more incongruous by the minute. He had exalted change in everything but himself. He had leaped centuries ahead in inventing a new world to live in, but he knew little about his own part in that world. Given time, he might be expected to bridge those gaps normally; but by his own hand, he had destroyed even time. Communication, transportation, and war no longer waited on time. Whatever bridges had to be built and crossed would have to be built and crossed immediately.

The purpose of that editorial, I am afraid, was somewhat misunderstood. It was said that I had written a farewell to man, that I had defined a predicament from which there was neither retreat nor escape. Such was not my intention, and I have only myself to blame for not having made my purpose clear. I believed there were rational grounds for hope— tremendous hope—and I said so, but I made the mistake of bearing down so heavily on the danger that by the time I tried to discuss the possibilities of meeting the new danger, the dominant mood of the editorial had been established in the minds of many readers.

I am no pessimist. I doubt that any man knows enough to be a pessimist. Neither am I a reckless optimist. I do not think that things necessarily come out all right in the end if left to themselves. I do not believe that any nation or any people enjoys a natural immunity against catastrophe or a special dispensation against disaster. Survival depends on ideas and action; and before we decide what the ideas are or what the action is to be, it is essential that we become supremely aware of the danger and resolve to meet it. It was in that spirit that I wrote the editorial, which seemed to me a logical expression

333

YEARS OF THE MODERN

of everything I had learned during the process of my "re-education." Far from subtracting from an affirmative, activist philosophy built around the plastic nature of history, atomic fission added something: the powerful ingredient of urgency. I never wavered in my confidence in the *capacity* of man to eliminate war and build a just peace, as well as to make whatever changes in himself that were dictated by the new problems and opportunities; what I tried to do was to emphasize that capacity rested on decision, and *decision* on *recognition* of the challenge.

On the political level, one of the most compelling reasons for urgency was that time was working against us. With each passing day after the end of the war, the classic and natural causes for tension and conflict between two giant nations outside a power vacuum would assert themselves unless some way could be found of eliminating the competition for power and security. When the United States and Russia looked at each other across this vacuum, the struggle to fill it would be on in earnest unless a world organization were invested both with preponderant force and a judicial structure which would be able to command the confidence of the world's peoples.

Another fact that bristled with urgency in the first year of the Atomic Age was that the nature of the new weapons had obliterated the prospects of an adequate military defense. In the absence of world armament-control as part of world government, the new weapons would be directed less by wisdom or knowledge than by fear and suspicion. Each nation would live nervously from one moment to the next, not knowing whether the designs or ambitions of other nations might prompt them to attempt the conclusive lightning-blow. The ordinary and inevitable differences among nations which

334

might in themselves be susceptible of solution might now become the signals for direct action, lest an enemy deliver the first and decisive blow.

Two months before Hiroshima, it seemed regrettable, but not unnatural, that the delegates at San Francisco should fail to invest the United Nations with the power of world law. Nor did it seem strange that the United States should propose the veto, and indicate its unwillingness to submit itself to a higher sovereignty. Russia, as the other great power, was no less anxious to avoid binding commitments, and served notice that her foreign-policy objectives were not to be made subordinate to the Charter.

But Hiroshima made San Francisco ancient history. It was as though a man-made ice age were descending, reducing all man's political bickerings and quarrels to a preposterous thimbleful alongside the universality of the threat. For the issue was not nations but man; and the peoples of the world were waiting for leadership which would enable them to break out of the old level on which they argued and fought, and onto a new level of awareness and responsibility equal to the danger and the opportunity.

At least that was what you thought about and dreamed about in 1945.

As I write these notes in 1949, against the background of a steady and almost relentless deterioration in the health of the world during the past four years, and with deep apprehensions about the consequences of such continued deterioration, I realize that the prospects of establishing a world government backed by the spirit of universalism are much remoter than they were after Hiroshima. Whatever common ground may have existed at the end of a common victory is now largely non-existent. The sides have been drawn and the question of the day seems to be not "whether," but "when."

Late as it is, however, I believe that peace is still possible. But first, a general statement may be in order:—

If I believed that peace could be achieved only at the expense of principle, I would be against peace. If I believed that peace meant surrender to evil, I would be against peace. l say this though I have seen an atomic bomb explode sixteen miles away; though I have seen dozens of dead cities, their insides hollowed out by dynamite and fire; though I have seen the faces of the dead in war and the faces of the damned whose bodies, but not whose minds, survived. I say this though I know that the next war will see America's cities join the long procession that began with Rotterdam and Coventry and London and Berlin and ended with Hiroshima and Nagasaki.

I believe it is possible to avert this war, and to avert it with honor. If I did not believe this, whatever lessons I may have learned in my re-education thus far would have been wasted. For these lessons, in their distilled form, say that man need not lose command of his destiny, that he has deep within him the resources of courage, conscience, and the spirit to shatter his predicament, and that he can transcend the complexities and perplexities that bedevil his existence if he can but raise a standard high enough for everyone to see and rally around. The world today hungers for ideals—not for supposedly "practical" ways out; for the curse of the twentieth century has been a grueling, biting, unrealistic materialism seeking sanction by calling itself "practical." The nation, or rather the people, that will define the ideal of a world government backed by the spirit of universalism as a basic both for survival and fulfillment will attract to itself such massed support everywhere as will dissolve what now appear to be the ineradicable components of disaster. It may be that the leaders of one or more nations will be able to blacken that ideal for their own peoples. No matter. The preponderance of mankind will respond at once and the rest in due course.

In saying this, I recognize that the procedures of peace are not enough. Peace that is merely non-war will be stagnant and without purpose. Government by itself can only provide a field for progress or decay; the making of world law is not the end but the beginning. The end is the supreme development and release of conscience, manifesting itself not only as a brake on conduct, but as a source of majestic inspiration in human affairs—on the individual and group both.

EPILOGUE

In philosophy, the fact, the theory, the alternatives, and the ideal are weighed together. Its gifts are insight and foresight, and a sense of the worth of life; in short, that sense of importance which nerves all civilized effort. Mankind can flourish in the lower stages of life with merely barbaric flashes of thought. But when civilization culminates, the absence of a coordinating philosophy of life, spread throughout the community, spells decadence, boredom, and the slackening of effort.

Every epoch has its character determined by the way its populations react to the material events which they encounter. This reaction is determined by their basic beliefs—by their hopes, their fears, their judgments of what is worth while. They may rise to the greatness of an opportunity, seizing its drama, perfecting its art, exploiting its adventure, mastering intellectually and physically the network of relations that constitutes the very being of the epoch. On the other hand, they may collapse before the perplexities confronting them. How they act depends partly on their courage, partly on their intellectual grasp. Philosophy is an attempt to clarify those fundamental beliefs which finally determine the emphasis of attention that lies at the base of character.

Mankind is now in one of its rare moods of shifting its outlook. The mere compulsion of tradition has lost its force. It is our business—philosophers, students, and practical men —to re-create and re-enact a vision of the world, including those elements of reverence and order without which society lapses into riot, and penetrated through and through with unflinching rationality. Such a vision is the knowledge which Plato identified with virtue. Epochs for which, within the limits of their development, this vision has been widespread are the epochs unfading in the memory of mankind.

—ALFRED NORTH WHITEHEAD,
in *Adventures of Ideas*

THE

CONTRIBUTORS

Henry Steele Commager

Allan Barth

Walton Hamilton

Alvin Johnson

David Riesman

Marshall Studio

J. K. Galbraith

Harvard Crimson Photo

Perry Miller

The Album

Harrison Brown

Erwin D. Canham

C. T. Lanham

Sumner Welles

Norman Cousins

THE CONTRIBUTORS

HENRY STEELE COMMAGER

Born and raised in the Middle West, studied at the University of Chicago and the University of Copenhagen. Taught history at New York University 1926-38, and at Columbia University since 1939. He has also been Pitt Professor of American History at Cambridge University.

Professor Commager is the author of many books in American history, among them a biography of Theodore Parker, and a study of Majority Rule and Minority Rights. Perhaps his most widely read book is *The Growth of the American Republic,* written in collaboration with Professor S. E. Morison. He is a member of the War Department Committee on the history of the war, contributor to numerous magazines, and editor of the *Rise of the American Nation,* which will be published in forty volumes.

ALAN BARTH

Born in New York City, 1906. Graduate of Yale, 1929. Began newspaper career in 1935 on Texas papers. Came to Washington, D.C., in 1938 as correspondent for the McClure Newspaper Syndicate. Since 1943 member of the editorial staff of the *Washington Post.* War service included editing of reports for O.W.I.'s Bureau of Intelligence.

Contributor to many national publications. Received Sigma Delta Chi award for distinguished service in American journalism, as well as a Heywood Broun Award. Nieman fellow at Harvard, 1948-49.

WALTON HAMILTON

Born at Hiwassee College, Tennessee, 1881. A list of colleges and universities at which he has taught would encompass, geographically, almost the entire United States.

It would be difficult to place Mr. Hamilton in any accepted educational category—he has been described as "an intellectual wanderer in quest of an education he has not yet attained."

His last years as a professor were spent at Yale Law School; his achievements there are well known. Mr. Hamilton is now engaged in private law practice in Washington, D.C.

ALVIN JOHNSON

Born in 1874 on a homestead in northwestern Nebraska. Graduate of University of Nebraska, 1897. After serving in the Spanish-American War he took his doctorate at Columbia University.

Following several years as an editor of the *New Republic*, he became one of the founders of the New School for Social Research, of which he was director from 1922 to 1946. One of his great works was in connection with the editing of the *Encyclopaedia of the Social Sciences*.

DAVID RIESMAN

Born in Philadelphia in 1909 and graduated from Harvard in 1931. Attended Harvard Law School and served as clerk to Justice Brandeis. Entered private practice in Boston. Professor of Law at the University of Buffalo.

After five years of legal teaching and research, Mr. Riesman returned to practice as an assistant district attorney. During the war he performed executive work at Sperry Gyroscope Company. In the spring of 1946 he returned to teaching at the University of Chicago.

He has spent the last several years at Yale directing a research project on political apathy and American character structure.

J. K. GALBRAITH

A Canadian by birth, Dr. Galbraith received his doctorate at the University of California in 1934. Subsequently he taught economics at Harvard and Princeton and published many articles on agricultural economics and industrial organization.

In 1940 he was appointed assistant to Chester Davis, and in 1941 was put in charge of price control in the Office of Price Administration. He continued as the nation's "price fixer" until 1943. From 1944 until 1948 he was a member of the board of editors of *Fortune*. In 1945 he served as director of the United States Strategic Bombing Survey and drafted its famous report. Dr. Galbraith returned to Harvard in 1948.

PERRY MILLER

Born Chicago, 1905. Educated in public school; ran away from home in 1923. Spent following three years as an actor, a seaman, and a factor in the Belgian Congo. As a result of these experiences, he entered the University of Chicago, taking his Ph.D. in 1931.

He has taught American literature at Harvard, first as instructor and then as professor. From 1942 to 1945 he saw war service in England, France, and Germany. Though his published works are mostly devoted to studies of early New England literature, his interests are wide, particularly in the field of American education. At present Professor Miller is spending a year as visiting lecturer at the University of Leiden.

HARRISON BROWN

Born in Sheridan, Wyoming, 1917. B.S. in chemistry, University of California, 1938. Ph.D., Johns Hopkins University, 1941.

In 1942 he joined the staff of the Plutonium Project at the University of Chicago as research associate; was transferred to Oak Ridge in 1943 as assistant director of chemistry. In 1946 he was appointed to the Institute for Nuclear Studies at the University of Chicago where he is now an associate professor.

Dr. Brown is executive vice-chairman of the Emergency Committee of Atomic Scientists, headed by Albert Einstein and Harold Urey.

He received the $1000 award of the American Association for the Advancement of Science in 1947.

ERWIN D. CANHAM

Born in Auburn, Maine, 1904. Graduated Bates College, 1925. Rhodes scholar, Oxford, England. While still at Oxford, Mr. Canham acted as reporter for the *Christian Science Monitor*, thus beginning an association that has continued to the present time. In 1932 he served as chief of the *Monitor's* Washington Bureau. He returned to Boston in 1945 and assumed his present post of editor-in-chief.

Mr. Canham has received a great number of important assignments for the United States government. During the year 1948-49, he was president of the American Society of Newspaper Editors.

C. T. LANHAM

Born Washington, D.C., 1902. Graduated from West Point in 1924. Rose to present position of Brigadier General in 1945. General Lanham has had a long and varied career in his profession. His services both as a combat leader in the past war and more recently as a military writer and speaker are well known. In the public mind he is perhaps best remembered for his personal leadership of his regiment in the initial assault on the Siegfried Line. For this he received the Distinguished Service Cross.

In 1948 General Lanham was transferred by special request to the Office of the Secretary of Defense, where he has served until recently as Director of the Staff, Personnel Policy Board.

SUMNER WELLES

Born New York City, 1892. Graduated Harvard, 1914. Began his long diplomatic career as secretary to the U. S. Embassy in Tokyo. Devoted many years to improving Inter-American relations. On several occasions served as Assistant Secretary of State. In 1937 he was appointed by President Roosevelt as Under Secretary of State, a position he held with distinction until his resignation in 1943.

In recent years Mr. Welles contributed a widely read column to the *New York Herald Tribune* and other news-papers on international affairs. He is the author of *The Time for Decision* and *Where Are We Heading?*

NORMAN COUSINS

Norman Cousins has been editor of *The Saturday Review of Literature* since 1939. His interest in the early histories of Greece and America found expression in a book, *The Good Inheritance*, published in 1941. A companion volume on the aphorisms of democracy appeared under his editorship the same year. In 1945, his editorial, "Modern Man Is Obsolete," was expanded into a short book.

He lives with his wife and four daughters in Norwalk, Connecticut, where he is moderator of the local Town Hall meetings. He also serves as State Chairman of the Governor's Commission on Education.

INDEX

345

Emerson, Ralph Waldo, 11, 191; *quoted*, 192, 316-17
Equality, 27-28, 29, 105
Escape from Freedom (Fromm), 124n
European Federation, 305-6
European Recovery Program; *see* Marshall Plan
"Every Man in His Humour," doctrine of, 40
Evolution, 6, 7, 193

Faraday, Michael, 208
Farrell, James, 312
Fascism, 108, 165, 289
Federal government, 37, 41, 60, 154-55, 157, 158-59, 160, 161, 164, 166, 167, 168-69, 170, 172, 194, 196, 197, 212 powers of, 42-45, 46-47, 51, 52-53, 105
Federal Reserve Board, 77
Federal Trade Commission, 77
Federalists, 21, 325
Fermi, Enrico, 222
Feudalism, 66-67, 119, 130
Fine, Benjamin, 196
Food and Agricultural Organization, 305
Ford, Henry, 74
Ford Motor Company, 40
Foreign policy, 12, 53, 59, 82, 141, 235, 250, 251-52, 262, 295-97, 301-2
Four Freedoms, 286
Fragment on Government (Bentham), 64
Franklin, Benjamin, 16, 68, 72

Free speech, 20, 22, 54, 55, 56, 57
Freedom, 43-44, 56, 57, 58, 59, 117, 119, 120, 166-67, 181, 182, 190, 199, 250, 256, 263, 267, 273, 274, 286, 300, 301, 308, 315, 321
Freeman, Edward Augustus, 4
Freud, Sigmund, 67, 119, 121, 127
Fromm, Erich, 124n, 143

Galileo, 208
Gallup, Dr. George, 235
Gandhi, 313-16, 322
Gay, Dean Edwin, 103
General Education in a Free Society, 187
George, Walter, 49-50
Germany, 54-55, 165, 291, 292, 293-95, 299, 328
Gibbon, Edward, 209
Gibbs, Willard, 16
Godwin, William, 120, 121n
Government sanctions, 90
Great Britain, 3, 10, 12, 17, 18, 24, 27, 29, 53, 55, 96, 109, 151, 155, 161, 165, 189, 288, 293, 294, 304
Great Transformation, The, (Polanyi), 120n
Greece, 22, 95, 322, 326
Greeley, Horace, 29
Greene, Graham, 11
Group Psychology and the Analysis of the Ego (Freud), 127

Hague Conferences, 287
Hahn, Otto, 222